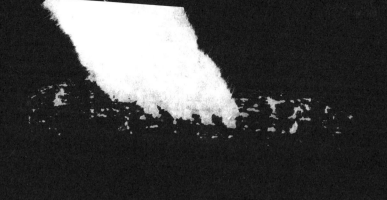

D1621176

WIDENING THE SCOPE OF COGNITIVE THERAPY

The Therapeutic Relationship, Emotion, and the Process of Change

Jeremy D. Safran, Ph.D.

JASON ARONSON INC.
Northvale, New Jersey
London

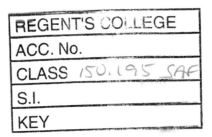
This book was set in 11 pt. New Baskerville by Alabama Book Composition of Deatsville, Alabama and printed and bound by Book-mart Press, Inc. of North Bergen, New Jersey.

Copyright © 1998 by Jason Aronson Inc.

10   9   8   7   6   5   4   3   2   1

Library of Congress Cataloging-in-Publication Data

Safran, Jeremy D.
   Widening the scope of cognitive therapy : the therapeutic
relationship, emotion, and the process of change / Jeremy D. Safran.
      p. cm.
   Includes bibliographical references and index.
   ISBN 0–7657–0138–3 (alk. paper)
   1. Cognitive therapy.   2. Eclectic psychotherapy.   3. Emotions and
cognition.   4. Psychotherapist and patient.   5. Therapeutic
alliance.   I. Title.
RC489.C63S245   1998
616.89′142—DC21   97–37557

Manufactured in the United States of America on acid-free paper. Jason Aronson Inc. offers books and cassettes. For information and catalog write to Jason Aronson Inc., 230 Livingston Street, Northvale, New Jersey 07647-1731. Or visit our website: http://www.aronson.com

To my daughter, Ayla

Contents

PART II: EMOTION IN COGNITIVE THERAPY

PART III: RUPTURES IN THE THERAPEUTIC ALLIANCE

PART IV: PSYCHOTHERAPY INTEGRATION

PART V: AN INTERVIEW

Preface

The title of this collection of papers, *The Widening Scope of Cognitive Therapy*, was inspired by a classic article written by the psychoanalyst Leo Stone (1954) in which he explored the need for flexibility among analysts, especially when working with populations that do not benefit from standard procedures. Since the early days of my graduate career in clinical psychology, I have been impressed with the need to widen the scope of cognitive therapy by integrating theoretical and technical principles from other therapeutic traditions. The themes that I have been most concerned with are the therapeutic relationship and the role of emotion in the change process.

My interest in the therapeutic relationship can be traced back to the fascination I had as an undergraduate for the writings of Harry Stack Sullivan, the father of the interpersonal tradition. Sullivan was a notoriously difficult writer, and many dislike his style. But I have always been taken with his unique sensibility and his penchant for pithy phrases, such as: "We are all more simply human than otherwise," and "The supply of interpretations greatly exceeds the demand for them."

Chapter 1 of this book reflects my early interest in the implications of Sullivan's thinking for cognitive therapy. I had written a draft of this article while still a graduate student and had sent copies to both Donald Kiesler (whose writings in the interpersonal tradition had been an important influence on me) and Marvin Goldfried, neither of whom I knew at the time. Both were extremely supportive and encouraging, and this played no small role in inspiring me with the confidence to continue writing in this area. Chapter 2 was an attempt to flesh out some of the theoretical principles articulated in Chapter 1, and to spell out some of the technical principles deriving from them.

Shortly after writing this chapter, I read Guidano and Liotti's *Cognitive Processes and Emotional Disorders,* which influenced me in two major ways. First, it stimulated me to think in greater depth about the structural organization of cognitive processes and to reread George Kelly. This, in turn, was one of the influences that led me to write Chapter 3 in collaboration with Michael Vallis, Zindel Segal, and Brian Shaw, who were then colleagues of mine at the Cognitive Therapy Unit at the Clarke Institute of Psychiatry in Toronto. A second important impact of Guidano and Liotti's book was to stimulate me to reread John Bowlby's work, which was one of the important influences that inspired Chapters 4 and 5. Another important stimulus for these two chapters was my attempt to think about schema theory in a more clinically meaningful fashion. This interest was catalyzed, in part, by an invitation from Zindel Segal to participate in a panel on schema theory, which he had organized at the Society for Psychotherapy Research Conference. This led me to develop the idea of the interpersonal schema, which subsequently came to play an important role in my thinking.

In the area of emotion, I was influenced tremendously by my collaboration with Les Greenberg, who was an important mentor and collaborator for many years, and who remains a good friend. I met Les while still in graduate school at the University of British Columbia. In those days, the clinical psychology program there had a rather traditional behavioral program with little interest in experiential approaches (or the therapeutic relationship for that matter). Les, a junior faculty member in the Counseling Department, had a background in client-centered and Gestalt therapy. Although this made him suspect among my respectable behavioral professors, I found that my discussions with him helped to clarify important things about the role of emotion in therapy that my behavioral education was unable to. I also participated in two Gestalt therapy groups that he led (I subsequently had more extensive training in Gestalt therapy with Harvey Freedman, a protégé of Fritz Perls, who co-founded the Toronto Gestalt Institute), and this experiential learning influenced my thinking in a way that no mere theoretical discussion could have done.

Chapters 6 and 7 were written in collaboration with Les Greenberg at approximately the same time as one another. I have selected these two pieces, rather than others we co-authored, because they form a complementary set, with Chapter 6 directed to a cognitive behavioral audience and Chapter 7 initially written for a psychoanalytic audience interested in cognitive therapy. Chapter 8, written a number of years later, was a response to an invitation to write an "opinionated essay" on the topic of emotion in cognitive therapy for a book that Paul Salkovskis edited on contemporary trends in cognitive therapy. One of the points I make in this chapter (and that I believe is still true) is that although it has become more common for cognitive therapists to speak about the importance of emotion, the potential implications of emotion therapy and research for clinical practice have yet to be fully realized.

Chapter 9, co-authored with Peter Crocker, Shelly McMain, and Paul Murray while I was still at the Clarke Institute, is the first article I wrote on the topic of ruptures in the therapeutic alliance. It is difficult to trace the exact origins of my interest in this topic, but I remember that when I first started practicing psychotherapy, I was very much impressed with the significance of sessions in which I had been able to work through problems in my relationship with clients. I also remember experiencing an immediate feeling of resonance when I later came across Kohut's writing on empathic failures. The consistent research finding that the therapeutic alliance is the best predictor of treatment outcome was another influence. Finally, I imagine that the determinants of my interest in the topic go back much further to my own personal struggles around negotiating the needs for agency versus relatedness with others.

Chapter 10 was originally stimulated by various questions that colleagues had raised in response to Chapter 9 and to my presentations on the topic at the Society for Psychotherapy Research. For example, are patient expressions of anger or negative sentiments always indicative of problems in the alliance? Are there differences between alliances taking place early in therapy versus those taking place late in treatment? Are certain basic preconditions necessary in order to be able to work through ruptures in the alliance? I am particularly grateful to Ed Bordin for stimulating my thinking on these issues and for encouraging my interests in the area.

Chapter 11, my favorite chapter in the book, is an attempt to cast the topic of alliance ruptures within a broader theoretical and philosophical framework. I wrote a first draft of this chapter while still at the Clarke Institute and completed it at Adelphi University in New York. This move to a more psychoanalytic milieu no doubt played some role in influencing the increased emphasis on psychoanalytic theory in the chapter. At the same time, my interest in Otto Rank and his psychology of the will (elaborated in this chapter) dates back to my undergraduate days. My interest in Sándor Ferenczi's work began about a year before I moved to Adelphi and was stimulated by a wonderful book by André Haynal that explores the political factors underlying Ferenczi's marginalization by the psychoanalytic movement and traces his influence on many important contemporary psychoanalytic ideas.

Chapters 12 and 13 focus explicitly on the topic of psychotherapy integration. While all of the previous chapters are attempts to integrate principles from different therapeutic traditions, these final chapters examine philosophical, sociological, and psychological issues relevant to the enterprise of psychotherapy integration. They were stimulated, in part, by personal experiences of trying to introduce psychodynamic and humanistic ideas to cognitive-behavioral colleagues and cognitive ideas to psychodynamic colleagues and students. Chapter 12 was initially an invited contribution to the first issue of the Argentinean journal *Revista de Clínica Psicológica*. I owe a special debt of gratitude to Hector Fernandez Alvarez and his colleagues at the Aigle Center in Buenos Aires for their warm support, friendship, and intellectual stimulation, and for introducing me to the ideas and politics of South American psychology.

Chapter 13, written in collaboration with Stan Messer, critiques common approaches toward psychotherapy integration from a postmodern perspective. It highlights the human tendency to establish our own identities through the marginalization of the other, and how this gets played out in the relationship between proponents of different therapeutic traditions. I have been consistently struck by how ready therapists are to respond to other theoretical traditions and their associated worldviews and epistemological biases with dismissiveness, condescension, or moral indignation. This has always seemed to me to be particularly ironic given the fact that, as therapists, one of our primary tasks is valuing, accepting, and working to understand the uniqueness of the other.

I don't think I have ever had as much difficulty getting a paper published as I did with this one. We went through endless rounds of revisions, with at least one reviewer in every round criticizing it for being nihilistic or for rejecting the importance of scientific methodology. I hope the final version makes it clear that we are not taking either of these positions. Instead we make use of developments in contemporary philosophy of science to articulate a stance that is theoretically and methodologically pluralistic but still allows for making rational choices between alternatives.

Chapter 14 consists of an interview with me conducted by Christine Maguth Nezu and Lisa DelliCarpinni for the *Behavior Therapist*. I am grateful to them for helping me to articulate my thoughts.

In addition to the various people I have already acknowledged, I would like to thank Michael Moskowitz, Judy Cohen, Lenora Hume, and the rest of the staff at Jason Aronson for helping me to bring this book into existence. And finally I want to express my love and appreciation to my wife, Jenny, for her support and for her interest in my ideas and her constructively critical response to them.

Part I

The Therapeutic Relationship and Case Formulation

1

Some Implications of Sullivan's Interpersonal Theory for Cognitive Therapy

The objectives of this chapter are twofold. The first is to highlight the potential compatibility from a metatheoretical perspective between cognitive therapy and the tradition of interpersonal psychotherapy that originated with Harry Stack Sullivan. The second objective is to identify some of the ways in which cognitive therapists stand to benefit by recognizing this compatibility and, by drawing upon principles of interpersonal psychotherapy, to enrich their own practice.

As Wiggins (1982) noted, since Sullivan's time a small but persistent group of theorists have periodically urged others to consider seriously the clinical merits of an interpersonal perspective. In fact Kiesler and colleagues (1976) specifically discussed some of the potential payoffs for behavior therapists in conceptualizing the therapeutic relationship with principles derived from interpersonal and communications theory. These exhortations appear to have had little impact upon the writings of behavior therapists.

More recently, however, the tradition of cognitive behavior therapy has broadened and matured to the point where theorists writing from within the cognitive-behavioral camp are advocating a rapprochement between cognitive therapy and other therapeutic traditions (Goldfried 1980). A parallel development has been the growing tendency for cognitive therapists to draw upon principles of experimental cognitive psychology to provide a coherent metatheoretical framework for cognitive therapists (e.g., Arnkoff 1980, Bower 1978, Goldfried 1979, Greenberg and Safran 1981).

This development has set the stage for formulating principles of therapeutic change that are held in common by diverse therapeutic traditions, using concepts derived from cognitive psychology as a common language. Such an integration seems particularly desirable, given the general failure of psychotherapy research to demonstrate the superiority of one type of psychotherapy over another (Sloan et al. 1975, Smith and Glass 1977).

As a number of authors have argued (Carson 1982, Chrzanowski 1982, Kiesler 1982a,b), Sullivan's basic therapeutic concepts are remarkably contemporary by the standards of today's experimental cognitive psychology and mesh very easily with theoretical notions coming out of the social cognition tradition. Although many of Sullivan's ideas originated with Freud, they are embedded within the context of a cognitive metapsychology, which makes them easy to assimilate into the developing cognitive-behavioral tradition in a meaningful, integrated fashion. For this reason, the traditions of cognitive therapy and interpersonal psychotherapy are not plagued with the same type of metatheoretical differences that have hindered a more creative cross-fertilization between psychoanalysis and cognitive-behavior therapy. Since both interpersonal psychotherapy and cognitive therapy lend themselves well to cognitive formulations, the impediments to creative integration are greatly diminished. In the next section, I will outline a few of the key concepts in Sullivan's system in order to illustrate their compatibility with the contemporary cognitive tradition. I will then discuss some of the implications of these concepts for cognitive assessment, behavioral assessment, and the therapeutic relationship.

PERSONIFICATIONS AND SELECTIVE INATTENTION: KEY THEORETICAL CONCEPTS

One of the more central concepts in Sullivan's system is the personification. In Sullivan's system, the personification is essentially a cognitive template or structure directing interpersonal perception. There are two basic types of personifications: those that apply to the perception of the self and those that apply to the perception of others.

Both types of personification are developed through learning experiences and subsequently direct and organize the acquisition of new information about the self and others. This notion is very similar to the contemporary cognitive concept of schema, which, as Landau and Goldfried (1981) have proposed, can provide a useful unifying construct in the field of cognitive assessment.

Personifications of the Self

According to Sullivan, people come to accept certain characteristics and experiences as belonging to the self, while they see other characteristics and experiences as not belonging to the self or, in Sullivan's terms, belonging to the "not me." The personified self can thus be thought of as a collection of beliefs, generalizations, and assumptions about the self that an individual acquires over time. Personifications of the self function in a self-perpetuating fashion. New information that is consistent with the personified self tends to be admitted to awareness, whereas inconsistent information is not.

This notion is consistent with the concept of self-schema that has emerged in the social-cognition literature. Markus defined the self-schema as "cognitive generalizations about the self, derived from past experience, that organize and guide the processing of the self-related information contained in an individual's social experience" (1977). She demonstrated that individuals with well-defined self-schemas are better at recalling schema-consistent evidence than people with poorly defined self-schemas. They are also faster at identifying characteristics consistent with their self-schemas. Rogers and colleagues (1979) found that subjects who had viewed a list of adjectives tended to recall adjectives that were consistent with their self-schemas better than adjectives that were not. Swann and Read (1981a) demonstrated that subjects actively seek social feedback that confirms their self-conceptions in preference to feedback that is disconfirming. These and similar studies have demonstrated the operation of self-schemas or self-personifications.

Other studies have demonstrated the clinical relevance of these constructs. O'Banion and Arkowitz (1977), for example, demonstrated that socially anxious individuals recall more negative information about themselves than nonanxious individuals. Alden and Cappe (1981) found that unassertive individuals evaluate their own behavior more negatively than assertive individuals, even when judges rated their behavior as equally socially competent. Roth and Rehm (1980) found that depressed individuals rated themselves as displaying approximately twice as many unskilled as skilled behaviors, even though observers judged their skilled and unskilled behaviors as equally frequent. Derry and Kuiper (1981) demonstrated that depressed individuals are more likely than normals and psychiatric controls to recall depressively toned adjectives. Research of this type has demonstrated that personifications of the self can indeed play a significant role in perpetuating clinical problems.

Sullivan adds a developmental hypothesis to account for the existence of self-personifications. He theorizes that these personifications develop through the reflected appraisals of others. In brief, those characteristics of the self that are valued by significant others during important developmental periods become personified as the self, while others are not. The individual who is valued by his parents for being strong comes to personify himself as strong and not weak. Conversely, the overly protective parent who becomes anxious when his child demonstrates evidence of autonomy may facilitate the development of a personification of the self as weak.

Selective Inattention

Sullivan theorized that a major variable influencing the selective processing of information about the self is that information that is inconsistent with the personified self provokes anxiety, because nonpersonified characteristics have met with nonacceptance and anxiety in the past. The cognitive processes that are employed to reduce this anxiety are termed *security operations* by Sullivan. One of the more important security operations is selective inattention (Sullivan 1940).

According to Sullivan, people actively avoid or become unaware of events that provoke anxiety. Because of this selective inattention, people are often unable to benefit from experience by learning new things about themselves. This construction of experience can be exacerbated by automatically engaging in behaviors that will reduce anxiety by eliciting confirmatory, rather than unconfirmatory feedback.

Sullivan's concept of selective inattention stands up well in the light of today's experimental psychology. In contemporary cognitive psychology, it is taken as given that the contents of awareness are always determined by an active selection of a subset of the full array of potential information available to the individual (Kahneman 1973, Neisser 1976). Moreover, there appears to be a strong consensus, based upon experimental evidence, that information that is not processed in focal awareness may still be processed outside of awareness and may influence both perception and behavior (see Shevrin and Dickman [1980] for an excellent review of this research).

In addition, there is a body of evidence demonstrating that the threshold for the perception may be raised for emotionally laden stimuli (Dixon 1971, Kostandov and Arzamanov 1977, Shevrin 1973). It appears then that Sullivan's concept of selective inattention may be a theoretically viable one, warranting further attention by cognitive therapists.

The Personifications of Others

Sullivan believed that people tend to organize information about new acquaintances on the basis of expectations developed through interactions with people in the past. It is thus not uncommon for

people to distort their perceptions of new acquaintances in a
fashion consistent with their previous learning experiences. A
woman who had a tyrannical father may tend to see all men as
tyrannical. A man who had a rejecting mother may tend to see all
women as rejecting. Sullivan (1954) referred to these distortions in
the perception of the characteristics of other people as parataxic
distortions. Although Sullivan's concept of the parataxic distortion
originated in the psychoanalytic notion of transference, once again
an extremely important concept has been reformulated in terms
of general cognitive organizing principles. Cantor and Mischel's
(1977) research on the influence of prototypes on interpersonal
perception provides another example of the convergence between
Sullivanian thought and the contemporary social cognitive tradition. Cantor and Mischel argue that traits serve as normative
conceptual schemata that guide the processing of information
about other people. They are essentially cognitive heuristics that
simplify the processing of social information. Consistent with this
formulation, they demonstrated that subjects' memory for social
information is incorrectly biased in a fashion consistent with traits
previously ascribed to fictitious characters.

A number of other studies have demonstrated that manipulating subjects' expectations about the characteristics of another
person can bias the fashion in which relevant information is
processed. Zadny and Gerard (1974), for example, had students
observe a videotape in which a student stumbled and dropped a
number of items. Prior to viewing the film, subjects were told that
the student was either a chemistry major, a music major, or a
psychology major. On a subsequent memory test, subjects were
better able to recall dropped items that were consistent with the
student-actor's academic discipline or major (for example, a slide
rule for the chemistry major). Rothbart and colleagues (1979)
found that subjects had significantly better recall for descriptions of
behaviors that were consistent with traits initially ascribed to groups
of men than for both inconsistent and unrelated behavioral descriptions. Cohen (1981) had subjects view a videotape of a woman who
had previously been described as either a waitress or a librarian. The
videotape consisted of a staged interaction between the woman and

her husband, which had been designed to portray features consistent with both waitress and librarian stereotypes. Subjects were found to have better recognition memory for stereotype-consistent features than for inconsistent features. Safran and Segal (1987) provided subjects with information about an individual to shape their expectations that he would be either a domineering or an agreeable character. Following this, subjects viewed a videotape of a social interaction in which this individual displayed an equal number of domineering, agreeable, and neutral behaviors. It was found that subjects formed impressions of the individual that were consistent with their initial expectations. Moreover, using a modified version of Newtson's (1973) unitizing methodology, it was demonstrated that subjects attended selectively to segments of the interaction that were consistent with their initial expectations. Thus a growing body of research is providing evidence of the cognitive mechanisms through which personifications of others operate.

THE COGNITIVE-INTERPERSONAL LINK

The concepts discussed so far appear to be reasonably cognitive in nature—in fact, so much so that one might ask what is distinctively "interpersonal" about Sullivan's perspective. The answer to this question lies in the most fundamental tenet of interpersonal psychotherapy, which states that "maladaptive behavior persists over lengthy periods, because it is based upon perceptions, expectations, or constructions of the characteristics of other people that tend to be confirmed by the interpersonal consequences of the behavior emitted" (Carson 1982). There is thus a recognition of the circular and reciprocal nature of the relationship between the individual's cognitions, his own behavior, and his environment. The individual who always anticipates hostility from others may characteristically behave in a hostile fashion. This elicits hostile behavior from others, which in turn confirms his expectations. The depressed individual tends to withdraw, thus making it difficult for others to establish contact and confirming his depressive expectations.

As Meddin (1982) has noted, it is not that cognitive therapists are generally unaware of the importance of interpersonal relationships, but rather that they fail to examine systematically the interplay between cognitive and interpersonal factors. It might also be added that there is certainly no theoretical reason for cognitive therapists to avoid an exploration of the full implications of the link between these two realms, since this type of analysis is entirely consistent with the principle of reciprocal determinism (Bandura 1978) generally accepted by cognitive behaviorists.

Sullivan maintained that all individuals are characterized by certain regularities in the nature of the social interactions in which they typically engage. The personifications that an individual develops of both self and others have an important causal role in determining these repetitive patterns. Individuals who are relatively well adjusted tend to personify both self and others in a fairly flexible fashion. They are able to accept a wide range of attributes or characteristics as belonging to the self and are more flexible in the personifications or prototypes they employ in their perception of other people.

In contrast, individuals who are relatively maladjusted are more rigid in their personifications of both self and others. The self may, for example, be defined as exclusively submissive and agreeable, while dominant or quarrelsome characteristics may be seen as belonging to the "not me" (Sullivan 1953). Others may be inflexibly personified as dominant. Alternatively, others may be personified as either dominant or submissive, with no allowance for more subtle gradations between these two extremes.

Personifications of both the self and others inevitably impact upon the individual's interpersonal behavior. The self-personification becomes linked to interpersonal behavior in the following fashion. Because information that is incongruent with the self-personification is anxiety-provoking, individuals tend to behave in a fashion that elicits information that is congruent with the self-personification. They also tend to avoid situations likely to yield incongruent information. The individual who rigidly personifies himself as weak and dependent will behave in a manner that tends to demand a dominant response from others. Moreover the more rigidly he personifies himself in this way, the more likely he is to avoid individuals who do not respond in a complementary fashion. In addition, individuals who find it difficult to respond to him in a dominant fashion will tend to avoid him. There are thus a number of ways in which personifications of the self shape the individual's interpersonal experience and perpetuate themselves. This type of perspective on the link between the self-personification or self-schema and interpersonal behavior appears to be one missing from cognitive therapy. Because it has some potentially important clinical implications, it should at the very least be given further consideration as a potential working hypothesis and a topic for empirical investigation. (Along these lines, Swann and Read [1981b] have demonstrated empirically that subjects will intensify behaviors that elicit self-image confirming feedback from others when they are told that others have self-image inconsistent impressions of them.)

Personifications of others also function in a self-fulfilling manner and shape social interactions. As stated earlier, the individual who sees all others as hostile may meet this perceived hostility with his own hostility, thus eliciting hostility even where none existed in the first place. The depressed person may expect rejection from others and may actually promote it by withdrawing in anticipation of rejection. Coyne (1976) has demonstrated that communications from depressed individuals are likely to be experienced as aversive by others and tend to elicit withdrawal and rejection. This perspective on the link between expectations about the characteristics of others and interpersonal behavior, while central to the Sullivanian tradition, has begun to be discussed in the cognitive-behavioral literature (e.g., Coyne 1982, Meddin 1982).

In the 1970s and 1980s cognitive behaviorists became increasing sophisticated at assessing cognitive variables that play an important role in clinical problems (e.g., Kendall and Hollon 1981). It is now important for them to think carefully about the link between cognitive and social factors. The discussion thus far suggests that in the cognitive realm there are two crucial types of schemata to assess: personifications of the self and personifications of others. It also suggests that there are certain crucial interpersonal behaviors to assess—those that play the role of eliciting behavior from others that confirms dysfunctional personifications. Sullivan referred to these characteristic patterns of interpersonal behavior as *dynamisms*. (It should be noted that Sullivan employed the term *dynamism* to refer more generally to any enduring psychological pattern, whether overt or covert in nature.) This notion of recurring interpersonal patterns in an individual's life is basic to the interpersonal approach. In fact, Sullivan (1953) defined personality as "that relatively enduring pattern of recurrent interpersonal situations which characterize a human life" (p. 111).

Having accurately assessed the dynamisms that lead to unsatisfactory interpersonal relationships, the therapist can provide the client with feedback to help him modify these patterns. Moreover, he or she can formulate hypotheses as to the nature of the personifications that would give rise to specific dysfunctional dynamisms. It is important to remember, however, that the therapist cannot always rely on the client's self-report as a guide to which dynamisms are important. The very fact that a specific dynamism continues to be a problem for a client suggests that the client may not be aware of that dynamism or its impact on other people. As Lazarus (1980) has pointed out, this is particularly likely to be the case, since

> Frank, forthright, and honest feedback is a rare commodity. Social protocol often demands a degree of tact and diplomacy that hinges on hypocrisy. Even good friends are often loathe to provide one with honest feedback, lest the other person take offence, and when loved ones do offer feedback, their perceptions are bound to be biased and may often be questioned. [p. 283]

How then is the therapist to obtain the type of data necessary to conduct this vital type of behavioral assessment?

THE THERAPIST AS PARTICIPANT-OBSERVER

One possibility would be to interview significant others. While this can potentially be of some value, it must be remembered that their perceptions may be biased and that moreover they may be in the habit of responding to the client's dysfunctional behaviors automatically, without ever carefully or accurately analyzing the reason for their responses. Another possibility would be actually to observe the client interacting with other people. By observing the way in which people respond to the client and isolating the client behaviors and communications that precede personification-confirming social responses, the therapist would be able to assess the relevant dynamisms. This possibility is often not practical, of course.

A viable option, however, is for the therapist to become skilled at observing and assessing the nature of the interaction between the client and himself or herself. Sullivan referred to the therapist as a *participant-observer*, to emphasize the fact that the therapist can never be a completely impartial, uninvolved observer of the client's behavior. He or she cannot avoid becoming part of the interpersonal field that shapes both the client's behavior and his or her own. In his words, "the psychiatrist has an inescapable, inextricable involvement in all that goes on in the interview; and to the extent that he is unconscious or unwitting of his participation in the interview, to that extent he does not know what is happening" (Sullivan 1954, p. 19). The therapist must thus acknowledge that he or she is part of the interpersonal field and at the same time become a keen observer of both the client's behavior and his or her own subjective reactions to the client. The most important diagnostic information available to therapists regarding their clients' characteristic interpersonal styles and impact upon other people is thus their own automatic reaction toward individual clients. This follows naturally, since the therapist is simply another human being in interaction with the client, a person who is likely to respond to the client as other people will. Therapists' own feelings and behaviors in therapy thus provide them with clues, on the basis of which hypotheses about their clients' respective interpersonal styles are advanced (Carson 1982, Chrzanowski 1982, Kiesler 1982).

This formulation suggests that cognitive-behavior therapists typically neglect some of the most important assessment information available to them—namely, their own feelings and reactions (Kiesler et al. 1976). It also suggests that the traditional cognitive behaviorist is in grave danger of helping clients maintain their maladaptive behaviors and dysfunctional expectancies about human relationships by virtue of inattention to his or her own behaviors. Cognitive therapists who are unaware of the dominating responses that submissive clients elicit from them can implement a masterful depression-management program and at the same time confirm the clients' belief that others must take care of them. Therapists who are unaware of the competitive response that some clients pull from them may devise a thoroughly appropriate stress inoculation for a client and at the same time confirm that client's belief that the world is inhabited by hostile, competitive people who must be dealt with in a hostile, competitive manner.

The basic point here is that therapists must have the skills to recognize the impact that clients have upon them, to provide the client with appropriate and utilizable feedback and to "unhook" themselves from the reflexive interaction pattern with the client (Kiesler 1982a,b). Of course, effective cognitive-behavior therapists may already be operating in this way to some extent. Even if this is the case, it is nevertheless still important to begin discussing this type of therapeutic activity explicitly and to begin subjecting it to critical scrutiny.

THREE PROBLEM AREAS FACING
COGNITIVE THERAPISTS

A variety of procedures have been recommended for increasing treatment compliance, ranging from increasing therapist attractiveness (Goldstein et al. 1966) to reducing incongruities between expectations about therapy and the actual treatment provided (Goldfried and Davison 1976) to employing self-management programs that clearly place the responsibility for change in the hands of the client (Mahoney and Thoresen 1974). The adoption of an interpersonal perspective provides new insight into the management of treatment noncompliance by viewing the situation from a radically different perspective. The very phrase *treatment compliance* suggests that the problem is formulated within the context of a medical model of service delivery. The notion is that the therapist prescribes a treatment in the same way that a physician prescribes medication, and the problem then becomes one of whether the client complies with the prescription.

When the therapeutic transaction is formulated within the context of an interpersonal perspective, however, it seems apparent that this medical analogy is inappropriate. The client comes to therapy because she is in distress. This does not mean that she is initially interested in modifying her self-personification. In fact, all her security operations are operating precisely to avoid circumstances and to screen out information that may be inconsistent with the sense of self she brings with her into therapy (Sullivan 1954). There is a very real sense, then, in which the client has a vested interest in not doing things that contradict her belief systems about herself and the rest of the world. In fact, despite her best intentions, the client engages the therapist in an interaction with the objective of confirming the validity of the personification she brought into therapy. The therapist's task thus becomes not simply to prescribe a therapeutic activity, but actively to use the therapeutic relationship to disconfirm the client's dysfunctional expectations about interpersonal relationships. According to Sullivan (1954), the therapist must maintain a keen awareness for minute changes in the mood or rhythm of the therapy interview, for these changes may signify the fact that the client's self-esteem has been threatened and that she is responding with security operations. These operations result in a deterioration of communication between client and therapist. At such times it is essential for the therapist to clarify what events may have threatened the client's self-esteem and to help reduce the client's anxiety to a manageable level. The accurate assessment of occurrences that have threatened the client's self-esteem and motivated security operations provides the therapist with valuable information about the nature of the client's self-personification and the type of experiences that are relegated to the "not me." A vital point to note here is that changes in the client's personifications are best achieved when the client's anxiety is kept at a manageable level, since only then will anxiety-provoking information be admitted to awareness. The therapist must thus be adept at monitoring the client's anxiety level and providing her with appropriate reassurance to increase her sense of self-esteem, allay anxiety, and decrease security operations.

Viewed from the perspective of interpersonal psychotherapy, instances of client noncompliance are no longer seen simply as obstacles to effective psychotherapy. Instead they become viewed as events that provide the therapist with vital information about the client and the style of relating to significant others in his or her life. Such events enable the therapist to formulate hypotheses about the dysfunctional patterns of living in which the client engages. These hypotheses can then be evaluated by offering feedback to the client in a tentative form. In this fashion, therapeutic impasses are transformed into the real breakthroughs of therapy.

For example: A client comes into therapy who initially seems extremely eager for the approval of the therapist. After the first few sessions it becomes apparent that whenever the therapist asks him to complete a homework assignment, the client finds some excuse for not completing it. Moreover, while not directly expressing hostility toward the therapist, the client appears to adopt a somewhat indirect, sullen manner. The therapist finds herself becoming frustrated and trying more and more to control the client's behavior. At this point she stops and decides to discuss what is going on and to disclose some of her feelings toward the client. She does this in a nonthreatening manner by focusing upon her own feelings of powerlessness and frustration, rather than by accusing the client. She then asks the client to engage with her in a collaborative effort in order to examine his contributions to the interaction. It emerges that the client wants the therapist's approval and feels belittled when asked to do homework assignments. Because he does not want to lose the therapist's approval, he has not told her about any of these feelings directly. The more the therapist tries to control him, the more his expectations are confirmed that she will not respect his autonomy. He thus feels an even greater need to be rebellious. The therapist then asks the client if he has experienced this type of pattern with other people, and the client responds that he has. The therapist and client then investigate the similarities between the present and the other relationships and begin to explore the nature of the expectations that the client has about relationships as well as more direct ways of asserting his autonomy.

While it is beyond the scope of this chapter to go into details about the management of therapeutic process from the perspective of interpersonal psychotherapy, detailed accounts are available elsewhere (e.g., Sullivan 1954). The essential point is that interpersonal theory does provide a perspective on psychotherapy process that is lacking from current cognitive-behavioral traditions and that would potentially be of immense value in clarifying the nature of clients' noncompliance with treatment.

TREATMENT MAINTENANCE

A second major challenge pinpointed by cognitive-behavior therapists is the identification of factors promoting treatment generalization and maintenance (Marlatt and Gordon 1979, Wilson 1980). Behavioral clinicians in search of procedures for enhancing treatment maintenance have alternately emphasized the importance of focusing upon cognitive variables or environmental factors. While operant conditioners and token economists have long maintained that the most effective way to maintain behavior changes is through changes in the environment (e.g., Atthowe 1973), cognitive therapists have focused upon modifying expectations of self-efficacy (Bandura 1977) or shaping the way in which future treatment relapses will be construed (Marlatt 1978). More recently, cognitive therapists taking a systems perspective have discussed the importance of blocking family interactions that maintain and exacerbate the client's dysfunctional behaviors (Bedrosian 1981).

The value of adopting an interpersonal perspective to psychotherapy is that the causal link between cognitive, behavioral, and environmental factors is clearly specified, and it becomes clear that it may well be necessary to intervene at all three foci. As Lazarus and colleagues (1982) have argued, it is vital that we avoid assigning primacy to any one link in the circular chain. This is true on both theoretical and practical levels. Behavioral changes that are processed in a distorted fashion because of rigid personifications may not last long. Conversely, cognitive changes may be temporary in nature, if not supported by confirming information from the environment. This touches on a critical point.

An interpersonal perspective of psychotherapy suggests that a vital first step for the therapist is to determine which particular pattern of interpersonal behaviors emitted by the client is likely to provoke undesirable social consequences. The precise nature of these behaviors or dynamisms may not be immediately apparent to the therapist, and it is for this reason that a careful assessment of the impact of the client on the therapist is conducted (Kiesler 1982). A failure to conduct a careful assessment of this type may result in a failure to modify behaviors that are instrumental in maintaining a dysfunctional expectation-behavior-environmental consequence loop.

A brief example may be useful to illustrate this point. A 26-year-old male graduate student comes to therapy complaining of a general sense of depression. The therapist employs a multicomponent therapeutic program consisting of scheduling pleasurable activities, assigning mastery and pleasure tasks, and identifying and modifying automatic thoughts (Hollon and Beck 1979). During the course of treatment, the therapist often tends to feel condescended to or put down by his client but attempts as best he can not to let these feelings interfere with the treatment and proceeds to the best of his ability. After ten sessions, the client appears to have made some changes. He is engaging in more pleasurable activities and has identified and has begun to change some key automatic thoughts relating to his fear of rejection by others. He is feeling less dysphoric and decides to terminate therapy. Five months later, he returns to therapy complaining that, despite the realization that his fears of rejection act as self-fulfilling prophecies and despite an attempt to be more sociable, he cannot seem to form and maintain satisfying relationships.

Had the therapist in this case paid greater attention to his feelings of discomfort with the client in therapy, he might have developed some valuable hypotheses about the specific behaviors in which the client engages that tend to distance and alienate people. Moreover, providing the client with feedback about his impact upon the therapist might have paved the way for the examination of additional automatic thoughts that had not emerged in therapy. While this example is, of course, somewhat simplified, it does provide some illustration of the fashion in which focusing upon the therapeutic relationship can provide the therapist with valuable information that may be useful in enhancing treatment generalization and maintenance.

THE ROLE OF AFFECT IN COGNITIVE THERAPY

The third area to be discussed is more conceptual than practical in nature. Nevertheless, addressing this conceptual issue may have some important practical implications for the type of therapeutic interventions employed. Mahoney (1980) has argued that cognitive therapists have adopted an overly restrictive view of affective experience, in viewing emotions as epiphenomena only to be controlled, rather than experienced. At the same time, considerable empirical evidence is accumulating that suggests that the traditional cognitive view of emotions as the direct causal product of cognitions is faulty (Cacioppo et al. 1979, Craighead et al. 1979, Lapoint and Harrell 1978, Safran 1982a,b, Sutton-Simon and Goldfried 1979). In the more traditional behavioral camp Rachman (1981) has argued that cognitive interventions may be of limited value if, as Zajonc (1980) has suggested, there is something primary and irrevocable about emotions. Rachman (1981) has also drawn clinicians' attention to a number of helpful therapeutic procedures that involve expressing rather than controlling emotions, and suggests that this type of "emotional processing" warrants further exploration and clarification.

Safran and Greenberg (1982a) have argued that difficulty in consciously experiencing certain types of emotions can be central to a variety of clinical problems. One example is the unassertive person who does not become aware of his anger or resentment and expresses it in a passive-aggressive manner. Another example is an individual who feels hurt by somebody else's actions but responds with anger and indignation rather than some acknowledgment of his own vulnerability. The experience of appropriate emotions can be a functional process that motivates adaptive behavior (Plutchik 1980). For example, the experience of anger can motivate an individual to protect himself. The experience of affection can motivate one to establish a bond with others. Sullivan's concept of the personified self clarifies the way in which an individual's early learning experiences can constrict the range of emotions an individual is able consciously to experience. An individual who rigidly personifies himself as strong cannot acknowledge feelings of weakness. A person who rigidly personifies himself as agreeable has difficulty experiencing anger. It is thus important for the therapist to assess accurately the individual's self-personification in order to clarify how the client distorts both internal events and external experience. An important benefit for cognitive therapists in adopting a Sullivanian perspective on the development of the self-personification is that a framework is provided within which the clinical role of denial or distortion of emotional experience can be conceptualized. Inner experience can be biased and distorted by rigid personifications in the same fashion that information about others can be.

It may be clinically important for the therapist to assess the nature of such distortions where they exist and to help the client learn to experience potentially adaptive emotions that are typically obscured (Safran and Greenberg 1982a). For these reasons, the Sullivanian perspective on personifications of the self and security operations can provide an important complement to cognitive therapy by providing theoretical constructs that permit therapists to broaden their conception of the role of affective processes in psychotherapy. This in turn will set the stage for developing procedures for more accurately assessing clients' affective experiences and for facilitating awareness of previously unattended-to emotions.

CONCLUSIONS

In this chapter, it has been argued that the tradition of cognitive therapy would be enriched by the adoption of certain therapeutic principles and clinical procedures derived from the tradition of interpersonal psychotherapy originated by Sullivan. This does not mean random eclecticism in which therapeutic procedures are borrowed from other therapy traditions without regard to underlying principles but, rather, a systematic theoretical integration between cognitive therapy and interpersonal therapy. Because of the inherently cognitive nature of many Sullivanian formulations, this type of integration is greatly facilitated. Moreover, the basic assumption of a continuous causal loop between expectations, behaviors, and social consequences is held in common by both traditions. This integration should not entail an indiscriminate acceptance of all Sullivanian formulations, but rather a careful examination of the principles and procedures that are most theoretically consistent and therapeutically useful.

The exploration of the interface between Sullivanian theory and cognitive therapy provides an overall theoretical perspective that helps to specify the nature of both cognitive variables and interpersonal behaviors that are important potential targets for therapeutic assessment and modification. Both *self-personifications* and *personifications of others* are cognitive structures that should be focused on in therapy. Both can be conceptualized as cognitive schemas or templates that bias the processing of a variety of different types of information through a process of *selective inattention*. Although this bias may stem in part from a general information-processing style that favors confirmatory evidence (Nisbett and Ross 1980), Sullivan's system holds that *anxiety* may also motivate this process. This assumption has important clinical implications, for it suggests that the therapist must be skilled at monitoring and reducing the client's anxiety level when attempting to facilitate change in his personifications.

The concept of *dynamisms* has been borrowed from Sullivan in this chapter to refer to maladaptive interpersonal behaviors and communications propelled by existing personifications and functioning to perpetuate them. These behaviors constitute another important target for therapeutic intervention. An accurate assessment and skilled utilization of the process of the *therapist–client relationship* can be a fundamental tool for assessing and changing dysfunctional personifications and dynamisms. The therapist must always be cognizant of his role as a *participant-observer* in the therapeutic interaction. The adoption of certain interpersonal principles can provide an illuminating perspective on three important issues currently confronting cognitive therapists: (1) therapeutic compliance, (2) therapeutic generalization and maintenance, and (3) the role of affect in cognitive therapy.

2

Assessing the
Cognitive-Interpersonal Cycle

In Chapter 1, I discussed a number of ways in which Harry Stack Sullivan's conceptions of interpersonal psychotherapy are compatible with the contemporary cognitive behavioral tradition, and I described some specific ways in which the incorporation of principles and practices derived from the Sullivanian tradition would potentially broaden and enrich both the theoretical and practical scope of cognitive behavior therapy. Because the primary objective of that chapter was to bring Sullivan's interpersonal theory to the attention of cognitive therapists and to stimulate an interest in interpersonal conceptualizations, certain aspects of Sullivanian theory were either simplified or neglected.

The first objective of this chapter is to expand upon and clarify certain aspects of Sullivanian theory that were presented in a more simplified fashion in Chapter 1. The second objective is to present a more detailed account of the manner in which interpersonal and cognitive approaches can be interfaced in practice, bearing in mind the clarifications that have been made.

HOT INFORMATION PROCESSING IN THE REAL
WORLD: ANXIETY AND THE DEVELOPMENT
OF THE SELF

While it is true that formulations such as self-personification, personification of others, and selective inattention are essentially "cognitive" in nature, there is an important respect in which these concepts differ from comparable concepts emerging from the social cognition literature. Cognitive information-processing theory, in general, deals with the way in which people process information from the environment in a nonemotional context. It is thus a theory of "cold" information processing. As Folkman and colleagues (1979) and Safran and Greenberg (1982b) have argued, this may limit its applicability to clinical situations. Sullivan, in contrast, is very much concerned with "hot" information processing in an emotional context. In his model, self-schema consistent and inconsistent information receive differential processing, not only as a by-product of a normal information processing confirmatory bias (Nisbett and Ross 1980), but also because inconsistent information arouses anxiety in the individual, who subsequently does whatever he can do to minimize this anxiety and restore his sense of security and self-esteem.

Because this notion is so central to Sullivan's model, I will outline it in greater detail. Sullivan spoke about three aspects of the personified self: the *good me*, the *bad me*, and the *not me*. The *good me* consists of those feelings, psychological experiences, and character-istics that the individual values and feels good about in himself. The *bad me* consists of those feelings and characteristics that the indi-vidual believes to be part of who he is, but that he devalues or feels bad about. The *not me* consists of those feelings and characteristics that the individual views extremely negatively, and that are cogni-tively symbolized as a part of personal experience only in a very primitive, rudimentary, and elementary fashion (Sullivan 1953). For example, an individual may value those aspects of himself that he sees as strong (*good me*), may feel bad about those aspects of himself that he sees as angry (*bad me*), and may not acknowledge to himself that he ever feels weak (*not me*).

According to Sullivan, personifications of the self are learned by the child through interactions with significant others as he develops. Those feelings, experiences, and potential aspects of the self that are viewed positively and are rewarded by significant others become personified as the *good me*. Thus, for an example, a young child who is rewarded by his parents for independent behavior comes to value those aspects of his self that are associated with independence. Those feelings and characteristics that are not valued by significant others, however, also become devalued by the child. They come to be personified as either the *bad me* or the *not me*.

The determining factor here is the degree of anxiety that becomes associated with the feeling or experience. Anxiety is a central explanatory concept in Sullivan's system, and he uses this term in a specialized way to designate all forms of emotional distress related to a loss of self-esteem (Chapman 1978). Anxiety is thus a noxious tension, which is inversely related to the experience of feeling good about oneself. According to Sullivan, the young child experiences anxiety whenever a significant other disapproves of him. Anxiety can also be directly transmitted in social interactions. Thus, for example, the mother who feels tense and anxious when she is breast-feeding her child can transmit the experience of anxiety to the infant. Sullivan maintains that the experience of anxiety obstructs the perception and understanding of experience. Anxiety thus makes it difficult for the individual to accurately perceive and process that which is occurring both around him and within him. When the degree of anxiety that the child experiences in a social interaction is moderate in intensity, the child personifies associated experiences as the *bad me*. He processes these experiences and accepts them as part of the self but views them as bad. When the anxiety becomes extreme, associated psychological experiences cease to become fully personified as part of the self and thus become the *not me*.

In Sullivan's framework, the individual is fundamentally an interpersonal being; therefore, his basic feeling of well-being and security in the world is thus integrally linked to the manner in which he is valued or perceives himself to be valued by other people. As long as he is able to view himself in a manner that is consistent with his personified *good me,* he experiences a sense of self-esteem and security in the world. When, however, this picture of himself is threatened by feelings, thoughts, or feedback that are consistent with the way in which he has come to personify either his *bad me* or his *not me,* the individual experiences anxiety and a loss of self-esteem and security.

The particular character of the experiences that will precipitate anxiety in later years is thus determined by the child's early learning experiences with significant others. According to Sullivan, people are constantly acting to maintain their self-esteem and sense of security and to minimize the experience of anxiety as much as possible. Psychological processes and behaviors that function to maintain the individual's self-esteem and to restore his sense of security when it is threatened are referred to by Sullivan, simply enough, as *security operations.*

One of the major security operations takes place through a process of selective inattention. Experiences that are associated with anxiety are attended to and processed less fully than those that are not. The more intense the anxiety, the less processing the related experience receives. It is this attenuated processing that is responsible for the fact that the *not me* is personified only in a rudimentary fashion.

Selective inattention thus controls the contents of focal awareness. Consistent with contemporary cognitive theory, Sullivan (1953) recognizes that selective inattention has both adaptive and nonadaptive consequences:

> This control of focal awareness results in a combination of fortunate and unfortunate uses of selective inattention. The sensible use is that there is no need of bothering about things that don't matter, things that will go all right anyway. But in many cases there is an unfortunate use of selective inattention, in which one ignores things that do matter; since one has found no way of being secure about them, one excludes them from awareness as long as possible. [p. 233]

It is important to note that Sullivan employed the concept of selective inattention in a fairly broad sense to refer not only to the specific situation in which the individual selectively ignores sensory information from the environment but also to any situation in which the individual fails to draw obvious inferences from either his own or other people's actions. (Sullivan 1953). He also categorized behaviors that function to avoid dealing with anxiety-arousing topics as forms of selective inattention. Examples of such behaviors are changing the topic, becoming confused, and becoming preoccupied with topics that distract from the area associated with anxiety.

In addition to selective inattention, Sullivan spoke about a variety of other security operations, such as avoiding interpersonal situations to minimize anxiety, blaming others or other events for one's problems, actual dissociation (disowning one's experiences), transforming anxiety into other emotions (e.g., experiencing anxiety as anger or apathy), and thinking about and behaving toward others in a critical or derogatory fashion so that one's perception of one's own value becomes enhanced relative to one's perception of the other (Sullivan 1953, 1956).

ANXIETY AND THE THERAPEUTIC PROCESS

Because of these security operations, valuable opportunities for learning new things about the self and others are lost. This has important implications for the therapeutic process, which were alluded to in Chapter 1, but which were not spelled out in detail. The concepts we have been discussing suggest that many dysfunctional belief structures are maintained at least partially by a need to minimize anxiety, and that the process of confronting these beliefs and assumptions in therapy can generate anxiety. In fact, on the basis of Sullivanian theory, one would predict that to the extent that a belief can be modified simply by providing disconfirming evidence, without arousing substantial anxiety, it suggests that the belief may not be central to the person's view of himself or the world.

It is thus important to have some notion of overall cognitive organization, which recognizes that (1) not all belief structures are equally central in the individual's organization of knowledge about himself and the world, (2) those belief structures that are most central will be most difficult to change, and (3) challenging more central belief structures will arouse more anxiety than challenging less important belief structures.

Guidano and Liotti (1983), for example, speak about two types of cognitive changes that can take place in the therapy: "peripheral changes" and "central changes." According to them, "a peripheral change coincides with the reorganization of the client's attitude toward reality within the limits allowed by the maintenance of his or her attitude toward self." In contrast, they view a "central change" as "the modification of the attitude toward oneself that follows the restructuring of personal identity" (p. 97). They argue that although peripheral changes may result in some reduction of distress and improvement in the client's adaptation to his environment, in many cases, changes of this type will be short-lived, or of limited value.

It is thus important to have some way of distinguishing between central and peripheral cognitive structures. Because challenging more central structures is likely to result in more anxiety than challenging peripheral structures, increases in the client's anxiety level and concomitant mobilization of security operations are important to monitor for diagnostic reasons. According to Sullivan (1953), "There is bound to be anxiety, and in fact the anxiety probably serves as pain and tenderness do in a physical diagnosis, being used by the doctor as a guide to the outlining of diseased areas" (p. 120).

In discussing Sullivan's clinical style, White (1952) states: "To Dr. Sullivan, tonal variations in the voice were frequently dependable clues to shifts in the communicative situation. He also was alert for other slight manifestations of anxiety, such as a change of subject, or not comprehending what the analyst has said, or a question that did not bring a response" (p. 123). In *The Psychiatric Interview*, Sullivan (1954) describes a number of other such clues, including peculiar misunderstandings or mistaken interpretations of the interviewer's questions, stereotyped verbal expressions that are not particularly communicative, mannerisms, stereotyped gestures, postural tension, contortions of the face, fatigue, habitual qualification of statements, failure on the client's part to remember what he was talking about, and complete blocking.

For the cognitive therapist, shifts in communication of this type should function as markers to probe for the client's feelings and cognitions immediately preceding the shift. For example, the therapist notices that while he is pursuing a particular line of inquiry, the topic subtly shifts. At this point the therapist might stop the client and say: "I noticed that first we were talking about one thing and then you began to talk about something else. What was going through your head, just before that happened?"

Alternatively, rather than probing for cognitions following a communication shift, the therapist may wish to file the information away and use it to generate hypotheses about the nature of the client's self-personification. For example, the client who becomes confused while discussing anger may personify anger as part of his *bad me.*

Let me be clear at this point that I *am not* making any claim such as "cognitive therapists are not sensitive to their clients' nonverbal behaviors." In fact, I have no doubt that effective cognitive therapists are sensitive to their clients' nonverbal behaviors. What I am stating is that Sullivanian theory suggests that monitoring the client's anxiety level and security operations on an ongoing basis is the essence of good therapy and that its importance cannot be overemphasized. It is also important to emphasize that changes in the communicative situation can be sufficiently subtle to elude easy detection. As I will argue in the next section, it is thus important for therapists to become skilled at monitoring their own feelings and reactions, since they provide important clues regarding the nature of their relationship with clients at any given time. This self-monitoring process thus helps the therapist to generate hypotheses about what the client is experiencing. It should also be emphasized that the therapist must vigilantly monitor himself for security operations that may be masking anxiety. When he does become aware of such anxiety he should ask himself, "What particular interaction of my own sensitivities and my client's behavior are responsible for my anxiety?" As Sullivan (1954) states, "The psychiatrist has an inescapable, inextricable involvement in all that goes on in the interview; and to the extent that he is unconscious or unwitting of his participation in the interview, to that extent he does not know what is happening" (p. 19).

In addition to serving an important diagnostic function, monitoring subtle shifts in the communicative situation provides the therapist with guidelines for modulating his own comments and behavior to avoid needlessly threatening the client's self-esteem and mobilizing his security operations. This is essential because (1) the excessive mobilization of security operations will impede an accurate cognitive assessment, and (2) excessively high levels of anxiety will militate against the possibility of new learning, and changing important dysfunctional cognitive structures. As Sullivan states: "Skill therefore addresses itself to circumventing these security operations without increasing their scope; this amounts to avoiding unnecessary provocation of anxiety without, however, missing data needed for a reasonably correct assessment of the problem" (White 1952, p. 119).

Another useful guideline for circumventing the client's security operations is that an accurate assessment of the client's self-personification on the basis of all the data that have emerged over the course of therapy can help to develop hypotheses about what type of areas are likely to be "secure areas" and what type of areas are likely to be sensitive areas that should be handled with increased tact. Data for this type of assessment can be obtained from biographical information, self-descriptions, statements of beliefs and values, observations of general affective style (e.g., the client who rarely expresses fear is likely to personify the experience of fear as part of his *bad me*), and the observation of areas associated with mobilization of security operations.

Other guidelines for circumventing security operations in therapy can be found in an article by Wachtel (1980), in which he discusses a number of general principles involved in wording comments in a manner that decreases their threat value. For example, the comment "I think you're feeling very angry at me, and the boredom is a cover" has an implicitly accusatory message. In contrast, the statement "I wonder if you're staying silent because you feel that you'd better not say anything if what you're feeling is anger," rather than accusing the client of hiding something, conveys the message that it's all right to be angry, and that if the client is not expressing anger, he is probably doing it for psychologically important reasons.

Making the Cognitive-Interpersonal Link

One of the most effective means the therapist has of assessing the nature of the interpersonal behaviors of the client that are most socially dysfunctional is to monitor his own emotional reactions and behavior tendencies that arise in response to the client. This follows directly from Sullivan's postulate that the therapist is a *participant-observer* in interaction with the client, who will tend to respond to the client in a manner similar to that of other people. It is essential for the therapist to become aware of the client's characteristic interpersonal pull and to unhook himself from the interaction in order to disconfirm the client's dysfunctional expectations about interactions. Kiesler (1982a) has done an excellent job of operationalizing this process, by specifying a number of procedural steps. He argues that in addition to unhooking himself from the interaction with the client, it is useful for the therapist to metacommunicate about the impact that the client has on him. It is important for the therapist to pinpoint for the client, as specifically as possible, the particular client behaviors and communications that create this impact, since increased specificity will maximize the usefulness of the feedback for the client.

Kiesler (1982a) provides the following example of such a communication. Having identified certain client behaviors that seem to be distancing him, the therapist says to his client:

> I realize it's important for you to be cautious and rational in what you do or say to others, and I agree that it is important in many situations. Yet it seems in our sessions you sometimes send messages you don't intend to send as a result of this caution.

For example, you often show long, silent pauses with me after I've said something to you, and frequently a quick smile flashes on and off. Several times when you did that I thought you were really disagreeing with what I was saying, or were thinking my comment was a little stupid. But I found out later that that wasn't the case, that actually you were feeling a little stupid about yourself. . . . I wonder if others might misread you sometimes in the same way, feeling that you are disapproving of them, which is not your intent at all. [p. 289]

Kiesler then adds that by bringing the impact of this behavior to the client's attention, he can help the client to change a behavior that is distancing people in everyday life—in this particular case, by making them feel foolish and irritated.

In addition to pinpointing and providing feedback to the client about the interpersonal impact of dysfunctional behaviors, the process of pinpointing dysfunctional interpersonal behaviors can provide the cognitive therapist with markers indicating the need for cognitive exploration. A central tenet of a truly *cognitive-interpersonal* perspective is that cognitive activities, interpersonal behaviors, and repetitive interactional or *me–you patterns* are linked together and maintain one another in an unbroken causal loop, which will be referred to here as the *cognitive-interpersonal cycle*. The assessment of any one aspect of this cycle facilitates the assessment of the remaining aspects. Thus, as I will illustrate, the correct identification of important dysfunctional behaviors paves the way for the exploration of associated cognitive activity. Conversely, the identification of important automatic thoughts can facilitate the further identification of maladaptive security operations and interpersonal behaviors. The possibility of effective therapeutic intervention is maximized when all aspects of the cycle have been thoroughly assessed. It is thus important for the clinician to thoroughly assess the type of cognitive activity that gives rise to or supports the pinpointed dysfunctional interpersonal behavior on a long-lasting basis, because it may be difficult to modify the behavior if he does not concurrently modify the cognitive activity that supports it.

In the above illustration, for example, the therapist who has

pinpointed the behavior that has the negative impact could inter-
rupt the interaction the moment the client becomes silent and
smiles, and say: "I'm aware that when I asked you that question, a
smile flashed on and off your face, very quickly. What was going
through your mind when that happened?" If the client is not
immediately aware of the relevant cognitive activity, the therapist
can have the client intentionally engage in the relevant behavior, in
order to provide himself with behavioral cues that may trigger the
associated cognitions. In the above situation, if the client appears to
be registering disapproval or condescension on his face, it is
probable that some aspect of his cognitive activity corresponds to his
communicative behavior. In other words, it is unlikely that experiencing a sense of foolishness has arbitrarily become paired with
looking scornful.

In terms of the Sullivanian framework, which was discussed
earlier, one hypothesis would be that the client does indeed
experience a scornful feeling toward the therapist, but that this is at
least in part a security operation, which functions to raise the client's
self-esteem when he feels foolish. The best way to evaluate the
veracity of such a hypothesis is to explore the client's cognitive
processes in collaboration with the client, in as nonthreatening a
fashion as possible.

Once the therapist has conducted a comprehensive assessment
of the dysfunctional cognitive activity that is linked to the relevant
dysfunctional interpersonal behavior, he can begin to modify this
cognitive activity at the same time that he is giving feedback about
the impact of the dysfunctional behavior, and remaining unhooked
from the dysfunctional interactional pattern.

In this particular case, it would be vital for the therapist to
access the client's feelings of being foolish, and related automatic
self-defeating thoughts, before he could begin challenging them. It
is important to emphasize that these cognitions might not emerge
without the therapist first taking the intermediate step of exploring
and listening to the client's scornful and disapproving thoughts and
feelings in an accepting fashion. This is because acknowledging
automatic thoughts related to the feeling of being foolish may
initially be too anxiety-provoking for the client. The process of

listening and accepting the client's scornful thoughts, however, helps him to feel secure enough to begin exploring feelings and cognitions that are associated with his *bad me*.

Before proceeding to a second example, let me briefly summarize and amplify upon the steps involved in assessing the cognitive-interpersonal cycle.

1. The therapist explicitly identifies the characteristic feelings and responses that the client evokes in him.
2. The therapist explicitly identifies the particular client behaviors and/or communications that evoke these responses. It is important to remember here that, as Kiesler (1982a) has noted, many of these behaviors or communications can occur on a nonverbal or paralinguistic level (e.g., a client evokes feelings of protectiveness in the therapist when he speaks in a soft, fragile-sounding voice).
3. Once the therapist has identified the relevant behaviors in the client, the therapist begins to explore automatic thoughts that accompany or precede the behaviors. It is important to probe for automatic thoughts as close as possible in time to the appearance of the relevant behavior, because this is when they will be most easily accessible.
4. Once some of the automatic thoughts and beliefs have been identified, the therapist can assign a variety of different homework tasks. These assignments serve the dual function of heightening the client's awareness of what particular behaviors are problematic for him, as well as gradually increasing his awareness of the dysfunctional cognitions that are linked to these behaviors.

One type of assignment consists of monitoring the behaviors that have been pinpointed and using their occurrence as a cue to begin monitoring cognitions. This can help the client to conduct a more detailed assessment of the relevant cognitive activity. A second assignment consists of intentionally engaging in the pinpointed behaviors and then observing what type of automatic thoughts tend to be linked to these behaviors. This assignment is particularly useful when the client has difficulty monitoring the dysfunctional behavior, and it functions as well to help the client gain some sense of control over the behavior. A third assignment consists of monitoring the automatic thoughts that have been identified in therapy, and then observing what types of behaviors are linked to them. In addition to heightening the client's awareness of the link between the pinpointed behaviors and the relevant automatic thoughts, this third intervention can serve the function of helping him to identify other me–you patterns that may not have been pinpointed in therapy but may nevertheless be problematic. Once the client has a clear sense of what the dysfunctional beliefs and automatic thoughts are, as well as what the dysfunctional behaviors are, he can begin to challenge his cognitions and modify his behaviors at the same time.

The following case will illustrate the implementation of these steps. A 35-year-old man presented in therapy with feelings of general dysphoria and dissatisfaction with life. In the first session, the therapist was aware of a general feeling of confusion and frustration in himself but was unable to identify the cause. In the second session, the therapist experienced the same feelings as well as a growing sense of irritation with, and distance from, the client. He was able to pinpoint the fact that his feelings of frustration, confusion, and distance seemed to be related to his client's style of continuously sidetracking the conversation, thus making it difficult to stay on any one topic. The therapist then discussed the impact that the sidetracking had upon him in a nonthreatening fashion and related it to the way in which other people seemed to maintain a distance from his client. This was then related to his client's feelings of loneliness and isolation.

The therapist then waited for the next incident of sidetracking in the interview, and at that point began probing for feelings and thoughts that his client was experiencing. His client indicated that he was experiencing some anxiety. In response to the therapist's continued probing, the client indicated that he was afraid that the therapist might get too close to him. The therapist asked his client what he imagined the therapist would think of him if he got closer. The client replied that he imagined the therapist would think that he was "weak" and that he was "a baby." He also imagined that if he discussed his real feelings, the therapist would be bored and wouldn't listen.

The therapist continued to probe for automatic thoughts and in this manner was able to access a variety of specific fears and automatic thoughts that were associated with his client's sidetracking behavior. In addition, he was also able to explore a number of aspects of his client's self-personification. It emerged that his client personified any feelings of weakness or vulnerability as part of his *bad me*. He believed that it was essential for him to always be reasonable, strong, and in control of himself and the situation. At the end of the session, the therapist assigned his client the task of monitoring his sidetracking behavior and associated thoughts over the week.

When the client returned the following week, he had been very successful at monitoring his cognitions. The session was spent exploring the emotional impact that these cognitions had upon him and identifying the situations in which these cognitions were most likely to occur. At the end of the session, the therapist assigned the client the task of monitoring the identified cognitions and observing the corresponding behaviors, using the common precipitating situations that had been identified as cues. When he returned to therapy the following week, the client reported that he was distancing people not only by sidetracking but also by speaking in a very formal voice.

This case provides a second illustration of the manner in which the cognitive therapist can interface the process of metacommunicating with the client about his dysfunctional me–you patterns with exploring the cognitive processes that are linked to and support those patterns. There are a number of observations worth making about this illustration:

1. If the therapist had not used his own feelings and action tendencies diagnostically, he may not have pinpointed a me–you pattern, which turned out to be a major problem for his client.
2. If the therapist had not metacommunicated with his client about this pattern and unhooked himself, he would have

confirmed his client's negative expectations that people would find him boring and uninteresting, and would reject him.

3. If the therapist had not explored the cognitive processes that were linked to the me–you pattern, the fears that supported them would still persist, thus making it more difficult to change them.

4. If the therapist had not used the pinpointed me–you pattern as a point of departure for cognitive assessment, he might have had difficulty assessing some very important automatic thoughts. This is true both because the behavior was creating an obstacle to the cognitive assessment process and because the relevant cognitive processes were most readily accessible when the client was sidetracking.

CONCLUSIONS

In summary, I have argued that a full assessment in the context of a cognitive-interpersonal therapy requires that the therapist conduct a comprehensive exploration of both the specific interpersonal behaviors and me–you patterns that impair the client's interpersonal relations, and the particular cognitive activities that are linked to them. The assessment of this cognitive-interpersonal cycle must be conducted in full awareness of the fact that cognitive information-processing activity in the real world is "hot cognition" and that the therapist must use his skills to, in Sullivan's terms, circumvent the client's security operations, in order to obtain the relevant data.

As Sullivan (1954) stated in his inimitable way:

Anyone who proceeds without consideration for the disjunctive power of anxiety in human relationships will never learn interviewing. When there is no regard for anxiety, a true interview situations does not exist; instead there may be just a person (the client) trying to defend himself frantically from some kind of devil (the therapist) who seems determined (as the client experiences it) to prove that the person (the client) is a double dyed blankety-blank. This can be a spectacular human performance, but it does not yield psychiatric data relevant to therapeutic progress. [p. 108]

A final point I have made is that the assessment of any one aspect of the cognitive-interpersonal cycle can facilitate the assessment of other aspects. Thus, the explicit identification of subtle, but nevertheless dysfunctional, behaviors and paralinguistic communications can facilitate the exploration of associated cognitive activity. Conversely, the identification of important automatic thoughts can facilitate the discovery and exploration of recurring dysfunctional interactional patterns that are linked to them. For this reason it is valuable for the therapist to be guided in case conceptualization by the recognition of the complete interdependence of cognitive and interpersonal realms.

In attempting to clarify some aspects of Sullivan's system that were presented in a more simplified fashion in Chapter 1, I am all too aware that I may have neglected other aspects of the system that are just as important. In particular, I am concerned that some of the cognitive implications of Sullivan's theorizing may have been emphasized at the expense of some of the more interpersonal aspects of his work. My hope is that Sullivan himself would feel that these aspects, although perhaps somewhat neglected, are not entirely forgotten, and that in his view, the unfortunate consequences of my selective inattention would not outweigh the fortunate consequences.

3

Assessing Core Cognitive Processes in Cognitive Therapy

Jeremy D. Safran, T. Michael Vallis,
Zindel V. Segal, and Brian F. Shaw

In the course of therapy the cognitive therapist works to identify, explore, and intervene with a variety of client ideation. As a result, therapists are frequently in a position of having to select specific cognitive targets from among several alternatives. In this paper we consolidate relevant theory and research and propose technical guidelines to facilitate the selection of intervention targets. The central thesis of this paper can be stated as follows: Certain cognitive variables are more central to the client's problems than others, and for this reason the process of identifying these variables is vital. This process is facilitated by an understanding of the way in which cognitive processes are organized and structured.

The idea of choosing appropriate cognitive targets for intervention on the basis of an adequate case conceptualization is not a novel one (e.g., Beck et al. 1979). Nevertheless, our experience in training therapists has convinced us that many cognitive therapists, particularly when learning the approach, have considerable difficulty choosing appropriate cognitive targets for intervention and would benefit from a clear articulation of relevant theory and guidelines.

We will begin with a brief review of the relevant theoretical literature. We will then attempt to integrate this theory with a number of theoretical considerations that we consider relevant to the practice of cognitive therapy. Following this we will articulate a number of technical guidelines to facilitate the selection of cognitive targets. In the final section, we will review relevant research and suggest future research directions.

RELEVANT LITERATURE

A number of cognitive behavioral therapists have begun to distinguish what can be referred to as *core* or *central* from *peripheral* cognitive processes. Mahoney (1982), for example, argues that cognitive processes are hierarchically structured. According to him, higher-level cognitive processes can be thought of as tacit organizational principles that shape lower-level cognitive processes. Mahoney maintains that these higher-level processes can be thought of as more core or central with respect to overall cognitive organization, and that core cognitive processes are more difficult to change than peripheral cognitive processes. He hypothesizes that this resistance to change may be due to their chronological primacy in the development sequence.

Guidano and Liotti (1983) also distinguish between central and peripheral cognitive changes. They maintain that beliefs vary with respect to how central they are to the individual's overall cognitive organization. Real and durable therapeutic changes are said to result from the modification of central beliefs. Modification of peripheral beliefs may result in a temporary reduction of distress but not in durable change. According to Guidano and Liotti, central beliefs are those pertaining to the self. Deep change (i.e., significant change that is maintained) results from a change in attitude toward the self. Such change is obtained through the development of new rules that determine one's self-worth. Peripheral beliefs are not directly connected with the experience of the self. They do not reflect an individual's self-knowledge or the tacit rules that guide one's experience of oneself.

More recently, Meichenbaum and Gilmore (1984) have proposed the existence of superordinate cognitive structures that they refer to as "core organizing principles." These core organizing principles are conceptualized as hypothetical constructs that are useful for purposes of understanding coherence and thematic unity in an individual's thoughts, feelings, and behavior. According to Meichenbaum and Gilmore, these principles often operate at a tacit level and must therefore be inferred on the basis of consistency in emotional or behavioral responses to specific types of situations. Core organizing principles are thus distinguished from other cognitive structures by virtue of their predictive utility in understanding an individual's emotional and behavioral responses across a range of situations.

It is interesting (if not humbling) to note that the articulated distinction in cognitive behavioral theory between core and peripheral cognitive processes was anticipated by George Kelly by approximately two decades. According to Kelly (1955): "Core constructs are those which govern a person's maintenance processes—that is, those by which he maintains his identity and existence" (p. 482). In other words, core constructs are those that are related to the individual's basic identity in the world or fundamental sense of self. Kelly defines peripheral constructs by default as "those which can be altered without serious modifications of core structure" (p. 483).

Kelly's organizational corollary states: "Each person characteristically evolves for his convenience in anticipating events, a construction system embracing ordinal relationships between constructs" (p. 56). He believed that cognitive structures are organized in a hierarchical fashion such that lower-order or subordinate structures are subsumed by superordinate structures that are more central or core in nature. For example, the dimension of good/bad may be superordinate to and subsume the dimension of intelligent/stupid, which may in turn be superordinate to another construct. This type of hierarchical organization has important implications for therapeutic change because any modification of a subordinate construct will not be disruptive to the entire system. In contrast, a cognitive change in a superordinate construct will be more disruptive to the overall construct system because it implicates changes in constructs subordinate to it.

The primary motivating variable in Kelly's system is the need to construe and interpret events adequately. According to Kelly, "Anxiety is the recognition that the events with which one is confronted lie outside the range of convenience of one's construct system" (p. 495). Individuals experience anxiety when they feel that their currently operating constructs or cognitive structures do not permit them to interpret and anticipate events adequately. Because anxiety represents the awareness that one's construct system does not adequately reflect the events at hand, it is a precondition for revising one's belief system. If anxiety becomes too intense, however, cognitive reorganization cannot take place. The individual faced with the prospect of modifying a core, relatively superordinate construct may maintain the status quo rather than risk disrupting the overall system and experiencing intense anxiety.

In contrast, peripheral constructs can be modified without changing other peripheral constructs, or those that are more central and superordinate to them. Challenging peripheral constructs thus does not precipitate as much anxiety as the modification of core constructs. While peripheral constructs can be changed without the immediate availability of alternative constructs to replace them, it is essential to have alternative constructs available before core constructs can be modified. The availability of alternative constructs reduces the anxiety level and makes change possible.

Finally, Kelly maintains that the therapist can never assume in advance that a particular cognitive structure is either central or peripheral. A construct or belief that initially appears to be peripheral may subsequently emerge as central for an individual. As Neimeyer (1985) asserts, Kelly's personal construct theory, while offering a less well-developed model of specific cognitive events than cognitive behavioral theory, offers a correspondingly more elaborate model of cognitive structure. In subsequent sections of this chapter we will explore some of the implications of integrating this type of idiographic perspective with the practice of cognitive therapy.

This brief review suggests that it may be clinically useful to adopt the perspective that cognitive processes vary with respect to how central or peripheral they are. To summarize the major principles articulated thus far: (1) core cognitive processes are related to the definition and experience of the self in some fundamental way, (2) peripheral cognitive processes are subsumed by, or derived out of, core cognitive processes, (3) core cognitive processes can be distinguished by their ability to predict an individual's emotional and behavioral responses to a wide range of situations, and (4) an attempt to modify core cognitive processes is likely to evoke more anxiety than the modification of peripheral cognitive processes. In the next section we will attempt to integrate the principles with considerations relevant to the practice of cognitive therapy.

INTEGRATION AND CONCEPTUALIZATION

A clarification of cognitive behavioral terms may be useful at this point. We will refer to two levels of dysfunctional cognitive processes in this chapter: automatic thoughts and dysfunctional attitudes. Automatic thoughts are the directly accessible cognitive material that reflects the client's ongoing negative self-evaluation. These thoughts occur almost instantaneously and are habitual and plausible to the individual. Such evaluation is an ongoing process in which constituent elements such as past memories, present perceptions, and related affect combine to construct a sense of self in the present. The self can thus be seen as a process rather than as a stable or concrete entity. Therapeutic change consists of helping the client to become aware of how he or she is constructing the self in the moment and then helping to change this process of construction.

Dysfunctional attitudes are tacit, higher-level rules that are abstracted to describe the principles guiding the client's self-evaluation. Dysfunctional attitudes are less directly accessible than automatic thoughts. They are maladaptive, higher-level or organizational principles that must be inferred on the basis of conscious cognitive activity and observable behavior.

In order to clarify any potential confusion at this point, let us make it clear that we are not equating automatic thoughts with peripheral cognitive processes and dysfunctional attitudes with core cognitive processes. Automatic thoughts can be thought of as the surface-level manifestation of dysfunctional attitudes. These underlying attitudes themselves, however, vary with respect to how central they are to the individual's overall cognitive organization.

In our experience, therapists who are learning cognitive therapy often become enamored with technical interventions for changing thoughts, while the importance of conceptualizing the client's thinking from an organizational/hierarchical perspective is overlooked. There is a tendency for therapists to target easily accessible automatic thoughts or dysfunctional attitudes for intervention, without progressing to more central or core issues. Novice therapists often work to identify the specific content of negative thoughts surrounding an upsetting situation and apply specific interventions such as identifying distortions associated with these thoughts. As therapy progresses in this fashion, symptomatic change occurs, but core beliefs are not necessarily addressed. What seems to be missing in these cases is a plan, based on a conceptualization of core cognitive processes.

In some cases the failure to assess core cognitive processes adequately can result in treatment failure. Liotti (1984), for example, provides the illustration of the therapist who errs by treating an agoraphobic client with relaxation procedures, without realizing that one of the client's core beliefs is that he must always be in control, and without realizing that the relaxation procedure is seen as a threat to that control.

The assessment of core cognitive processes involves a process of accessing a constellation of automatic thoughts that are associatively linked for the individual and subsequently inferring the tacit rules that guide this self-evaluative process. For example, one depressed client typically accessed the following constellation of automatic thoughts when she became upset: "This is awful, I can't cope, I'm out of control." The tacit rule or assumption implied in this constellation was: "If I am not always strong and in control then others won't respect me." In therapy it emerged that a wide variety of events (some of which were topographically dissimilar) readily elicited this same constellation of automatic thoughts from her. It was not uncommon for this client to be self-critical in other ways as well (e.g., "I'm stupid, I'm unattractive, I'm incompetent"). The constellation of automatic thoughts that was activated most commonly for this woman and that appeared to be associated with the greatest degree of emotional distress once activated, however, related to the "in control" issue. The assessment of core cognitive processes thus requires that the therapist attend to patterns and thematic redundancies in the client's automatic thoughts. This process necessitates an evaluation not only of the primary dimensions of the client's self-evaluation but also of the dimensions that are most problematic for the individual.

Careful assessment is thus required to access a core constellation of automatic thoughts that will provide both the therapist and the client with clues as to the tacit rules associated with this constellation. It is vital that the therapist work out, in collaboration with the client, the specific rules implicit in self-evaluation. This very process of working with the client to make tacit rules explicit is an important part of the therapeutic process in that it helps the client begin to develop a metaperspective on the biases in his/her information-processing activity. It is important therapeutically for the client to have a concrete, meaningful understanding of how these two are linked. The first step in targeting core cognitive processes is to conduct a comprehensive assessment of an individual's negative self-evaluative activity and higher-level constructs.

The position we are advocating here can be contrasted with cognitive frameworks such as self-statement modification (Meichenbaum 1977). In our view, the assumption that all negative automatic thoughts have equal salience and import, and can simply be replaced by a more adaptive internal monologue, is ill-founded. Dealing with automatic thoughts in a random or isolated fashion may provide some momentary relief for the depressed or anxious client. We hypothesize, however, that lasting change more likely derives from fully assessing and modifying the central, idiosyncratic constellation of negative automatic thoughts and associated assumptions.

The approach we are describing here can also be contrasted with Ellis's (Ellis and Greiger 1977) approach. Although it might be argued that Ellis works at the level of core constructs by challenging irrational beliefs, his approach does not involve an exploration of the higher-level constructs in terms that are idiosyncratic for each client (cf. Neimeyer 1985). The approach we are suggesting here involves the modification and reorganization of fundamental beliefs through a process of gradually and systematically inferring core beliefs on the basis of their surface manifestations (i.e., automatic thoughts) and then altering or reorganizing these core belief structures by empirically evaluating their surface manifestations and then tying these surface referents back to the core beliefs.

Horizontal versus Vertical Exploration

In therapy sessions cognitive therapists work to elicit the client's perception of situations. Therapists are encouraged to probe for the meaning and implication of events upsetting to the client. This process of exploration can be categorized into two types. The first type of exploration, *horizontal exploration*, involves a survey or exploration of a variety of automatic thoughts without reference to the degree of centrality for the person. The objective is to sample a range of automatic thoughts relevant to a specific situation. In this way therapists can gain useful information but may or may not identify core cognitive processes. Horizontal exploration is useful for showing the client the relationship between mood and automatic thoughts and for conducting a general survey of the range of negative thinking relevant to a given situation. *Vertical exploration*, on the other hand, involves helping the client to articulate his or her automatic thoughts with specific attention to the central-peripheral dimension. In response to a particular negative automatic thought, the therapist pursues the meaning of the event vis-à-vis the self.

Vertical assessment involves a detailed assessment of the individual's idiosyncratic way of construing events and the individual's perception of the self. The reason we continue to explore rather than challenge the early automatic thoughts is that we want to assess the individual's negative self-evaluative activity in its totality. It is assumed that this method of inquiry will lead to an understanding of the more central, higher-level constructs or assumptions. For example, a client who failed an exam at a university accessed the automatic thought: "I can't handle university." At this point the therapist could have challenged this belief or encouraged the client to examine evidence relevant to this belief. Instead she decided to engage in a process of vertical exploration. In response to the therapist's probes, a constellation of automatic thoughts emerged that revolved around the client's beliefs that he was not smart enough. The client at this point spontaneously recalled two memories of situations in which he had felt humiliated and worthless because he felt he had "been stupid" at the time. As he recounted these memories, he became visibly more emotional. Further exploration revealed that these feelings of intellectual inferiority and associated feelings of worthlessness cut across a number of problem situations for the client. It also emerged that he believed that his value as a person was completely dependent upon his intellectual performance. In this situation had the therapist intervened when the first automatic thought emerged, she may not have accessed the entire chain of self-evaluative cognition and higher-level constructs that underlay the client's distress.

To further illustrate the relevant issues, consider the following example. The client is a 25-year-old male who is being treated with cognitive therapy for depression, apathy, and chronic procrastination. He has been considering applying for admission to a university but has been blocked in this respect by his chronic procrastination. In the session from which the segments are extracted the therapist works with the client to identify the core cognitive processes associated with procrastination. The client begins by telling the therapist that he had intended to arrange to have his transcripts forwarded to the university the previous day. He indicates that he lay in bed thinking of telephoning the transcript office but was unable to mobilize himself to do so. The therapist asks him if he recalls how he was feeling at the time and to describe any relevant thoughts or images.

C: I see a picture of some of the people that I have to contact to try to get something moving on this, and I see them hating me. They see me as a nuisance.

T: Uh huh. Can you actually visualize those people?

C: I can see, I can see a face of one woman that I have to deal with, yeah. Yeah. Oh yeah, I can see her, yeah. You know.

T: Uh huh. OK. So you can hear her and her reaction. She's thinking you're a nuisance.

C: Uh huh, yeah.

T: Yes . . .

C: That I'm sort of, just a troublemaker, a sort of punk trying to stir up trouble, and that there's this—"Sorry you've got your answer and that's all there is to it." That's her reaction.

T: Uh huh.

C: And that she's sort of actually conniving in case I should manage to get to someone higher up than her. She's gonna connive. I mean it's a ridiculous fear I suppose . . .

At this point note that the client spontaneously begins to challenge or invalidate his own subjective construal. A possible intervention would consist of encouraging the client to continue challenging his unrealistic fantasy. Instead, the therapist intervenes to prevent the client from prematurely invalidating his own subjective construal and to continue accessing information relevant to a more comprehensive assessment of his core cognitive processes.

T: But very real for you.

C: Yeah, very real. Yeah.

T: OK. So, here's this woman and . . . you're very good with imagery, I think . . . you're able to get an image of her, of this woman. She's conniving . . .

C: Uh huh, right. (Client laughs.)

T: You laugh right now but it's real . . . right?

C: Yeah, real for me. Yeah.

T: She sees you as being kind of a punk.

C: Ha ha, yeah. Yeah. (Client laughs.)

T: And again, you laugh a little bit. It seems . . . what—a little . . . ?

C: Yeah, it's funny when I hear things that I say, read back to me.

T: Uh huh.

C: Why do I laugh there? Hmm. Because it really . . . when I hear it from you, it isn't accurate. She's not like that. She wouldn't think of me as a punk at all, but then yet, then yet, from another point of view when I say it, it's really what I mean.

T: Uh huh.

C: Peculiar.

T: Yes. It's very real for you at the time, right?

C: Yeah. Yeah.

T: And then somehow or other when you hear me say it, you kind of step outside, very quickly.

C: Yeah, yeah, and just. "Oh, that's ridiculous," you know.

T: Uh huh.

C: "Of course she doesn't see me as a punk, you know."

Once again, the client begins to question the reasonableness of his subjective construal. The therapist brings this to the client's attention and encourages him to suspend his critical judgment for the moment, in order to obtain a more comprehensive assessment.

T: Uh huh. So before you step outside—

C: Yeah . . .

T: Because I think you're very good at that . . . I'm going to ask you to try and just stay with the, you know, your subjective experience for a while, OK?

C: Got ya.

T: OK. So here's this woman, you kind of look at her, umh, and you know, you have thoughts like, "She's going to think that I'm a punk and I'm trying to create trouble." Can you elaborate on that imagery at all?

C: Hmm hmm, hmm hmm—Well I can't really elaborate on the image but on the action . . . like I'm lying here in bed and the thought occurs to me, "This is what I've got to do. I've got to phone this woman," ah—It's funny, after describing all this, suddenly it doesn't seem as surprising to me, that what happens is that I stay in bed for another hour.

At this point the client begins to see the impact of his subjective construal process on his emotions and behavior. By continuing the process of assessment, rather than prematurely intervening, the therapist is helping the client to gain a tangible appreciation of the role of his own cognitive activity in shaping his experience. This enriches the therapist's understanding of the relevant cognitive processes and contributes to the process of decentering.

T: So you have a somewhat better idea of what's going on in your head now.
C: Yeah. I can see when I was lying there in bed thinking . . . "I should call the transcript office," the other part of me was saying "no way . . . I'm not going to call that woman."
T: Can you make a case for not talking to that woman?
C: You bet I can!

At this point the client proceeds to elaborate upon his automatic thoughts and catastrophic images in a less inhibited way. He articulates an elaborate fantasy in which the clerk threatens to send the wrong transcripts to the university. He describes feelings of complete helplessness and powerlessness in the face of her threats. Then the client continues:

C: And suddenly, it's like I'm wrong and she's in the right. I can imagine her saying "I'm going to call the principal." And it's like I've got to hang up and run and hide.
T: So it's as if you're a powerless child who's done something wrong.
C: Yeah. I'm in the wrong. And I'm gonna get squashed like a bug. And I have no defense, no defense at all.

Here the client begins to more fully access negative self-referent ideation. The vividly metaphorical statement "I'm gonna get squashed like a bug" testifies to the emotional immediateness of the material for the client. The therapist has now accessed a constellation of automatic thoughts and images that revolve around a fundamental perception of the self as a powerless child victimized by powerful and malicious adult figures.

In the next session the therapist worked with the client to explicate dysfunctional attitudes or tacit rules that were linked to the cognitive constellation that had emerged. Relevant tacit rules that emerged might be stated in simplified form as: "It is essential for me to have other people's approval," and "I must not show it if I am angry with others." However, it is only within the context of the detailed assessment of the client's subjective construal process that the idiosyncratic flavor of these rules is revealed. For him, it is essential to have other people's approval because he sees himself as a powerless child. It is dangerous for him to express his anger because he fears retaliation by malicious, larger-than-life adversaries. The abstracted dysfunctional attitudes thus take on their full meaning only in context of the whole core cognitive constellation in which they are embedded.

In subsequent sessions the therapist was able to work with the client to successfully challenge various aspects of this constellation using standard cognitive behavioral interventions. Once the entire constellation of negative automatic thoughts and associated assumptions has been explored, the therapist may choose to intervene by testing or challenging any given aspect of the constellation. If this is done in the context of the comprehensive type of exploration we have just discussed, we hypothesize that there is greater potential for change. If the client has explored and made explicit for himself the entire cognitive affective chain and associated higher-level constructs, the process of shifting his perspective or reevaluating one aspect of the constellation helps him to see the potential modifiability of the rest of the chain. For example, in the previous illustration, once the detailed exploration of core cognitive processes has taken place, challenging the client's fears of retaliation can help him to modify his perception of himself as a powerless child. Any given aspect of the entire cognitive constellation is thus embedded within the context of an entire web of meaning. If this web of meaning is clearly articulated, the process of challenging one element can help to loosen associated constructs.

In contrast to the above approach, an intervention that consists of simply challenging one automatic thought in isolation may not help the individual to revise or critically evaluate basic, more fundamental constructs or assumptions. Moreover, the therapist who intervenes prematurely (i.e., focuses on a peripheral automatic thought) will not obtain information that is vital for the true understanding of the nature of the construct system that underlies any particular automatic thought.

While the adequate assessment of core cognitive processes is an important part of good cognitive therapy, we do not believe that the therapist must always intervene by explicitly challenging dysfunctional attitudes, nor do we suggest that a therapist should challenge an automatic thought only if he or she believes that it is linked to a core or central dysfunctional belief. It is possible, for example, that effectively challenging an automatic thought may facilitate the process of decentering or recognizing that one plays an active role in constructing reality, even if that automatic thought is relatively peripheral in nature. What we *are* advocating, however, is the notion of informed intervention. Guided by an understanding of the core constructs and assumptions for a particular client, the therapist can more effectively intervene at whatever level seems appropriate at a given point in a session.

Guidelines for Targeting Core Cognitive Processes

In this session we will systematically articulate some of the guidelines that are implicit in the theoretical discussion and clinical illustrations presented above.

Self-Referent Cognitions. The first theoretical guideline suggested by a number of authors (Guidano and Liotti 1983, Raimy 1975) is that core cognitive processes tend to be related to the self. In other words, the cognitive processes of greatest importance in cognitive therapy are those that involve some evaluation of the self or that evaluate the impact of an event on the perception of self. This does not mean that distortions in the processing of information about the self are the only important distortions in Beck's (1976) negative cognitive triad. What it does mean is that from a clinical perspective both dysfunctional expectations about the future and distorted processing of current experiencing should ultimately be evaluated in terms of their impact upon self-perception.

In terms of specific guidelines for the practicing cognitive therapist, we suggest that automatic thoughts or dysfunctional assumptions that are not self-referent in nature are less likely to be central than those that are self-referent in nature. It may be useful for the therapist to engage in a process of vertical exploration with the objective of accessing the underlying, more central cognition. For example, a therapist who was working with a client who was troubled by severe heterosocial anxiety was engaged in the process of exploring the automatic thoughts his client had in the context of telephoning a woman to ask her for a date. In response to the therapist's probe, the client reported the automatic thought, "She'll reject me, and think that I'm a fool." At this point, guided by the self-reference principle, the therapist engaged in a process of vertical exploration. The therapist asked a series of questions designed to ascertain the meaning of this predicted event for the client vis-à-vis his self-perception (e.g., "What does this mean about you as a person?"). In response to these probes, the client accessed the following series of thoughts: "She will find me unattractive," "I will never meet a nice woman," "I'm unlovable." In contrast to the first set of automatic thoughts that emerged, the therapist might have probed for a list of automatic thoughts, regardless of the principles of vertical exploration and self-reference. In this case the client might have reported the following thought: "Women are all cold and rejecting." While the therapist could conceivably have intervened by encouraging the client to examine evidence relevant to this belief, we hypothesize that the client's negative self-perception was more central and thus more pivotal to the change process.

Common Themes. Certain important common themes have been observed to arise across a variety of types of clients. It is presumably in recognition of this that therapists such as Ellis have attempted to enumerate commonly held irrational beliefs. Major common themes identified by Ellis in his work are concerned with issues of lovability and competence (e.g., "Without the love and respect of others, I am worthless," and "I must be competent at everything I do").

Beck and his associates (e.g., Beck 1983) hypothesize that there are two major types of dysfunctional attitudes characteristic of depressive individuals. According to them, individuals whom they refer to as sociotropic base their self-worth on the love and respect demonstrated by others. These individuals tend to be oriented to the interpersonal domain. In contrast, individuals who are designated as autonomous are thought to base their self-worth on achievement and thus are oriented to accomplishments. We believe that it can be useful for the therapist to bear in mind that concerns related to personal lovability and competence are common for people and to keep these themes in mind during the assessment process. Moreover, studies that attempt to empirically establish the attitudes that are central in the cognitive organization of particular client types can be useful (e.g., Reda 1984). However, while information acquired in a nomothetic fashion can help the therapist decide where to begin looking when assessing for core cognitive processes, it is vital that he approach every client in an idiographic fashion.

Cross-Situational Consistency. The self-evaluative cognitions that are important to focus on with any particular client are likely to be consistent across situations. It is important, therefore, for the therapist to observe patterns or regularities in the client's automatic thoughts or dysfunctional attitudes. Similarly, the therapist should be alert to consistencies in the types of situations or events that distress the client. These consistencies are useful clues for the identification of central cognitions. For example, if a client is frequently upset by certain interpersonal interactions, one might hypothesize that this individual bases her self-worth in part on being positively evaluated by others.

Once the therapist has formed a hypothesis about the themes of the automatic thoughts reported by the client, the therapist should look for disconfirmatory, as well as confirmatory, evidence that the theme is characteristic of the client. If a given automatic thought is consistent across several situations, this would serve to confirm the therapist's hypothesis. Cognitions that are highly characteristic of an individual's self-evaluative thinking are more productive targets than others.

Process Markers versus Content Markers. All the guidelines for targeting core cognitions that we have discussed so far have focused on *what* the client reports. Another means of targeting core cognitions is to pay attention to *how* the client speaks about his or her experience. Safran and Greenberg (1982a,b), for example, have discussed the importance of accessing "hot cognitions" or emotionally laden thought rather than "cold cognitions." It is important to access hot cognitions in therapy because the more important cognitive processes may be accessible only in the affective state that is characteristic of the client when he or she is experiencing problems (Greenberg and Safran 1984b). This hypothesis is consistent with Bower's (1981) findings that the accessibility of cognitions is mood-dependent. The work of Teasdale (e.g., Teasdale and Fogarty 1979) on the effects of manipulated mood on the recall of affect-consistent words also corroborates this hypothesis. Similarly, Beck et al. (1979) have stated that it is important for the therapist to be sensitive to affective shifts during a session. These shifts are thought to be valuable markers of important cognitive activity. The observation that an automatic thought appears to be "hot" is useful because a change in affect may indicate that the associated cognition is important to the client. The affective reaction may be due to the fact that one has tapped into an associative network of related memories, images, and emotions (Greenberg and Safran 1986a, Lang 1985, Lang et al. 1983, Safran and Greenberg 1986).

Learning from Ineffective Strategies. The therapist's conceptualization of the case evolves as a trial-and-error process. It is essential that the therapist be prepared to modify his or her understanding of the client's cognitive organization as a function of experience. It is not at all uncommon in cognitive therapy for the specific intervention strategy employed by the therapist to be ineffective. When techniques fail, important information concerning core cognitive processes might be available. Attempting to identify the reasons why a given strategy did not work can be an aid to gaining an understanding of core beliefs that might underlie the person's distress.

Consider the following example:

> A 45-year-old male client with compulsive personality features and an emotionally overcontrolled style habitually felt agitated and irritated with other people. The therapist discerned a common theme in which the client became upset when, in his perception, people "took him for granted" and left him emotionally "short-changed." After an initial assessment, the therapist hypothesized that core cognitive processes for this man revolved around a dysfunctional belief that he had to have other people's support in order to be worthwhile. Guided by this conceptualization the therapist attempted to help the client modify this attitude and to scale down unrealistic expectations of other people. In response to this intervention the client became sullen and agitated.
>
> Prior to the next session the client telephoned to cancel. He maintained that life was not worth living and that he was contemplating suicide. At this point the therapist consulted with her supervisor. After listening carefully to the audiotape of the previous session, the supervisor hypothesized that the therapist had incorrectly assessed the nature of the client's core cognitive processes. He hypothesized that the client's actual core cognitive processes revolved around the belief that his value as a person depended on his ability to take care of himself and to not show any needs. It was further hypothesized that as a consequence of this the client had difficulty directly communicating his needs to other people and was thus constantly in the situation of finding himself disappointed and bitter when his needs were not met. Finally, it was hypothesized that by attempting to help the client see that his expectations of other people were unrealistic, the therapist had supported the client's tacit belief that he had no right to have needs. As a result of this the client become even more depressed. Moreover, he became angry with the therapist, whom he saw as siding with all the

other people in his life and whom he perceived as challenging his right to have needs.

Guided by this formulation, the therapist's intervention in the next session was substantially different than it had been in the previous session. Instead of challenging ideas related to the belief that he needed other people's support to be a worthwhile person, the therapist proceeded to challenge ideas related to the belief that he was a "bad" or "worthless" person if he needed things from other people. As a result of this session the therapeutic alliance improved and the client's mood improved substantially.

This outcome suggested that the second hypothesis about the nature of the client's core cognitive processes was more accurate than the first hypothesis. In this example, it should be noted that the client's belief that he had no right to have needs as a person was not easily accessible. Indeed, the tacit nature of this attitude may at least in part be responsible for the initial error in formulation. However, the fact that the intervention guided by the initial hypothesis about the nature of the client's core cognitive processes had unpredicted and undesired results provided the therapist with valuable information on the basis of which a more adequate conceptualization could be generated.

Strategies targeted at specific cognitions may also be ineffective because of the functional nature of the cognition. That is, the specific cognition (e.g., an agoraphobic who maintains that "it's dangerous out there") may be resistant to change because it is derived from a more central thought about the self (e.g., "I can't cope"). Often initial client reports are external to the self (i.e., they are not self-evaluative) and represent post hoc explanations to preserve a sense of the self (see Guidano and Liotti 1983, who present a similar idea, which they label the "protective belt").

Finally, it is important to remember that as Kelly (1955) has argued, those cognitions that are most central for an individual are also likely to be those that are most resistant to change. The modification of superordinate constructs is more anxiety-provoking than the modification of subordinate constructs. Unexpected resistance to a particular intervention should thus alert the therapist to the possibility that he may have unwittingly challenged a relative core belief.

RESEARCH AND FUTURE DIRECTIONS

The empirical validation of the ideas presented in this paper represents an important step in advancing both the theory and the practice of cognitive therapy. For example, studies might investigate the comparative efficacy of core versus peripheral interventions within different treatment domains. Research on the assessment of core and peripheral cognitions is a necessary first step, however, in order to provide the requisite specificity that would enable an empirical confirmation of the above formulations. We are aware of no studies that deal with the issue directly. However, some available research using the Dysfunctional Attitude Scale (DAS) (Weissman and Beck 1978) is relevant, albeit in an indirect manner.

Two studies using this scale suggest that elevated DAS scores observed in remitted depressed clients are associated with a recurrence of depressive symptoms or relapse within six months to one year after discharge (Rush et al. 1984, Simons et al. 1984). These findings are important, because they suggest that a reduction in depressive symptomatology may not be maintained if the client's dysfunctional attitudes are not adequately modified. They do not, however, distinguish between those dysfunctional attitudes that are core and those that are peripheral. It is possible for two clients to obtain identical DAS scores by endorsing very different items.

A more recent study by Reda (1984) adopts a somewhat more differentiated perspective. He utilized this same instrument in an effort to identify "permanent cognitive constructs" in depression. He reports that a number of items on this scale are persistently endorsed by depressed clients during the episode and remain elevated one year later, whereas other items are no longer endorsed once the episode is over. His conclusion is that these persistently held beliefs are descriptive of the core cognitive style in depression. The next logical research step will be to adopt an even more idiographic approach to the assessment of dysfunctional attitudes and to devise a means of distinguishing between core and peripheral dysfunctional attitudes for *individuals* in a more reliable fashion. It may well be that paper-and-pencil measures such as the DAS are inadequate for this task, because they cannot tap idiosyncratic attitudes and higher-level constructs (Segal 1984). Another difficulty may be that clients at the beginning of therapy may not yet have articulated to themselves some of the core, tacit rules that guide the processing of information.

A potentially useful approach in this context has been adopted by social anxiety researchers. These researchers are becoming increasingly interested in moving beyond the assessment of readily accessible thoughts (e.g., Glass et al. 1982) to an elucidation of the individual's system of meaning that guides the processing of information in social situations (Arnkoff 1980, Schlenker and Leary 1982). The thrust of this work is to assess the tacit rules that operate on incoming and stored information, and contribute to the cognitive distortions, selective attention, or memory bias observed in clinical situations (Merluzzi et al. 1981, Merluzzi and Rudy 1982).

Goldfried and colleagues (1984), for example, utilized multidimensional scaling in an attempt to map differences in tacit rules between high and low socially anxious males. They found differences between these two groups in their construal of social situations, with anxious subjects giving the highest weighting to the dimension of "chance of being evaluated," whereas nonanxious subjects weighted intimacy twice as heavily as the "chance of being evaluated." This methodology may provide an avenue of describing the salient, core dimensions associated with specific problem situations. For our purposes, the important finding here is not so much the between-group differences in the process of construal but rather the methodology of assigning relative weights (saliency) to tacit rules. This methodology will potentially allow a test of the hypothesis that core processes for an individual will be those that are most strongly weighted.

Another potentially useful methodology is suggested by Luborsky's (1984) research on the core conflictual relationship theme (CCRT) in psychodynamic therapy. In brief, the CCRT was developed as a procedure for measuring the presence of and changes in pervasive, dysfunctional relationship patterns in the context of psychotherapy. The CCRT is assessed by dividing a clinical transcript into a series of relationship episodes and then having independent clinical judges rate specific theme components (e.g., the client's intention, the response from the other) that they see occurring redundantly across a client's relationship episodes. Inter-rater reliability is assessed by comparing the ratings of the judges. While it is beyond the scope of this chapter to describe this methodology in greater detail, the essential point for our purpose is that despite the fact that the raters are making relatively high-level inferences about abstract themes and intrapsychic processes that clients are often unable to articulate themselves, adequate reliability of ratings can be established.

Once the constructs proposed in our formulation have been satisfactorily operationalized, the next logical step would involve testing the relative efficacy of interventions targeted at a core or peripheral level. This process could be initiated by comparing within-session changes resulting from the application of the two types of intervention. The most compelling evidence, however, will come from treatment comparisons where the effects of core versus peripheral interventions on symptom remission and risk of relapse could be evaluated. Empirical research will play a vital role in the validation and refinement of the theory advanced in this chapter. The future of such research is dependent upon the development of innovative methodologies such as those described above.

4

Toward a Refinement of Cognitive Therapy in Light of Interpersonal Theory: I. Theory

There is a growing recognition among cognitive therapists of the importance of the therapeutic relationship (e.g., Arnkoff 1983, Goldfried 1982, Jacobson 1989, Safran 1984a,b, Wilson 1984). This recognition stands in marked contrast to earlier cognitive behavioral writings that deemphasized the importance of this variable in the change process. While many cognitive therapists now recognize the importance of the therapeutic relationship, however, cognitive behavioral theory still lacks a systematic theoretical framework to clarify the relationship between what have traditionally been thought of as relationship factors and technical factors in therapy, and to guide the use of the therapeutic relationship (Lambert 1983, Sweet 1984, Wachtel 1982).

There is also a growing body of empirical evidence indicating that cognitive formulations of emotional disorders pay insufficient attention to the role of interpersonal and environmental variables. Coyne and Gotlib (1983), for example, following a thorough review of research relevant to the role of cognition in depression, concluded that cognitive models of depression overestimate the role that cognitive processes play in precipitating and maintaining depression, and fail to recognize that the negative cognitions of depressed individuals may accurately reflect negative environmental realities, or undesirable life circumstances. Krantz (1985) reviews a large body of evidence suggesting that depressed individuals possess social skills deficits and are more likely than nondepressed individuals to experience relationships characterized by avoidance and rejection. Beidel and Turner (1986) review an overlapping body of evidence and conclude that cognitive behaviorists overestimate the role that cognitive processes play in both psychopathology and therapeutic change.

A number of authors have described the importance of incorporating an interpersonal perspective into cognitive therapy. Meddin (1982), for example, suggests that traditional cognitive behavioral interventions be combined with strategies more typically employed by marital and family therapists. Similarly, Bedrosian (1981) suggests that cognitive therapists focus on family relationships as well as on the cognitive processes of the depressed individual. Krantz (1985) argues that in addition to challenging negative or biased information-processing styles it may be useful to encourage clients to join support groups or create new social networks that will help to provide positive information that will contradict the negative information provided by old social circles.

These are all examples of a technically integrative approach. This approach recognizes that both cognitive and interpersonal factors play an important role in clinical problems and thus suggest the use of interventions taken from both traditions. The selection of interventions is, however, not guided by an integrative conceptual perspective.

The approach to be outlined in this chapter is, in contrast, conceptually integrative in nature. This approach recognizes that both cognitive and interpersonal spheres are important and attempts to develop an integrative theoretical framework for purposes of understanding the relationship between cognitive and interpersonal realms in normal psychological development, as well as in the development and maintenance of emotional problems.

The perspective to be outlined is not proposed as a new model of psychopathology nor as a new theory of change. Instead it is intended as a conceptual and technical refinement of cognitive behavioral theory and practice through the systematic integration of a number of concepts, propositions, and hypotheses derived from interpersonal theory. I am referring here to the theoretical tradition that traces its roots back to the seminal contributions of Harry Stack Sullivan (1953, 1954, 1956) and has been elaborated on by a variety of contemporary theorists such as Anchin (1982), Beier (1966), Carson (1969, 1982), Cashdan (1973), Leary (1957), and Wachtel (1977). Most directly influential on the current perspective, however, have been the contributions of Kiesler (1982 a,b, 1983, 1986, 1988).

The reader will also find that much of the thinking in the perspective to be outlined here is compatible with certain contemporary developments in psychodynamic theory, particularly those that are more interpersonal in nature (e.g., Gill 1982, Luborsky 1984, Sandler and Sandler 1978, Strupp and Binder 1984, Weiss et al. 1987). This is not surprising; these theorists have also been an important influence on the current perspective. What distinguishes the present approach, however, is an attempt to articulate the central theoretical concepts in a framework that is compatible with cognitive theory and that is amenable to empirical investigation.

FORMULATING THE SCHEMA CONCEPT FROM A COGNITIVE-INTERPERSONAL PERSPECTIVE

The schema concept has become a central theoretical construct in cognitive models of psychopathology and psychotherapy. A schema can be defined as a *generic cognitive representation* that the mind extracts in the course of exposure to particular instances of a phenomenon (Bartlett 1932). This generic knowledge structure guides both the processing of information and the implementation of action.

Theorists' conceptualizations of what schemas are and what exactly is contained within a schema vary widely. The fact that there is no one definition of the schema is not a problem in and of itself. This multiplicity of definitions is referred to by theorists as the modularity hypothesis (Brewer and Nakamura 1984). This hypothesis asserts that different hypothetical constructs are necessary for clarifying the way in which information is processed in different domains.

What does constitute a problem, however, is that clinically oriented theorists often are not clear about what exactly they mean when they use the term schema. Because the schema concept is acceptable coinage in the cognitive sciences it is tempting for psychotherapy theorists to employ it in order to confer scientific respectability on ill-defined concepts. Thus clinical theorists as diverse as Beck (1976) in the cognitive tradition, Kernberg (1976) and Horowitz (1979) in the psychodynamic tradition, and Rice (1984) in the client-centered tradition employ the schema concept without clearly defining the term or specifying precisely what type of knowledge is represented schematically.

The concepts of cognitive psychology provide the researcher with tools to test certain hypotheses about the way in which knowledge is represented. It is important to recognize, however, that using the schema concept does not eliminate the necessity of clarifying what type of knowledge representation is worth focusing on in the context of psychotherapy.

The schematic structure that has received most attention from cognitive therapists is the self-schema. A scrutiny of the clinical literature on self-schemas reveals that this construct is not employed in a uniform fashion by theorists. One common usage of the self-schema concept in clinical theory derives from research and theory in the social cognition domain. In this tradition, self-schemas are defined as "cognitive generalizations about the self, derived from past experience, that organize and guide the processing of self-related information contained in an individual social experience" (Markus 1977). Research guided by this conceptualization has focused upon the self-referent processing of adjectives (Kuiper and Olinger 1986).

A second common usage of the self-schema concept has evolved out of a more clinically oriented tradition. In this view, the self-schema is conceptualized as a self-worth contingency. Beck and his associates have been the major proponents of this perspective in the cognitive therapy tradition (Beck 1976, Beck et al. 1979). They view the schema as a tacit rule that guides the process of self-evaluation. The belief "I have to be perfectly competent at everything I do in order to be worthwhile as a person" would thus be seen by Beck and colleagues (1979) as an example of a depressogenic self-schema. Research guided by this conceptualization has employed paper and pencil measures such as the Dysfunctional Attitudes Scale (Weissman and Beck 1978) to assess for the presence of rigid and dysfunctional self-worth contingencies.

The notion that self-worth contingencies are clinically important has both theoretical appeal and empirical support (Kuiper and Olinger 1986). It is not, however, immediately apparent how this conceptualization is related to the schema concept as typically employed in cognitive psychology. While the social-cognition conceptualization of the self-schema as "cognitive generalizations about the self" is more closely tied to both theory and research in cognitive psychology, the restriction of researchers' attention to the fashion in which people currently represent the self imposes a somewhat narrow focus on our investigation of self-knowledge. The restrictiveness of this focus has been recognized by Markus (1983) and Markus and Nurius (1986) who suggest that the concept of self-schema be broadened to incorporate the idea of "possible selves." Possible selves are defined as an individual's ideas of what he or she might become, would like to become, and are afraid of becoming (Markus 1983). Markus and Nurius (1986) maintain that the expansion of the self-schema concept in this fashion establishes a rationale for the investigation of a variety of different components of self-knowledge such as rules, standards, and strategies that the individual uses to evaluate, guide, and control his or her own behavior.

This revised conceptualization of the self-schema appears to be more compatible with the notion of self-schema as a self-worth contingency, because a self-worth contingency *is* essentially a rule or standard that is employed to evaluate and guide one's own behavior. There thus appears to be some potential for reconciling the discrepant self-schema conceptualizations emerging from clinical and social-cognition literatures. By expanding the notion of self-schema in this fashion, however, the link with schema theory in cognitive psychology becomes more obscure. How can information such as possible selves, goals, plans, strategies, and rules for self-evaluation be regarded as part of a generalized information structure based upon past experience? If the schema concept is to be employed in a rigorous and consistent fashion in clinical theory, it will be necessary to address this question.

Schemas and the Acquisition of Real World Knowledge

The investigative paradigm that has been most commonly used in self-schema research—that of evaluating the processing of adjectives—represents both positive and problematic features of the cognitive sciences approach. On the positive side it involves making and testing rigorous predictions about the way in which knowledge is represented. On the negative side it involves the use of laboratory tasks that have limited ecological validity (Neisser 1976, 1981, Safran 1986, Safran and Segal 1987, Safran, Segal et al. 1990). The testing for biases in the processing of adjectives appears to lose sight of the very reason that Bartlett developed the schema concept in the first place—that is, to account for the fashion in which learning influences the way in which people deal with new instances in the *real* world. As Neisser (1976) has argued, this type of *lack of ecological validity* may stem from some of the basic assumptions of the information-processing approach.

Information-processing theory has been strongly influenced by the mind-as-computer analogy. This analogy has advanced cognitive psychology by facilitating the process of formulating and testing precise theoretical predictions about unobservable psychological processes. It fails to take into account, however, that there is a fundamental difference between the way in which computers process information and the way in which people acquire knowledge. In the real world people do not simply process static information. Instead, they actively mine the world for information by moving around, manipulating, and interacting with their environment (Gibson 1966, McArthur and Baron 1983, Neisser 1976, 1981, Safran and Greenberg 1986, 1987, 1988, Shaw and Bransford 1977). Information processing theory typically does not reflect this intrinsic connection between knowledge acquisition and action.

The Ecological Approach

An alternative in cognitive psychology to the information-processing approach can be found in the ecological approach to perception, initially developed by Gibson (1966, 1979). Although the application of the ecological approach was originally limited to perception, a growing number of proponents are beginning to explore the implications of this approach for both cognitive psychology in general (e.g., Shaw and Bransford 1977) and for social psychology (e.g., McArthur and Baron 1983). As I have argued elsewhere, the incorporation of some of the basic tenets of the ecological approach into mainstream cognitive theorizing can provide a useful corrective influence to information-processing theory (Greenberg and Safran 1987, Safran and Greenberg 1986, 1987, 1988). For this reason, I will briefly summarize some of these principles below.

The first is that one cannot study an organism out of context of its ecological niche (Gibson 1966, 1979). It is thus important to attempt to understand human functioning in real world settings rather than in artificial environments.

The second is that there is an intrinsic connection between knowledge and action, and that knowledge is acquired through action and for action (Gibson 1966, 1979, Mace 1977, Weimer 1977). It is thus a mistake to attempt to understand schematic processing in terms of the way in which static information is registered and processed. Instead, it is important to investigate the way in which information processing and action in the real world interact.

A final tenet is that all psychological processes should be viewed from a functional perspective. This tenet suggests that it is conceptually useful to inquire into what type of adaptive role a given aspect of human functioning has played in the history of the species.

Rather than viewing human beings as disembodied computing machines, it is important to regard them as biological creatures who have evolved specific features that play a functional role in the environment of ecological adaptedness (Gibson 1979, McArthur and Baron 1983, Shaw and Bransford 1977).

These propositions, which are central to the ecological approach, are metatheoretical assumptions that are not directly falsifiable. Instead, their scientific merit must be evaluated on the basis of their ability to generate productive research programs leading to the formulation of falsifiable hypotheses (Lakatos 1978, Weimer 1979). In the next session we will explore the way in which these principles can influence our attempt to clarify the type of schematic structures worth investigating in clinical psychology, and can facilitate the integration of cognitive and interpersonal perspectives.

Representations of Self–Other Interactions

If we examine the schema concept from an ecological perspective, and ask what kind of generic knowledge structures play a central role in the real world, it would seem that the encoding of static environmental features would be less important than the generalized representation of significant and survival-relevant interactions that have been experienced. A central postulate of the interpersonal perspective is that some of the more important survival-relevant events for human beings involve interactions with other human beings. Such a perspective starts with the assumption that there is a wired-in propensity for maintaining relatedness to others and that this wired-in propensity plays an important role in the survival of the species (Bowlby 1969, Greenberg and Safran 1987, Safran and Greenberg 1987, 1988, 1989, Schachtel 1959, Sullivan, 1953, 1956).[1]

---

1. This proposition is central to Bowlby's (1969, 1973, 1980) attachment theory, which is influenced by an ethological perspective. It is also compatible with the emphasis on evolutionary adaption characteristic of the ecological approach (McArthur and Baron 1983), although it is not typically held as an explicit proposition by ecological theorists.

Given the importance for survival purposes of maintaining relatedness to others, particularly in infants, it would seem to be particularly adaptive to be able to encode past experience in a way that maximizes this possibility. Consistent with this line of reasoning, Bowlby (1969, 1973, 1980) hypothesizes that human beings develop internal working models representing interpersonal interactions relevant to attachment behavior.

In the language of cognitive psychology, this type of working model can be conceptualized as an *interpersonal schema* (Safran 1986, Safran and Segal 1990) that is abstracted on the basis of interactions with attachment figures and that permits the individual to predict interactions in a way that increases the probability of maintaining relatedness with these figures. This type of schema is a *generalized representation of self–other relationships*, rather than a representation of self or a representation of others. It is thus intrinsically interactional in nature. As Bretherton (1985) argues, a person's beliefs about the self automatically imply certain beliefs about others, and vice versa.

A related concept has been proposed by Stern (1985). Drawing on Tulving's (1972) distinction between episodic and semantic memory, he theorizes that infants develop prototypical representations of interactions with attachment figures through a process of encoding specific interactional sequences in episodic memory. He suggests that over time, interactions that are similar in nature become averaged in memory, and the details that are specific to individual events become abstracted into a generalized representation in semantic memory.

According to Stern, these prototypical memories, or what he refers to as Representations of Interactions that have been Generalized (RIGs), are closely related to Bowlby's (1969) concept of the working model, but are more specific in nature. A working model thus consists of a number of RIGs that are assembled into a larger overall generalized representation of interactions with the attachment figure.

It may be useful, as Neisser (1976) suggests, to think of schemas of different orders of abstractness and generality as being embedded within one another, and as functioning in a hierarchical fashion. Bowlby's (1969) working model can thus be thought of as a higher-order, fairly general interpersonal schema that has a number of more specific interpersonal schemas, or RIGs, embedded within it. The growing evidence that individuals have multiple working models (Bretherton 1985) can also be understood in this fashion. An individual may have different interpersonal schemas for people who play different roles in their lives (e.g., authority figures, prototypical lovers), and these lower-level schemas may all be embedded within a higher-level more abstract and generalized interpersonal schema.

What type of information would be coded in those interpersonal schemas? As Main and associates (1985) point out, an individual's memory can be seen as guided by general-event schemas that organize experience in terms of reactions, goal paths, attempts, and outcomes. It is hypothesized that the specific information coded in memory includes goals, action plans, and if-then contingencies relevant to maintaining relatedness. It may thus be useful to think of an interpersonal schema as being somewhat like a *program for maintaining relatedness* (Safran 1986, Safran and Segal 1990). The perspective being advanced is that the basic goal of maintaining interpersonal relatedness is biologically wired in. The specific information, strategies, and principles that are employed in order to obtain this goal are learned.

Viewing the interpersonal schema as analogous to a program for maintaining interpersonal relatedness provides a framework for more fully understanding the relationship between cognitive and interpersonal realms. It also clarifies the fashion in which self-worth contingencies, goals, plans, and strategies can be coded as part of the same schematic structure. The various types of goals, plans, and strategies that Markus (1983) argues should be viewed as part of the self-schema can be viewed as coded information acquired on the basis of previous interactions, relevant to the maintenance of interpersonal relatedness.

In an interpersonal schema, self-worth contingencies function as implicit rules for maintaining relatedness. They are like *action rules* in a script (Abelson 1981). As Abelson (1981) suggests, these action rules are not necessarily consciously articulated by the individual. Thus, for example, the dysfunctional attitude, "I must be perfectly competent at everything I do," can be viewed as a tacit rule for maintaining relatedness that has been developed on the basis of maladaptive learning experiences with attachment figures.

Higgins (1987) refers to this as self–other contingency knowledge. Although the present conceptualization is consistent in certain ways with his self-concept discrepancy model of motivation, it goes beyond his model to attempt to clarify the relationship between this type of knowledge representation and schema theory.

A general issue regarding the coding of information in interpersonal schemas involves the question *how* or in *what form* information is represented. It is hypothesized that information relevant to attachment behavior has an important affective component to it (Bowlby 1969, Greenberg and Safran 1987) and that it is thus coded at least in part in expressive-motor form (Bucci 1985, Greenberg and Safran 1987, 1989, Safran and Greenberg 1987, Zanjonc and Markus 1984). The hypothesis is that interpersonal schemas are partially coded in the form of procedural knowledge that individuals experience as a currently felt sense when certain activating conditions occur.

If, however, as Leventhal (1984) theorizes, the emotional synthesis process involves processing at both expressive-motor and conceptual levels, the relevant information would be coded at least partially in conceptual/propositional form as well. It is thus hypothesized that interpersonal schemas are best conceptualized as cognitive-affective schemas that are coded at both conceptual and expressive-motor levels. While some aspects of an individual's interpersonal schema may be readily accessible in conceptual/linguistic form, other aspects may be more difficult to access symbolically. In theory, however, it would be both possible and important to access the expressive-motor level in therapy by working with clients in an emotionally alive fashion. Once this has taken place, the possibility of forming a conceptual representation of information coded at the expressive-motor level exists (Greenberg and Safran 1987, Safran and Greenberg 1987).

Maintaining Interpersonal Relatedness

We have hypothesized that interpersonal schemas allow the infant to maintain interpersonal relatedness by facilitating the prediction of interactions with attachment figures. The goal of maintaining interpersonal relatedness continues throughout the lifespan (Bowlby 1969). The particular interpersonal strategies that are employed, however, are shaped by interpersonal schemas that may not be appropriate to the present context even though they were historically adaptive for the infant. Thus, it is not unusual for an individual to act in a fashion that pursues a subjective sense of interpersonal relatedness that may in reality impede interpersonal relatedness.

It is hypothesized that people establish a subjective sense of potential interpersonal relatedness in a variety of ways. One way consists of engaging in life plan strategies designed to increase the probability of maintaining relatedness to others. For example, the individual whose parents valued intelligence may become an academic. The individual who was valued for supporting or nurturing members of his or her family may ultimately become a therapist. The individual who was valued for his or her ability to entertain may become a professional entertainer.

A second way consists of interactional maneuvers designed to maintain relatedness. For example, the previously described academic may speak intelligently when he or she wishes to establish a subjective sense of potential relatedness. A woman who was related to as a child in a sexual manner may behave seductively when she wishes to maintain a sense of potential interpersonal relatedness.

A third way consists of distorting the processing of information that threatens the individual's subjective sense of potential interpersonal relatedness. One can fail to attend to external feedback that threatens one's sense of interpersonal relatedness. For example, the individual who has learned that relatedness is contingent upon being warm and kind can fail to fully process or forget interactions with others providing feedback that he or she has been aloof or uncaring. One can also distort internally generated information that threatens one's subjective sense of interpersonal security and evokes anxiety. For example, the individual who learns that anger or sadness threatens interpersonal relatedness may fail to fully process expressive-motor behaviors consistent with these emotions (Greenberg and Safran 1984a, Safran and Greenberg 1986, 1987).

It is essential to recognize that the individual's goal is not necessarily one of maintaining relatedness to a specific person in a specific interaction, but rather, one of acting in a fashion that enhances his or her sense of potential relatedness in an abstract, generalized sense. In other words, the audience that an individual plays to is an internal one (Sullivan 1953). One may, for example, behave in an overtly aggressive and alienating fashion, yet still be satisfying one's own inner model of how a potentially loveable person must be, given his or her perception of the interpersonal world. Individuals who imagine the world to be inhabited by hostile and malicious creatures may feel they have no choice other than to be vigilant and hostile in return. Given their perception of the world, a combative stance may appear subjectively necessary and also commendable. If the circumstances appear sufficiently dire, one may to varying degrees relinquish the goal of maintaining interpersonal relatedness in reality, yet act in a fashion that one imagines would be accepted and approved of by some ideally understanding person. Solutions to the problem of interpersonal relatedness are thus often complex.

Sullivan (1953) employed the term *security operations* to designate various psychological and/or interpersonal operations that function to maintain one's self-esteem. From an interpersonal perspective, one's fundamental sense of security in the world is a function of one's sense of potential relatedness to others (Safran 1984a,b). One of Sullivan's (1956) central theoretical propositions was that self-esteem is ultimately an interpersonal phenomenon; one feels good about oneself if one is satisfying one's generalized cognitive representation of others. Sullivan viewed anxiety as the inverse of self-esteem. According to him, anxiety is evoked by the anticipated disintegration of interpersonal relationships.

Sullivan did not offer a thoroughly articulated explanation of the connection between anxiety and the disruption of interpersonal relationships. He did not, however, have at his disposal the knowledge available from current theory and research on attachment behavior, mother–infant interaction, and emotional development. In light of such current developments, it is hypothesized that anxiety functions as a biologically wired-in form of feedback about potential danger to the organism (Bowlby 1973, Greenberg and Safran 1987, Safran and Greenberg 1989, Safran and Segal 1990).

As Bowlby (1973) maintains, animals of every species are genetically biased to respond with anxiety to stimulus situations that serve as naturally occurring clues to situations that are potentially dangerous to that species. Because maintaining proximity to other human beings plays such an important role in the survival of the human species (particularly in the helpless infant that depends upon the caretaker for survival on a moment-by-moment basis), it is not surprising that the perception of a potential disruption in an interpersonal relationship would elicit an anxiety response in human beings.

It is thus reasonable to hypothesize that human beings are by nature perceptually attuned to detect any clues regarding the disintegration of interpersonal relationships and are programmed to respond with anxiety. Anxiety can thus serve as a cue that alerts people to avoid associated experiences and stimulus situations. Behaviors and experiences that become associated with the disintegration of relationships with significant others will subsequently evoke anxiety. Conversely, experiences and behaviors that are valued by significant others become associated for the individual with a sense of interpersonal security. It is hypothesized that through this learning process people develop various kinds of security operations, ranging from diverting attention from anxiety-provoking information, to controlling the conversation in order to avoid anxiety-provoking topics, to presenting oneself in a fashion that momentarily raises one's self-esteem (e.g., as intelligent or strong) (Safran 1984a, Sullivan 1953).

While the notion that people will engage in behavioral avoidance of anxiety-provoking stimuli has always been accepted by behavioral and cognitive behavioral theory, Sullivan's notion of selective inattention to anxiety-provoking stimuli (both external and internal) has not. The research on selective attention, however, certainly demonstrates that people have the capacity to screen out stimuli, and the research on perceptual defense, although not without its attendant controversies (F. Dixon 1971, N. Dixon 1981), suggests that the selective inattention to anxiety-provoking stimuli is a phenomenon warranting further empirical investigation and careful consideration in a clinical context (see Dixon 1981, Erdelyi 1985, Shevrin and Dickman 1980 for reviews of the relevant literature).

The Cognitive-Interpersonal Cycle

To this point we have explored the connection between the interpersonal schema and the psychological and interpersonal strategies that the individual employs to maintain a subjective sense of potential interpersonal relatedness. It has been argued that this subjective sense derives from a historically adaptive interpersonal schema that may be maladaptive in the present context.

A key question now remains to be addressed. How is it that a cognitive structure of this type can remain unchanged in the face of new interpersonal experiences? From an information-processing perspective the answer to this question is that information that is schema-inconsistent is not attended to or is discounted (Beck 1976, Nisbett and Ross 1980).

The ecological perspective on cognition, however, suggests that this answer is only partial. It fails to take into account the intrinsic connection between knowledge acquisition and action in the real world. The central postulate of an integrative cognitive-interpersonal perspective is that a person's maladaptive interactional patterns persist because they are based upon working models of interpersonal relationships that are consistently confirmed by the interpersonal consequences of his or her own behavior (Carson 1969, 1982, Kiesler 1982a,b, 1986, Leary 1957, Safran 1984b, Strupp and Binder 1984, Wachtel 1977). One's interpersonal schemas shape the perception of the interpersonal world and lead to various plans, strategies, and behaviors, which in turn shape the environment in a manner that confirms the working model. There is, thus, a self-perpetuating *cognitive-interpersonal cycle* (Safran 1984a, Safran and Segal 1990). As Strupp and Binder (1984) argue, the individual shapes his or her interpersonal world by both construing and constructing it. This type of conceptualization of neurotic problems has been well articulated by Wachtel (1977, 1987), who refers to it as a cyclical psychodynamic perspective.

As Mischel (1973) suggests, all individuals display certain consistencies in construal style and associated behavioral consistencies. It is, however, hypothesized that the psychologically maladjusted individual has relatively negative and rigid expectations about the characteristics of others and rigid and constricting beliefs about the way in which he or she must be in order to maintain interpersonal relatedness (Carson 1969, 1982, Kiesler 1982a,b, 1983). Thus, they possess rigid and constricting interpersonal schemas that restrict the range of their interpersonal behaviors. As Kiesler (1986) states:

> In interpersonal theory, abnormal behavior is defined as inappropriate or inadequate interpersonal communication. It consists of a rigid, constricted, and extreme pattern of interpersonal behaviors by which the abnormal person, without any clear awareness, engages others who are important in his or her life. The abnormal person, rather than possessing the flexibility of the normal individual to use the broad range of interpersonal behaviors warranted by different social situations, is locked into a rigid and extreme use of limited classes of interpersonal actions. [p. 572]

As a result, maladjusted individuals are more likely than psychologically healthy individuals to be characterized by a high degree of redundancy of patterns across a wide range of different interpersonal situations (Carson 1969, 1982, Kiesler 1982a,b, 1986, Leary 1957). The more maladjusted the individual is, the more likely it is that he or she will pull a similar response from a range of different people. As a result, the maladjusted individual has a more limited range of interpersonal experiences than the well-adjusted individual.

The ongoing debate in the cognitive literature on whether clinical problems are cognitive or interpersonal in nature (Coyne and Gotlib 1983, 1986, Krantz 1985, Segal and Shaw 1986) is fueled by a tendency to think of such deficits in rather gross, molar terms. This perspective fails to capture the subtlety of the cognitive and interpersonal deficits that often bring people into therapy, or the nature of the interaction between them.

Consider the following example. A young female inpatient was referred to therapy for treatment of severe depression. She presented in a very sensible, rational manner and was quick to generate balanced and reasonable accounts of any untoward events that occurred to her. For example, after a negative interaction with a nurse on the ward, she explained to the therapist that there was no need for her (the client) to take it personally or to blame the nurse because the nurse was under a lot of stress and trying her best. When speaking about painful memories, she would smile wistfully and maintain that it was important to get on with the future and not dwell in the past. She had a history of supporting and helping others who were in need, but acknowledged that others were not there to provide emotional support when she needed it. The prevailing feature of her interpersonal impact was a sense of strength, resourcefulness, and self-containment that made it easy to respect her from a distance, but difficult to feel really close to her. This interpersonal impact seemed to flow from all aspects of her self-presentation: her unwillingness to dwell on painful memories, her wistful smile, her constant reasonableness and evenhandedness, her concern about the interviewer's welfare, and so on.

Further assessment revealed that this resourceful and self-contained interpersonal style was linked to a belief that nobody would be there for her if she were needy and vulnerable and that the way to obtain the respect of others was to be strong and self-contained. This belief was in turn maintained by the fact that her interpersonal style discouraged other people from relating to her in a caring, supportive fashion.

An understanding of the fashion in which security operations function helps to further clarify the fashion in which dysfunctional cognitive-interpersonal cycles can operate.

For example: as a result of important developmental experiences, a young man comes to view the maintenance of interpersonal relatedness as contingent upon his being intelligent. When he feels anxious in interpersonal situations, he attempts to reduce this anxiety by speaking in a fashion that he construes as intelligent. This communication style, however, is viewed by others as unnecessarily pedantic, and distances them. In this situation the very operations that are employed to reduce the man's anxiety by increasing his sense of potential interpersonal relatedness have the impact of distancing other people from him. The more anxious he becomes, the more likely he is to engage in the very operations that are interpersonally problematic for him.

As these examples illustrate, the deficits that characterize clients are not necessarily gross, easily observable, cognitive distortions that show up easily in analogue experimental tasks, or gross interpersonal deficits that show up easily on standardized behavioral measures. Instead, they often involve subtle interactions between cognitive and interpersonal levels. These interactions consist of core beliefs (Safran et al. 1986) about self–other interactions, or interpersonal schemata that bias the perception of self–other interactions and are intrinsically linked to various dysfunctional interpersonal strategies, behaviors, and communications. Because of the intrinsic connection between cognitive and interpersonal levels, it is difficult to accurately assess the cognitive processes that are central to an individual's problems without an understanding of the interpersonal aspect of the cycle. A large component of interpersonal communication takes place at the nonverbal level (Ekman 1972, Kiesler 1982a,b, Mehrabian 1972); therefore, the interpersonal or behavioral link in a dysfunctional cognitive-interpersonal cycle is often particularly *subtle* in nature. For these reasons, assessing the nature of a specific dysfunctional cognitive-interpersonal cycle can be a challenging task.

RESEARCH IMPLICATIONS

In Chapter 5, I will examine some of the relevant clinical considerations in greater detail. Here, I will explore some of the implications, for research, of the perspective I have been articulating.

1. *Interpersonal Schemas.* While schema research in clinical psychology has tended to focus on the schematic processing of static characteristics, the current perspective suggests that it is important to focus on the schematic processing of dynamic interpersonal events in which the individual participates. The type of schematic structure worth investigating would thus be more like a script (Abelson 1981) than a schema for static information. This type of focus introduces methodological complications, but such obstacles are not insurmountable. Although we will not focus in detail on methodological issues here, we will briefly touch on this area for purposes of illustration. The reader who is interested in a more detailed exploration of these issues is referred to Safran and colleagues (1989).

One methodological lead is provided by Neisser (1981). In an attempt to find an ecologically valid method for investigating schematic effects on memory, Neisser employed a variant of a case study methodology to compare John Dean's memory for events taking place in meetings with Nixon around the Watergate affair against the criterion of actual transcripts of those meetings.

This type of approach has a greater chance of yielding information about the type of schematic processing relevant to real world interactions than more commonly employed laboratory research. The distinguishing feature here is the examination of memory biases about naturally occurring events in which the subject is actually involved.

The psychotherapy situation provides a naturally occurring laboratory for examining schematic effects on memory in an ecologically valid fashion. By using an established methodology to help generate hypotheses about the client's working model of interpersonal relationships (e.g., Luborsky 1984, Strupp and Binder 1984, Weiss et al. 1987), the researcher could generate hypotheses about the type of schematic effects on memory that are likely to occur. It would then possible to compare the client's memory of a specific therapy session against the criterion of recorded sessions.

A second methodological lead is provided by script theory (Abelson 1981). According to Schank and Abelson (1977), events in scripts differ in their centrality to the action flow. There is now experimental evidence that subjects can verify central events as belonging to a script faster than they can verify peripheral events (Abelson 1981). If interpersonal schemas follow the same processing rules as scripts, researchers may be able to obtain information about the structure of clients' interpersonal schemas by asking them to judge whether various events have taken place in their own therapy sessions, and by then measuring the speed with which such judgments are made.

A third lead is provided by Main and colleagues (1985), who attempted to assess the working models of 6-year-old children by showing them pictures of children undergoing separations from their parents and asking them how they imagined the children in the pictures would feel and act. They hypothesized that children with working models of the attachment figure as accessible would be able to imagine more active ways of dealing with the separations than those who had working models of attachment figures as inaccessible. When subjects' responses were classified in terms of the degree of security of attachment they reflected, a relationship emerged between security of attachment as measured this way and security of attachment as measured at an earlier age, using mother–child observational measures.

In a similar fashion it would be possible to assess the interpersonal schemas of adult subjects by either: (1) using a projective test focusing on separation themes; or (2) asking them to imagine themselves in various relationship-threatening interactions with significant others and probing for feelings, reactions, and probable interpersonal strategies.

A fourth lead is suggested by a pilot study conducted by Safran and associates (1988). In this study a questionnaire was developed to evaluate subjects' expectations of the way in which three different significant others (mother, father, and friend) would respond to a range of interpersonal behavior on their part. Sixteen different interpersonal behaviors were derived from Kiesler's (1983) interpersonal circle, one behavior representing each of the sixteen segments of the circumplex. This provided some assurance that a full range of possible interpersonal behaviors was sampled in a theoretically guided fashion. Subjects were then asked to indicate the type of response (e.g., disappointed, resentful, respectful, warm) expected from each of the three significant others to each of the behaviors and to rate the desirability of each response. Slightly different versions of the questionnaire were then administered to two independent samples (n=54 and n=45) of undergraduate subjects (small modifications in the questionnaire were made after the first administration).

When subjects were divided into high symptomatic versus low symptomatic groups on the basis of the SCL-90 (Derogatis 1977), it was found in both samples that high symptomatic subjects expected significantly more undesirable responses from all three individuals and that this pattern was more pronounced for some interpersonal behaviors (e.g., acting mistrustful, hostile, detached, trusting) than for others (e.g., acting dominant, competitive, submissive, warm).

In a follow-up study (Hill and Safran 1994), the revised questionnaire was administered to 216 college undergraduates, divided into high and low symptomatic groups on the basis of the SCL-90. Collapsing across interpersonal situations it was found, once again, that high symptomatic subjects expected responses that were significantly more undesirable than low symptomatic subjects. Furthermore, low symptomatic subjects expected responses that were significantly more friendly, sociable, and trusting than those expected by high symptomatic subjects. Finally, low symptomatic subjects expected more complementary responses (i.e., friendly responses) to friendly interpersonal acts than did high symptomatic subjects. In contrast, high symptomatic subjects expected more complementary responses (i.e., hostile responses) to hostile interpersonal acts than did low symptomatic subjects.

While this type of aggregate analysis of the data obscures important individual differences, future research using this type of questionnaire would allow the investigation of the idiosyncratic working models of either individuals or particular interpersonal types by examining the nature of the specific interpersonal behaviors to which they expect negative responses (e.g., one type of individual might expect negative responses to dominant or quarrelsome behaviors, whereas another might expect negative responses to submissive or affiliative behaviors).

2. *Interpersonal Flexibility and Psychological Health.* A second important research focus will involve the evaluation of hypotheses regarding the actual interpersonal patterns associated with psychological maladjustment. A first hypothesis warranting evaluation states that psychologically maladjusted individuals actually display less flexibility in their interpersonal repertoire than well-adjusted individuals.

Paulhus and Martin (1988) have developed a questionnaire that asks subjects how capable they are of performing each of sixteen different interpersonal behaviors chosen to sample the segments of Wiggins' (1979) circumplex model of interpersonal behavior. Interpersonal flexibility is evaluated on this measure by summing the subjects' ratings of how capable they are of performing each of the sixteen interpersonal behaviors. Using this index, a significant correlation was found between interpersonal flexibility and both self-report ratings of self-esteem and peer ratings of psychological adjustment.

A second research possibility would involve comparing the range in behavioral patterns actually displayed by psychologically healthy versus unhealthy subjects across a variety of interpersonal situations. Using a behavioral rating instrument such as Kiesler's (1984) Checklist of Interpersonal Transactions, it would be possible to compare the behavioral consistency displayed by adjusted versus maladjusted individuals across a range of different interpersonal situations.

A final research direction would involve evaluating the hypothesis that psychologically maladjusted subjects are more consistent than psychologically healthy subjects in evoking negative responses from others across a range of interpersonal situations. Preliminary evidence relevant to this hypothesis can be found in the literature demonstrating that depressed individuals evoke more negative feelings and aversive responses from others in both role playing and real life situations (Arkowitz et al. 1982, Coyne 1976, Kahn et al. 1985, Strack and Coyne 1983).

Further investigation of this issue could be explored by administering a rating instrument such as Kiesler's (1987) Impact Message Inventory (IMI) to a range of different people who interact with subjects classified as psychologically maladjusted in order to evaluate the degree of consistency in *precise feeling patterns and response dispositions* evoked in others. The quality (i.e., negative vs. positive) and degree of consistency in these responses could then be compared with the quality and degree of consistency in response ratings on IMI ratings obtained from a range of individuals interacting with subjects classified as psychologically healthy.

3. *Summary.* The above research suggestions are not intended as an exhaustive catalogue of research possibilities, or as detailed and definitive research blueprints. Implementing them will obviously involve working out various methodological "bugs." They are, however, intended as an illustration of the type of systematic research program that is necessary in order to empirically ground the theoretical perspective being advanced and to demonstrate verifiability of the relevant hypotheses.

CONCLUSIONS

In this chapter I have outlined a number of concepts that can be useful for purposes of integrating cognitive and interpersonal approaches to psychotherapy. I have argued that the bridge between cognitive and interpersonal traditions can be facilitated by incorporating a number of metatheoretical assumptions compatible with the ecological approach (Gibson 1979, McArthur and Baron 1983, Shaw and Bransford 1977) into an information processing perspective. These include the propositions that: (1) there is an intrinsic connection between cognition and action, (2) human beings are biological creatures who have adapted to their ecological niche through evolution, and (3) there is a wired-in propensity for maintaining interpersonal relatedness.

A proposal has been advanced for formulating the schema concept in terms that are more ecologically valid and more interpersonal in nature, and that can help to clarify the relationship between cognitive processes and interpersonal behavior. In this proposal, a particular type of schematic structure is held to be of central clinical importance. This schematic structure, which I have designated as an *interpersonal schema,* is conceptualized as a generic knowledge structure based on previous self–other interactions. It contains information relevant to the maintenance of interpersonal relatedness. Interpersonal schemas can be thought of as being analogous to programs for maintaining interpersonal relatedness.

Dysfunctional interpersonal schemas constitute the cognitive component of cognitive-interpersonal cycles in which dysfunctional interpersonal patterns are shaped by and maintain dysfunctional cognitive structures. Because of the subtlety and complexity of these cognitive-interpersonal cycles, it is important for clinicians to have a conceptual grasp of the nature of the relationship between cognitive and interpersonal realms.

5

Toward a Refinement of Cognitive Therapy in Light of Interpersonal Theory: II. Practice

In Chapter 4, a preliminary framework was articulated for incorporating certain concepts derived from interpersonal theory into cognitive theory in a systematic fashion. It was suggested that a framework of this type could enhance cognitive therapy theory by facilitating the clarification of the fashion in which cognitive and interpersonal processes interact in the development and maintenance of psychological problems and in the change process. The concept of the interpersonal schema was proposed as a construct useful for integrating cognitive and interpersonal perspectives. The interpersonal schema, which can be thought of as a cognitively oriented elaboration of Bowlby's (1969) internal working model concept, was defined as a generic representation of self–other interactions. Finally, it was hypothesized that interpersonal schemas activate and in turn are maintained by cognitive-interpersonal cycles in which people evoke schema-consistent responses from others.

    In this chapter a number of therapeutic implications of this perspective will be considered. It will be argued that the therapeutic relationship provides an important vehicle for both assessing and challenging core cognitive structures. Many of the concepts to be articulated and therapeutic suggestions to be offered are taken directly from other theorists (e.g., Carson 1969, 1982, Cashdan 1973, Kiesler 1988, Strupp and Binder 1984, Wachtel 1977, Weiss et al. 1987). What distinguishes the current approach is not the novelty of the component concepts, but rather the attempt to articulate a systematic theoretical framework to guide the integration of interpersonal and cognitive perspectives.

ASSESSING THE COGNITIVE-
INTERPERSONAL CYCLE

A number of cognitive behavioral theorists have begun to distinguish between what are referred to as core versus peripheral cognitive structures (Arnkoff 1980, Guidano and Liotti 1983, Mahoney 1982, Meichenbaum and Gilmore 1984, Safran et al. 1986). The precise definition of core cognitive structures varies from theorist to theorist. There is, however, a general agreement that they play a central role in organizing the individual's cognitive and behavioral processes.

Moreover, a number of theorists hypothesize that these core cognitive structures are related to the fundamental assumptions the individual holds about the self and the world (Guidano 1987, Liotti 1987, Kelly 1955, Safran et al. 1986). These theorists also hypothesize that core cognitive structures must be modified in order to bring about enduring change (Biran 1988, Guidano and Liotti 1983, Safran et al. 1986). In contrast, it is hypothesized that the modification of peripheral cognitive structures, while resulting in symptom remission, will leave the client vulnerable to relapse because the fundamental structures that predispose the client to the problem remain intact.

If these hypotheses are valid, it would seem vital for cognitive therapists to clarify the nature of these core structures more precisely and to have some way of accurately assessing them. With this objective in mind, the following proposition is now advanced. It is hypothesized that the core cognitive structures underlying clinical problems are interpersonal schemas. In other words, it is the individual's generic representation of self–other interactions that predisposes him or her to develop clinical problems and that ultimately must be modified if change is to be maintained. As discussed in Chapter 4, these interpersonal schemas are embedded within distinctive cognitive-interpersonal cycles in which characteristic construal processes lead to characteristic behaviors and communications. These in turn evoke schema-consistent responses in others.

Because of the intrinsic connection between cognitive and interpersonal levels, it is difficult to accurately assess the cognitive processes that are central to an individual's problems without an understanding of the interpersonal aspect of the cycle. Because a large component of interpersonal communication takes place at the nonverbal level (Ekman 1972, Kiesler 1982a, Mehrabian 1972), the interpersonal or behavioral link in a dysfunctional cognitive-interpersonal cycle is often particularly subtle. For example, a client may communicate with a slightly arrogant tilt of the head or a confrontative gaze that evokes irritation in people, or in a wooden or excessively vague fashion that elicits boredom and detachment, or with a tentative voice tone that evokes feelings of nurturance in others (Carson 1969, Kiesler 1982a). For these reasons, assessing the nature of a specific dysfunctional cognitive-interpersonal cycle can be a challenging task.

How is the therapist to identify the often subtle nuances in interpersonal style that constitute part of the client's dysfunctional cognitive-interpersonal cycle? While cognitive therapists have generally discouraged the therapeutic use of the transference, some have argued that the client's behavior in therapy can provide a useful sample of his or her problem behaviors (e.g., Arnkoff 1983, Goldfried and Davison 1976).

However, cognitive therapists still tend to ignore the fact that one of the most important clues available regarding the client's dysfunctional behaviors and communicational style is the therapist's feelings and action tendencies (Safran 1984a). As Sullivan (1953, 1956) suggested, the therapist can function as a *participant-observer* in the interaction with the client. The therapist responds to the client's interpersonal pull like others, yet is able to monitor his or her own feelings and response tendencies and to use them to generate hypotheses about the client's dysfunctional interpersonal style.

Kiesler (1982a, 1988) also suggests that the therapist can use his or her own feelings to help pinpoint specific client behaviors and communications that are problematic. These pinpointed behaviors and communications can be thought of as *interpersonal markers*[1] indicating useful points for cognitive exploration (Safran 1984a, Safran and Segal 1990). For example, the therapist notices that while she is pursuing a particular line of inquiry, the topic subtly shifts. At this point she might stop her client and say, "I noticed that first we were talking about one thing and then you began to talk about something else. What was going through your mind just before that happened?"

These interpersonal markers indicate unique and ideal junctures for cognitive exploration. It is likely that the occurrence of those interactional patterns that are most characteristically problematic for the client will be accompanied by those cognitive processes that play a pivotal role in the dysfunctional cognitive-interpersonal cycle. The client who distances people with his wooden tone will have best access to the associated cognitive processes when this behavior is particularly in evidence. The client who distances others with vagueness will have best access to the relevant cognitive processes when she is being particularly vague. The therapeutic employment of interpersonal markers of this type can be extremely useful for therapists because the correct identification and modification of core cognitive processes may be vital if change is to be maintained.

The use of the therapeutic relationship to assess the client's cognitive-interpersonal cycle can be illustrated with the following example: A young, intelligent graduate student has no intimate friends and comes to therapy complaining of interpersonal isolation

---

1. A marker is a term developed by Rice and Greenberg (1984) to refer to a distinctive client behavior or communication indicating a readiness for a particular kind of therapy intervention.

and feelings of loneliness. In the first few sessions the therapist becomes increasingly aware of his own feelings of distance from the client and a lack of warmth and engagement in himself. Through careful monitoring of his own feelings and the interaction between them and his client's behavior, he is able to identify certain fluctuations in his client's behavior and in his client's communication style that appear to be related to his own feelings of distance. He notes that at certain points in the interview, his client communicates in a particularly pedantic, intellectualized, abstract, and excessively qualified way, and that he feels most distant from him at those points.

Subsequently, by probing for his client's feelings and automatic thoughts at points when the *identified interpersonal marker* is most prevalent, the therapist is able to identify specific events and themes that trigger a negative self-evaluation and evoke anxiety in his client. For example, on one occasion the identified interpersonal marker is preceded by an interaction during which the therapist has responded emphatically to something the client has said.

Rather than follow his automatic inclination to withdraw from his client, the therapist metacommunicates to the client about his own reactions and helps him to explore his own feelings and automatic thoughts. In this particular situation it emerges that the client has been feeling warmly toward the therapist and is anxious that he will be rejected if he shows his feelings. Once this information is obtained, the therapist is able to work with the client to help him see the fashion in which his own self-criticism and anticipation of rejection have led to an interpersonal act with a distancing impact. He is able to help him challenge his automatic thoughts and devise ways of empirically testing his expectation that he will be rejected.

Exploration of cognitive activity associated with the identified marker on other occasions helps to clarify another important feature of the client's dysfunctional cognitive-interpersonal cycle. The client is able to identify a general feeling of anxiety and tension associated with an increase in his pedantic style, along with a desire to command the therapist's respect. This disclosure is consistent with previous evidence gathered in therapy that the client's self-esteem is very much linked to the perception of himself as being intelligent, knowledgeable, and verbally articulate. Information gathered by exploring cognitive activity associated with the identified interpersonal marker thus helps to further clarify the therapist's understanding of the client's core cognitive processes and the relationship between them and his problematic interpersonal style.

While the above example illustrates the fashion in which the therapist can use his or her own feelings and reactions to facilitate the assessment process, it must always be remembered that these feelings are not infallible indicators of problematic client behaviors. They may, in fact, reflect specific therapist sensitivities that are triggered by a specific client. Interpersonal theory hypothesizes that the probability that the therapist's reactions to the client parallel the reactions of others increases as the intensity and rigidity of the client's dysfunctional interpersonal style increase (Carson 1969, 1982, Kiesler 1982a, 1986, Leary 1957).

In the final analysis, however, it is *always* an interaction. As Sullivan (1954) remarked, "The psychiatrist has an inextricable involvement in all that goes on in the interview; and to the extent that he is unconscious or unwitting of his participation in the interview, to that extent he does not know what is happening" (p. 19). The ability and willingness to honestly acknowledge one's own role in the interaction is thus crucial (Gill 1982, Kiesler 1988, Strupp and Binder 1984).

The therapist's feelings and reactions and pinpointed interpersonal markers provide only starting points for further investigation. Ultimately, only a collaborative exploration with the client will clarify whether the particular interpersonal pattern that emerges in the therapeutic relationship and the particular cognitive processes that the client accesses in this context are relevant to the client's everyday problems (Safran and Segal 1990).

DISCONFIRMING DYSFUNCTIONAL INTERPERSONAL SCHEMAS

To the extent that one has rigid expectations of how others will be and rigid beliefs about how one has to be in order to maintain relatedness, one's interpersonal repertoire will be rigid and stereo-typed. Interpersonal theory hypothesizes that because behaviors invite or pull for complementary behaviors from others (Benjamin 1974, Kiesler 1983, Leary 1957), people with rigid interpersonal repertoires experience less diversity in their interpersonal experience than those with more flexible repertoires (Kiesler 1982a).

A corollary of this hypothesis is that the maladjusted individual has little opportunity to encounter new interpersonal experiences that will help to modify his or her interpersonal schemas. A major objective in interpersonal psychotherapy is for the therapist to intervene in a fashion that elicits new, adaptive, and noncharacter-istic behaviors from the client. This in turn will elicit new behaviors from the client's significant others, thus providing them with new interpersonal experiences (Kiesler 1982a, 1988). This objective is accomplished in a number of ways.

First, the therapist identifies the reactions that are evoked in her by the client. The therapist then "unhooks" herself from the client's interpersonal pull by consciously and intentionally refrain-ing from carrying through the automatically elicited action ten-dency (Kiesler 1982a, 1988). By not reacting to the client in a complementary fashion, the therapist provides the client with a new interpersonal experience and begins to elicit new interpersonal behaviors that are not characteristic of the client. For example, the therapist responding to the quarrelsome client without hostility exerts a pull for new behavior from the client.

A second mode of intervention consists of metacommunicating with the client about the reactions that the client evokes in the therapist and providing the client with feedback about the nonver-bal behaviors and paralinguistic communications that evoke these reactions (Kiesler 1982a, 1986, 1988). Clients are often unaware of the precise impact they have on others or the fashion in which they evoke these reactions. By providing feedback of this type, the therapist can help the client identify and subsequently change aspects of his or her communication style that maintain the dysfunc-tional interactional cycle.

In addition, the process of metacommunicating in this fashion facilitates the unhooking process by helping both participants in the interaction to step outside of it and explore it in a collaborative fashion. Moreover, pinpointing the relevant client behaviors and communications helps them to decenter from their immediate experience by beginning to see their own contributions to the interaction (Safran and Segal 1990).

Augmenting the interpersonal perspective with a cognitive emphasis can further illuminate the mechanisms through which in-session therapist behavior can bring about change and can provide additional guidelines for assessing what type of therapist interactional style will be maximally therapeutic. Therapists who correctly assess the nature of their clients' dysfunctional interpersonal schemas will have at their disposal important additional information that can guide them in understanding the impact of their behaviors on the client and in avoiding countertherapeutic behavior.

The integration of cognitive and interpersonal perspectives generates the following hypothesis. An important mechanism mediating the therapeutic impact of noncomplementary behavior is the experiential disconfirmation of dysfunctional interpersonal schemas. Thus, the therapist who refrains from responding to the hostile client with hostility may be disconfirming the client's belief that others will always be hostile toward him. The therapist who unhooks from the interpersonal pull to take charge of a client's life disconfirms the client's perception of himself or herself as a "helpless person who must be taken care of by others." The therapist who values and accepts the client even when the client is sad disconfirms the client's belief that he or she must always be happy in order to maintain relatedness to others. Thus, as Carson (1982) suggests, the client–therapist interaction provides an opportunity for ". . . generating perturbations in extant, maladaptive cognitive schemata and restructuring them into a more functional processing system" (p. 78).

An adequate assessment of core dysfunctional interpersonal schemas thus facilitates predictions about what type of interpersonal stance will be therapeutic in a more specific and refined way than the classical psychoanalytic prescription of therapeutic neutrality.

Conversely, failure to adequately assess a core interpersonal schema can result in unanticipated reactions to therapeutic interventions.

CONVERGENCE WITH OTHER PERSPECTIVES

The current perspective converges in some respects with the Mount Zion Group's (Weiss et al. 1987) view of the role that the disconfirmation of what they term pathogenic beliefs plays in psychodynamic therapy. They postulate that neurotic problems arise from these pathogenic or dysfunctional beliefs about interpersonal relationships that individuals develop as a result of maladaptive learning experiences with significant others. An example of a pathogenic belief would be the belief that one will be abandoned if one shows vulnerable feelings or that one will hurt others if one is independent.[2] They further hypothesize that clients in therapy unconsciously behave in a fashion that will test whether their therapists will confirm their pathogenic beliefs and that the disconfirmation of these beliefs is a central mechanism of change in psychodynamic therapy.

These hypotheses have now been evaluated in a series of studies. For example, Silberschatz (1987) demonstrated that the disconfirmation of pathogenic beliefs is significantly correlated with an immediate reduction in client anxiety, an increase in relaxation, and an increase in the extent to which the client confronts or elaborates bold or nontrivial material. Caston and associates (1987) found a relationship between the in-session disconfirmation of pathogenic beliefs and immediate increases in insight and the elaboration of nontrivial material. Silberschatz and colleagues (1986)

---

2. Eagle (1987) has previously pointed out the similarity between the concept of the pathogenic belief (Weiss et al. 1987) and Beck's concept of the dysfunctional attitude. He has also noted that pathogenic beliefs are dysfunctional attitudes of a particular type, that is, dysfunctional beliefs about interpersonal relationships. There is thus a close parallel between the concept of pathogenic belief and the concept of interpersonal schema as articulated in the current perspective.

found a relationship between immediate increases in client Experiencing Level (Klein et al. 1969) and the disconfirmation of pathogenic beliefs. They also found that good ultimate outcome was associated with a higher proportion of interventions disconfirming pathogenic beliefs to those confirming them. One particularly interesting finding is that the disconfirmation of pathogenic beliefs appears to play a role in the change process even when the therapist does not explicitly hold this hypothesis as a model of change (Weiss et al. 1987).

While the proposition that clients submit their therapist to transference tests either consciously or unconsciously is not a necessary component of the current position, the perspective that I am outlining *does* accord a central role in the therapeutic process to the disconfirmation of dysfunctional beliefs about self–other interactions through the therapeutic relationship.

There is also a similarity between the current view and Kohut's (1984) perspective on the mechanisms of therapeutic change. Kohut maintains that the central mechanism of therapeutic change in psychoanalysis is the process of *transmuting internalization.* According to him, the therapist, by providing the type of empathic, "mirroring" environment not provided by parents, helps the client to build new psychic structures. He further maintains that an important part of the change process often consists of empathically interpreting the client's reactions to inevitable lapses in the therapist's empathic behavior.

The current perspective recasts Kohut's formulation in a researchable framework. As Eagle (1984) argues, concepts such as transmuting internalization or "building structure" lack clear empirical meaning. A transmuting internalization may be understood in more cognitive terms, however, as the restructuring of a dysfunctional interpersonal schema through the provision of schema-inconsistent information at the experiential level. The concept of interpersonal schema helps to clarify in cognitive terms *the nature of the structure* that is being rebuilt—a generic cognitive representation of self–other interactions. In cognitive terms the internalization of the therapist is more readily understood as the development of a new working model of self–other interactions in which the generalized other is represented as potentially available.

A client's initial tendency to overreact to an experienced lapse in empathy can be understood in cognitive terms as what Beck (1976) refers to as dichotomous thinking (e.g., "either my therapist is completely empathic and available to me or he does not care"). This type of dichotomous thinking is fueled by the client's perception of self as inherently unlovable and of others as abandoning. Responding to an experienced lapse in empathy by withdrawing or acting in a hostile fashion may constitute an important component of a dysfunctional cognitive-interpersonal cycle, by precipitating the very abandonment that is anticipated.

DISTINCTIVE FEATURES OF AN INTEGRATIVE COGNITIVE-INTERPERSONAL APPROACH

Because the current approach has drawn heavily on Kiesler's (1982a, 1986, 1988) systematization of interpersonal therapy, there are obviously many similarities between the two approaches. There are, also, important similarities between the therapeutic approach outlined here and certain trends in contemporary psychodynamic thinking. The notion of the cognitive-interpersonal cycle is similar to Wachtel's (1977) cyclical psychodynamic perspective and to Strupp and Binder's (1984) conceptualization of the dynamic focus. It also bears some similarity to Luborsky's (1984) concept of the core conflictual relationship theme.

There are, however, some important features of the current approach that are distinctive products of the integration of cognitive and interpersonal approaches. While metacommunication about the therapeutic relationship plays a central role in most psychodynamic and interpersonal therapies, the current approach emphasizes a particular style of metacommunication. This involves the adaptation of cognitive techniques such as operationalizing expectations and reality testing (Beck et al. 1979) for exploring and challenging clients' dysfunctional interpersonal schemas. Although unhooking from the client's cognitive-interpersonal cycle may in itself challenge his or her dysfunctional beliefs about interpersonal relationships, the client may still fail to process schema-inconsistent information. It would seem reasonable to assume that the processing of information in the context of the therapist–client interaction follows the same rules of confirmatory biasing that information processing in other domains follows (Nisbett and Ross 1980).

It may be that any therapeutic metacommunication that is effective, whether it draws links between the current situation and others (as is more common in psychodynamic approaches) or focuses more intensively on different aspects of the current transaction (as is more common in Kiesler's approach) helps the client to clarify and test out dysfunctional expectations in the context of the therapeutic relationship (Safran and Segal 1990).

The client's subjective experience in session is regarded as a live sample of potentially relevant cognitive processing, and the emphasis is on exploring this material and helping the client to articulate his or her expectations as they emerge in the moment as clearly and explicitly as possible. The emphasis here is *phenomenological* rather than *interpretive* in nature.

The present approach articulates clear guidelines regarding optimal points in the interaction for exploring the client's cognitive processes. The notion of the *interpersonal marker* as a useful juncture for cognitive exploration is derived from the specific conceptual framework outlined here and in Safran (1990b) for clarifying the nature of the relationship between cognitive and interpersonal realms.

Once the client has articulated his or her expectations in the context of a specific therapeutic interaction, it is important for the therapist to maintain an ongoing exploration of whether the client experiences these expectations as being confirmed or disconfirmed. This process can be facilitated by encouraging the client to specify as clearly and concretely as possible what type of events would confirm the expectations and what events would disconfirm them. This process further facilitates the processing of schema-inconsistent information. In addition, the therapist can encourage the client to find *active ways* of testing the dysfunctional expectations that have been identified in session.

Weiss and colleagues (1987) theorize that clients unconsciously evaluate their pathogenic beliefs by submitting their therapists to transference tests. The current approach integrates this type of perspective with the stance of collaborative empiricism proposed by Beck and colleagues (1979), by encouraging clients to treat their perceptions as hypotheses and to *actively seek* ways of using the therapeutic relationship to evaluate hypotheses. The assumption is that promoting this type of active and intentional hypothesis testing will facilitate the change process by encouraging a conscious hypothesis testing set rather than leaving this process to chance.

Finally, the present approach reflects the cognitive behavioral emphasis on the generalization of changes to out-of-session situations. Thus, rather than assuming that learning that occurs through the therapeutic relationship will automatically generalize, clients are explicitly instructed to use out-of-therapy interactions to test expectations and beliefs that have been explored and evaluated through the therapeutic relationship. In this fashion, the client is encouraged to become an active collaborator in the therapeutic process and to continue the work between sessions.

The following example illustrates a number of the above principles. A careful assessment of a particular client's interpersonal schema suggested the presence of a belief that any suggestion of independence or emotional interest in other people by the client would be construed by the therapist as disloyalty and would lead to retaliation and abandonment. After explicitly clarifying the details of this working model in collaboration with the client, the therapist suggested that he generate a strategy for evaluating the accuracy of his expectation through action. The client suggested that he might try being more friendly with the clinic secretary. Once the client had developed this strategy, the focus switched to clarifying how the client would know whether his hypothesis had been confirmed or unconfirmed. Would the client be able to tell by evaluating the therapist's manner in the following session? Was there any possibility that he might misread the therapist's manner? In this fashion the client was encouraged to actively test out his dysfunctional belief and to be wary of his tendency to interpret events in a schema-consistent fashion. In subsequent sessions the client was encouraged to look for similar patterns in his relationships with other people and to generate other active strategies for evaluating this interpersonal working model between sessions.

THE RELATIONSHIP BETWEEN TECHNICAL AND RELATIONSHIP FACTORS

There has been a growing body of empirical evidence suggesting that the specific techniques associated with specific therapies are less important than therapy nonspecific factors such as positive qualities of the therapeutic relationship and the client's expectation that therapy will help. Lambert (1986) and Lambert and associates (1986) estimate, on the basis of their comprehensive reviews of the empirical literature, that while only 15 percent of the variance in outcome can be attributed to specific technical factors, up to 45 percent of the variance can be attributed to nonspecific factors. An illustrative study by Luborsky and colleagues (1985) found that while drug-dependent clients respond equally well to cognitive therapy plus drug counseling, supportive-expressive therapy plus drug counseling, and drug counseling alone, there were significant differences in the effectiveness of the individual therapists. The variable that was most highly predictive of outcome was the therapeutic alliance. This finding is consistent with the growing empirical evidence indicating the centrality of the therapeutic alliance to the change process. Orlinsky and Howard (1986), for example, in their comprehensive review of the research relating psychotherapy process variables to psychotherapy outcome, estimate that up to 80 percent of research relevant to the predictive value of the therapeutic alliance has produced significantly positive results.

This type of evidence is open to the interpretation that specific therapy techniques are unimportant and that it is the therapeutic relationship that is crucial to change. As Butler and Strupp (1986) point out, however, this interpretation is based upon the false assumption that specific and nonspecific factors are theoretically separable. As they argue, the traditional distinction between specific and nonspecific factors is based on the inappropriate assumption that psychotherapy is analogous to medical treatment. Unlike treatment through medication, however, wherein biological action is distinguishable in theory from the symbolic meaning of the treatment, psychotherapy techniques are intrinsically linked to the interpersonal context in which they take place. As Butler and Strupp (1986) point out, the impact of the therapist's intervention on the client will ultimately be determined by the meaning of that intervention to the client. The current conceptual framework suggests that this meaning will ultimately be mediated by the interpersonal schema that the client brings to bear upon the interpersonal situation. For example, a client who has an internal working model in which he or she is inadequate and others are critical may experience the cognitive therapist's attempt to examine the evidence relevant to a particular belief as invalidating and critical.

The exploration of factors leading to failed cognitive interventions and ruptures in the therapeutic alliance can lead to a deeper understanding of the client's internal working model of self–other relationships (Safran, Crocker et al. 1990, Safran and Segal 1990). These inevitable events should be seen as opportunities rather than as obstacles to therapy.

RESEARCH

There are two general types of research relevant to empirically evaluating the various propositions that have been advanced in this chapter. The first focuses on the evaluation of the efficacy of the therapeutic approach suggested. The second focus involves the evaluation of specific hypotheses regarding the process of change.

Outcome

Although evaluating the efficacy of the proposed approach may at first consideration appear straightforward, closer examination suggests that some obstacles be overcome. The most obvious approach would be to evaluate the relative efficacy of the proposed approach with a more traditional approach to cognitive therapy such as the protocol employed in the NIMH collaborative study on the treatment of depression (Elkin et al. 1989). The problem here, however, is the consistent failure of psychotherapy outcome research to find significant differences between treatments (e.g., Elkin et al. 1989, Luborsky et al. 1975, Sloane et al. 1975, Smith et al. 1980).

Various hypotheses have been advanced regarding the factors that make it difficult to demonstrate differential treatment efficacy (e.g., Kazdin 1986, Stiles et al. 1986), and I will not recount them all here. One particularly relevant factor, however, is that standard clinical trial studies obscure individual differences in outcome (Barlow and Hersen 1984, Chassan 1979, Kiesler 1966, Safran, Greenberg et al. 1988). Although the *average* client may show moderate gains in a particular study, in reality some clients do extremely well, others do moderately well, some do not change, and others deteriorate. The failure to find treatment differences may result, in part, from what Kiesler (1966) has termed the uniformity myth (i.e., the assumption that all clients are the same and benefit equally from all treatments). A clinical trial study that lumps together both clients who would be expected to benefit from a more traditional cognitive therapy and those who would not would have difficulty demonstrating the incremental utility of an integrative approach because many of them would be expected to do relatively well without it.

This type of methodological dilemma has prompted some psychotherapy researchers to follow Kiesler's (1966) recommendation to employ factorial designs to evaluate treatment by client type interactions. The problem with this approach, however, is that it assumes that the relevant client characteristics can be identified at the beginning of treatment. As Luborsky and colleagues (1980) conclude, it is often difficult to identify clients who will benefit from a particular treatment until therapy has commenced and an adequate sample of the client–therapist interaction is available. This fact has been partially responsible for stimulating researchers to move toward the investigation of the therapeutic alliance, rather than the static client characteristics, in an attempt to predict the outcome (Greenberg and Pinsof 1986).

For these reasons, rather than conducting a standard clinical trial study comparing cognitive therapy and the current approach, a better strategy may be to identify clients who either are not benefiting from standard cognitive therapy or are not establishing an adequate therapeutic alliance by a certain point in the treatment protocol. These clients would then be randomly assigned to either continue the standard treatment or shift to a therapeutic focus guided by the framework outlined in the current article.

Process Studies

Although the research design proposed above should be able to shed light on the efficacy of the current approach, it does not address the various hypotheses advanced regarding the mechanisms of change. In this section we will briefly consider a number of possible studies relevant to evaluating some of these hypotheses. A first important study entails the evaluation of the hypothesis that the disconfirmation of interpersonal schemas through the therapeutic interaction is an important mechanism of change. Weiss and colleagues (1987) have now conducted a number of studies demonstrating that "pathogenic beliefs" can be assessed reliably, and that therapist interventions which are rated reliably as disconfirming pathogenic beliefs are, as previously indicated, related to both immediate and ultimate outcome. It is beyond the scope of the present chapter to describe the elaborate methodology employed by Weiss and colleagues (1987), but there is sufficient similarity between the two theoretical approaches to permit the adaptation of their methodology to the present context. Collins and Messer (1988) have demonstrated that the basic Mount Zion Group methodology can be adapted to be used reliably with a different theoretical orientation. A first step would involve the adaptation of Weiss and colleagues' methodology to reliably assess dysfunctional interpersonal schemas and to evaluate the hypothesis that therapist interventions which are schema inconsistent are related to change.

A second related study would involve evaluating the hypothesis that the therapeutic alliance is mediated by whether the therapist

behaves in a fashion which either confirms or disconfirms the
client's core dysfunctional interpersonal schema. This could be
accomplished by dividing therapy sessions into high and low therapeutic alliance sessions on the basis of a validated measure of the
alliance and then comparing these two sessions types with respect to
the prevalence of interactions that are rated as schema disconfirming, using an adaptation of Weiss and colleagues' (1987) methodology. This type of study could be conducted either as a between
subjects or a within subjects design.

A third related study would involve evaluating the hypothesis
that one of the factors mediating the immediate outcome of a
traditional cognitive therapy challenging intervention (e.g., examining the evidence or considering alternatives) is whether that intervention is at an implicit level either confirming or disconfirming of
the client's core dysfunctional interpersonal schema.

As indicated previously, it is hypothesized that the impact of the
therapist's intervention is mediated by the client's perception of
the meaning of that intervention. This, in turn, is mediated by the
interpersonal schema that the client brings to bear upon the
interaction. This leads to the hypothesis that the positive impact of
a specific cognitive intervention will be mitigated if the client
perceives the therapist's action in a way which confirms his or her
dysfunctional interpersonal schema. This hypothesis could be evaluated by having independent raters evaluate the degree of cognitive
change taking place following every challenge intervention and
then rating the extent to which these interventions are schema
confirming or disconfirming using an adaptation of the methodology of Weiss and associates (1987).

A final research direction would involve evaluating the hypothesis that clients' interpersonal schemas change as a result of the
therapeutic approach described in the present article. This could be
accomplished by administering the type of interpersonal schema
questionnaire (Safran, Hill et al. 1988) described in Chapter 4 to
clients before and after treatment and evaluating whether change
on other outcome measures is associated with change on this
measure. A related investigation would involve evaluating whether
change on an interpersonal schema measure of this type is related

to maintenance of treatment gains at follow-up. If a questionnaire of this type provides a valid operationalization of an enduring cognitive structure that shapes information processing and interpersonal patterns, then those subjects who show significant changes on this measure should show more enduring changes in other areas than those who do not.

CONCLUSIONS

There has been a tendency in the cognitive behavioral literature to consider the therapeutic relationship to be less important than specific cognitive techniques. This is beginning to change as cognitive therapists increasingly recognize the importance of the relationship. There still, however, remains a tendency to view a good therapeutic relationship as more of a necessary condition for change than a mechanism of change. The current perspective, however, suggests that this view of things fails to recognize the inseparable nature of technical and relationship factors in the change process. By "unpacking" the concept of the therapeutic relationship, my intention has been to show how every cognitive intervention inevitably impacts on the therapeutic relationship and how any "relationship act" is ultimately a cognitive intervention. This type of clarification will hopefully help cognitive therapists explore the more subtle interpersonal aspects of the change process with the same type of conceptual rigor that has been applied to the cognitive realm.

Part II

Emotion in Cognitive Therapy

6

Hot Cognition and Psychotherapy Process: An Information-Processing/ Ecological Approach

Jeremy D. Safran and Leslie S. Greenberg

INTRODUCTION

The central theme that orients this chapter is the recognition that researchers and theorists in the psychotherapy field require and integrative perspective on cognition, emotion, and action to guide their thinking about the process of change in psychotherapy. In this chapter we will discuss a number of considerations relevant to the construction of such a model and briefly review alternative ways that theorists have chosen to think about the relationships among these three aspects of human functioning. Our objective will not be in any way to fully articulate a comprehensive model of the relationships among cognition, affect, and behavior, but rather to articulate a number of considerations relevant to the construction of such a model, in the hope that this process will be an impetus to the development of relevant theory and research in the future. In the process we will be talking not only about different approaches to conceptualizing the relationships among emotion, cognition, and behavior, but also about different metatheoretical perspectives on human functioning. Our impression has been that, all too often in the past, theorists have accepted certain theoretical assumptions without regard to the particular metatheoretical perspectives from which these assumptions derive and without consideration of alternative metatheoretical perspectives.

A further aim of this chapter is to refine the cognitive-behavioral conceptualization of emotion. After briefly discussing developments in the cognitive-behavioral conceptualization of the relationships among cognition, emotion, and behavior, we will explore the contributions that cognitive psychology has to make to our understanding of the role of emotional cognition or "hot cognition" in the psychotherapy process. Two different cognitive metatheoretical perspectives are compared: the information-processing metapsychology and the ecological metapsychology. This comparison is followed by a discussion of the value of integrating these metatheoretical perspectives in order to obtain a more comprehensive metatheoretical perspective of human functioning. We then outline our integrative model of emotional processing (Greenberg and Safran 1984b, 1986) in which emotion, cognition, and action are all viewed as interdependent aspects of a complex system that is involved in generating meaning. The role of emotion in psychotherapy is discussed, and we conclude with the presentation of a number of different types of therapeutic interventions that emerge from this integrative perspective.

THE COGNITIVE-BEHAVIORAL MODEL: ASSUMPTIONS ABOUT COGNITION, EMOTION, AND BEHAVIOR

The cognitive-behavioral model of emotion is sometimes represented in simplified form as the A-B-C sequence, originally articulated by Ellis (1962). In this model, "A" refers to the activating event, "B" refers to beliefs and corresponding internal dialogue, and "C" refers to the emotional consequence. While this model captures the central role accorded to cognitive mediating processes in cognitive-behavioral theory, it fails to represent a number of important theoretical refinements that have taken place in this model over the years.

Early cognitive-behavioral theory emphasized the causal role that conscious cognitive processes play in the production of emotion and behavior (Beck 1976, Ellis 1972, Mahoney 1974). Important tasks in the early years of cognitive-behavioral theorizing consisted of arguing for the superiority of mediational over nonmediational approaches and for the value of assuming that the relevant cognitive processes are conscious, rather than unconscious.

As the cognitive-behavioral tradition has developed, other theoretical issues have come to assume increasing importance. Bandura's (1978) argument about the need for a reciprocal determinist perspective cogently demonstrated the shortcomings of viewing the relationships among cognition, behavior, and environment in a unidirectional causal fashion. Zajonc's (1980) provocative article in *American Psychologist* has sparked a lively debate about whether it is reasonable to assume that cognition precedes emotion (e.g., Greenberg and Safran 1984a,b, Lazarus 1984, Mahoney 1984, Rachman 1984, Zajonc 1984).

In addition, some cognitive-behavioral theorists have begun to argue for the importance of expanding our definition of cognitive processes to include both conscious and unconscious cognitive processes (e.g., Kendall and Bemis 1984, Mahoney 1980, Meichenbaum and Gilmore 1984, Safran and Greenberg 1986a). A somewhat related development has been the criticism of those cognitive-behavioral approaches that tend to equate cognition with logical, conceptual activity and to ignore or underemphasize the role of perceptual activity in human functioning (Greenberg and Safran 1980, 1981). The tendency to adopt propositional logic as the sine qua non of human cognition has in the past left cognitive behaviorists open to criticism from those who assert that emotional problems persist even when clients know that their thinking is illogical or irrational (Rachman 1983, Wolpe 1978). As we will argue later, the exclusive identification of human recognition with propositional logic follows from the computer metaphor that has dominated the field of experimental cognitive psychology. While this metaphor has played a valuable and instrumental role in the development of cognitive psychology, it is important not to overlook its limitations. In the next section, we will examine in greater detail some of the implications of the computer metaphor for our understanding of human functioning.

THE CONTRIBUTIONS OF COGNITIVE PSYCHOLOGY

Over the years a number of theorists and researchers have urged cognitive-behavioral therapists to turn to the field of experimental cognitive psychology for new insights (e.g., Arnkoff 1980, Goldfried 1979, Greenberg and Safran 1980, 1981). What exactly does mainstream experimental cognitive psychology have to teach us about the relationship between emotion, cognition, and action? Unfortunately, as we have concluded elsewhere (Greenberg and Safran 1984b, 1986, Safran and Greenberg 1982b), traditionally cognitive psychology has had little to say about emotion. While the investigation of cognitive processes once again became a legitimate field of inquiry with the publication of Neisser's (1967) *Cognitive Psychology*, emotion was not until relatively recently granted equal status as a domain acceptable for scientific investigation. Moreover, as theorists such as Turvey (1977) and Weimer (1977) have argued, traditional cognitive psychology has had little to say about the relationship between cognition and action. These omissions seriously restrict the relevance of mainstream experimental cognitive psychology to the clinician, because problems in living always involve the interactions among cognition, emotion, and behavior. We are not the first to raise these concerns about mainstream cognitive psychology. Ulric Neisser, considered by many to be one of the fathers of cognitive psychology, has raised similar questions about the direction in which the field is heading. Neisser's (1976, 1980) criticisms focus upon the lack of ecological validity of much of the research that takes place in experimental cognitive psychology and on the tendency of experimental cognitive psychologists to study phenomena that are artifacts of artificial laboratory situations instead of the real phenomena of interest. While our current criticism is a more specific one (i.e., the failure of mainstream cognitive psychology to deal with the role of emotional processes and action in human functioning), this failure can be seen as a specific case of the general failure to investigate psychological phenomena in a holistic, ecologically valid context. While many cognitive behavior therapists are turning to experimental cognitive psychology for answers, we believe that it is important at this point to be somewhat circumspect and to ask ourselves what exactly mainstream cognitive psychology has to offer us as clinicians.

Information-Processing versus Ecological Perspectives in Cognitive Psychology

The failure of mainstream cognitive psychology to provide clinicians with the type of answers they need about the relationships among cognition, emotion, and action has led us to raise some more general and fundamental criticisms of mainstream cognitive psychology. As Neisser (1980) has pointed out, it is important to realize that there is not one cognitive psychology. It is important to distinguish between different metatheoretical perspectives in cognitive psychology. The predominant metatheory underlying cognitive psychology can perhaps best be described as the information-processing metatheory. Perhaps the most influential metaphor in this tradition has been that of people as computing machines. As Shaw and Bransford (1977) pointed out, the brain–computer analogy inherent in the information-processing perspective has many valuable features, but its shortcomings should not be overlooked. This analogy has helped to free many psychologists from the excessive restrictions of radical behaviorism by providing modeling techniques that allow us to make precise theoretical predictions about unobservable processes. Nevertheless, many aspects of human psychological functioning are not adequately captured by the brain–computer analogy. It is always best to remember that, as with any analogy, the brain–computer analogy is an approximate one, and that in reality there are various aspects of correspondence and noncorrespondence between human beings and computers. Again, as Shaw and Bransford (1977) point out, cognitive psychologists in pursuing the person–computer analogy

> tend to forget that humans and animals are active, investigatory creatures driven by definite intents through a complex, changing environment replete with meaning at a variety of levels of analysis. Thus we feel no tinge of theoretical compunction in blithely comparing such active, knowledge seeking beings with unconscious, static machines that lack a wit of natural motivation. Unlike humans and animals, who perceptually mine the world for information on a need to know basis, artificial systems can soak up information passively by being spoon-fed batches of alpha numeric characters that have been conceptually predigested by human programmers. . . . In such a sterile model of man, perceiving becomes a passive process and knowing a purposeless one, and as for action (that is purposive behavior), it remains non-existent. [p. 3]

Not all cognitive psychologists, however, subscribe to an information-processing metatheory. Perhaps the most serious metatheoretical contender is the ecological metatheory initially advanced by J. J. Gibson (1966). The ecological perspective focuses upon the interaction between the person and the environment in which he or she lives. Human beings are thus seen as organisms that live and operate in the context of specific environments and are adapted through an evolutionary process to their environmental niche. The ecological perspective is thus a *functional* perspective. It is concerned with understanding the adaptive significance of various aspects of human functioning in the context of the environment in which they have evolved. It is thus assumed that there is no way that we can begin to understand human psychological functioning without a detailed understanding of the environment in which this functioning takes place. The emphasis is thus much more upon the interface between people and their environment than it is upon information-transforming processes that are hypothesized to take place inside the individual's head.

Consistent with this, the emphasis of the ecological perspective is on the *acquisition of knowledge from the environment* rather than upon the processing of information about the environment. This may appear to be a subtle distinction, but in fact it is a very real and fundamentally important one. The information-processing perspective focuses upon the processing of information that the organism is presumed to register passively. (However, note that different information-processing theorists vary with respect to their assumptions about how active a role the individual plays in the processing of information.) The ecological perspective, however, does not make the types of distinctions that information-processing theory makes between different aspects of human functioning, such as perception, action, and cognition. Because the individual is conceptualized as an organism in interaction with its environment and the emphasis is upon the acquisition of knowledge about the environment, *action* is seen as part of the process of acquiring such knowledge. The assumption is thus that one cannot understand cognition independent of action. The separation of human functioning into action and cognition is thus an artificial one. Acting upon the world and acquiring knowledge about the world are parts of the same process.

Because the ecological perspective focuses upon the interaction of the organism with the environment and the assumption is that the organism is adapted to its ecological niche, it is also assumed that *perception* is the fundamental act through which the organism acquires information about the environment. In the traditional information-processing perspective, it is customary to focus upon perception in one sensory modality at a time. Thus, information-processing theory develops a model of visual perception or a model of auditory perception. In contrast, the ecological perspective emphasizes that perception takes place in all sensory modalities simultaneously. Thus, in the most radical form of the ecological approach (e.g., Gibson 1966), it becomes unnecessary to speak about higher-level cognitive processes that transform information into a form where it can be used by the organism. The assumption is that the organism becomes attuned to the environment so that the individual perceives meaning in the environment. The act of perception thus assumes a central role in the ecological perspective, and it is assumed that the focus of investigation should be at the point of interface between the organism and the environment (i.e., perceptual activity) rather than at some higher-level cognitive information-processing activities that are hypothesized to be taking place. Perception is conceptualized as more than an initial step in a chain of information-processing activity. It is hypothesized that meaning is inherent in the act of perception, and that knowledge of the world is acquired directly through simultaneous perceptual activity in all sensory domains.

From an ecological perspective it is thus seen as more parsimonious to assume that evolution has rendered a complex process of information processing unnecessary by designing perceptual systems that are adapted to extract meaning directly from the environment. As Shaw and Bransford (1977) state:

Hence, when asked where the buck of knowledge ceases to be passed, or where the epistemic regress ends, the ecological psychologist responds: At the beginning of the process; it starts with perception, the process upon which the intrinsic meaning of man's relationship to his world is founded. It is the perceiver who knows and the knower who perceives, just as it is the world that is both perceived and known. Neither memory, nor inference, nor any other epistemic process than perception intervenes between the knowing agent and the world it knows, for knowing is a direct rather than an indirect process. [p. 10]

A number of characteristics of the ecological perspective make it more suitable than an information-processing perspective for helping us to understand the role and nature of emotional processes in human functioning. Emotion is a fundamental aspect of what it is to be human. It is no less central to human functioning than are cognitions or behavior. A metatheoretical perspective based upon the person–computer analogy alone will necessarily be inadequate for purposes of understanding and modeling the functioning of a living organism that is in dynamic interaction with its environment, continuously acting, feeling, and thinking.

Our position is that an approach to investigation that attempts to understand the nature of cognitive processes by temporarily bracketing off action and emotion is bound to come up with a distorted understanding of the phenomenon of interest. Cognition, emotion, and behavior are in reality fused (cf. Greenberg and Safran 1984b). The implications of this assertion extend beyond the commonly held cognitive-behavioral position that there is a reciprocally determining relationship among cognition, emotion, behavior, and environment. The notion of reciprocal determinism, while conceptually useful, still assumes that each link in the multidirectional causal chain possesses an independent existential status. As Lazarus and colleagues (1982), however, aptly stated:

> Thoughts, emotions and motives are inferred from observations of the person, and we have noted how they often have the same referents. How we partition these concepts and punctuate theoretical sequences is often a matter of theoretical and methodological convenience. Yet we cannot lose sight of the fact that cognition, motivation and emotion are inferential processes, not entities, each with a separate and independent existence. For purposes of conceptual analysis, it is appropriate to distinguish among them. However, we must realize that in nature, that is, in the actual phenomena of human experience and action, they are usually fused and difficult to separate. To speak of such fusion is not a matter of conceptual sloppiness but a recognition of the necessity of putting the pieces back together into an organized whole. [p. 236]

For a number of reasons, then, we believe that mainstream cognitive psychology has not and will not fully meet the high hopes and expectations that clinical psychologists have had for it. To summarize, the adequacy of the information-processing tradition as a comprehensive metatheory is compromised by (1) the failure to take into account the fundamental role of motivation/emotion and perception in human functioning, (2) the tendency to regard perception in an overly restrictive fashion, (3) the absence of a biological/evolutionary and ultimately functional perspective, and (4) the failure to recognize that the practice of modeling some aspects of human psychological functioning while ignoring others provides a distorted picture of the phenomenon of interest.

In contrast to the information-processing approach, the ecological perspective emphasizes the role of biological/evolutionary factors in human functioning. In this respect it incorporates the type of neo-Darwinian perspective that has proved to be a powerful conceptual tool in contemporary ethology (Bowlby 1969, Lorenz 1973). As Dixon (1981) pointed out, a biological frame of reference can provide a much needed corrective influence to cognitive theory and research. Moreover, the ecological perspective eliminates the gap between epistemic processes and actions that has plagued theorists in social and cognitive psychology (Baron 1980). This is particularly important in the context of psychotherapy, where the ability to understand the relationship between cognitive change and action in the world is paramount. Finally, the ecological perspective provides a congenial framework for accommodating the type of affective-motivational considerations that are so central to psychotherapy. This is not to say that ecological theorists have dealt extensively with such considerations in the past; they haven't. As we shall see, however, the ecological emphasis upon in-wired perceptual adaptation and the complete interdependence between knowledge and action provides a useful framework for this purpose.

While we have been quite vehement in our criticisms of the mainstream information-processing approach, it is important not to throw out the baby with the bathwater. We believe that while information-processing metatheory has the above limitations, it also has some valuable features. Neisser's (1976) book *Cognition and Reality* provides an excellent example of a compromise position that attempts to combine the best features of an ecological perspective with the best features of an information-processing perspective. In this book Neisser adopts the ecological emphasis upon perceptual processing and interaction with the environment but also retains the information-processing concept of schema. He proposes that the individual acts upon the world through perceptual activity and that this activity revises expectations or schemata in an ongoing fashion. The individual acts upon the environment and is in turn acted upon by the environment. This ongoing modification of his or her expectations in turn continues to direct perceptual activity in an ongoing fashion.

Our objective is to advocate a middle-ground position, similar in some respects to that described above. Epistemologically the position we hold is best described by what Bhaskar (1979) has termed *transcendental realism*. This is a fallibilist realism in which knowledge is viewed as a social constructive process. At the same time, however, it is acknowledged that there is a real world that exists independent of cognizing experience. This results in a view of the cognitive system as constructive but as being able to be more or less accurate and to be continually striving toward greater fidelity of representation of what actually exists independent of the constructive process. In the next section, we will discuss some of the developments in information-processing theory that we believe can be usefully incorporated into this middle-ground position.

Recent Developments

A number of theoretical and empirical developments in the field of cognitive information-processing theory are useful for purposes of incorporating emotional into a more integrative view of human functioning and psychotherapy. Three such developments we will discuss are research and theory on unconscious information processing, associative network models, and schema models.

Unconscious Information Processing

One important development in the field of cognitive information processing that we believe is particularly relevant to the understanding of emotional processes in human functioning is the research and theory on unconscious information processing (Greenberg and Safran 1986, Safran and Greenberg this volume, Chapter 7). It is interesting to note that those theories of psychological functioning, which were initially developed to account for a variety of clinical phenomena (e.g., Freud 1896, Janet 1907), relied heavily upon the notion of unconscious motivation and the influence on behavior of information processing that occurs outside of conscious awareness. As Bowers and Meichenbaum (1984) point out, it is no surprise that theories developed initially to account for complex clinical phenomena relied upon formulations of the unconscious, given the apparent incomprehensibility of much "abnormal behavior" when viewed from a rational perspective. With the ascendance of the behavioral tradition in experimental psychology, theories dealing with unconscious processing fell into disrepute as did all mediational theories. When consciousness once again became a legitimate domain of inquiry, it is not surprising that one of the last areas of investigation to gain legitimate status was the domain of the unconscious. Given the fact that unconscious processes by their very definition seem to be nonamenable to direct observation and thus empirical investigation, unconscious processing was one of the last domains to gain legitimacy as a field for investigation. However, as more recent theorists and researchers have begun to recognize, it is impossible to have a viable theory of conscious information processing without having a theory of unconscious information processing (Bowers and Meichenbaum 1984, Dixon 1981, Mahoney 1980, Shevrin and Dickman 1980). One of the first areas of investigation in cognitive psychology to open the doors to the investigation of unconscious information processing was research on selective attention (e.g., Broadbent 1958, Kahneman 1973, Neisser 1967, Treisman 1969). Other active areas of relevant research have been the work on subliminal perception (e.g., Dixon 1981) and on implicit learning (e.g., Reber and Lewis 1977). We have reviewed this literature and discussed the importance of unconscious processing elsewhere (Greenberg and Safran 1986, Safran and Greenberg this volume, Chapter 7) and will limit ourselves here to noting the increasing recognition in cognitive psychology of the importance of unconscious processing in influencing people's perceptions and actions.

Associative Network Models

Another major theoretical and research development in the field of cognitive information processing that we find to be particularly relevant for purposes of understanding the nature of emotional processes in psychotherapy is the concept of semantic networks. As Johnson-Laird and colleagues (1984) point out, semantic network theories are essentially an evolution of a basic associationist model resulting from an attempt to frame such models for computers.

There is nothing new about the assumption that words and concepts vary with respect to the degree of associative relationship they have with one another. What distinguishes semantic network theory from simple associative theories, however, is the ability of semantic network theory to go beyond a simple model of word association to one of meaning. The inadequacy of a simple associationist model for purposes of understanding memory for meaning is illustrated by the following example taken from Johnson-Laird and colleagues (1984). The word *black* is strongly associated with both *white* and *night*. However, the nature of the relationship between *black* and *white* is very different from the nature of the relationship between *black* and *night*. An adequate model of meaning therefore requires the ability to distinguish between different kinds of concepts and different kinds of links between concepts. The development of computer modeling techniques provided theorists with the conceptual tools for labeling different kinds of concepts and different kinds of links between concepts. In semantic network models, the relationship between different items stored in memory is represented in terms of the degree of association between items in the network (represented by the length of the link or pathway), the nature of the association (represented by the label of the link), and the nature of the items that are associated (represented by the labels attached to nodes in the network). A number of different semantic network theories have been developed (e.g., Anderson and Bower 1973, Collins and Loftus 1975, Quillian 1968, Rumelhart et al. 1972).

These different network theories share a number of assumptions and are different with respect to certain assumptions. A common feature of all semantic network models, however, is that they provide a model of the organization of information in memory, which takes into account that there are different kinds of information stored in memory and different kinds of associations between information stored in memory. All semantic network theories are able to make predictions about the speed with which the activation of one element in a semantic network should activate elements in the network, and the notion of spreading activation of semantic networks is central to all semantic network theories.

Bower (1981) has extended the semantic network notion in order to take into account the relationship between emotion and various other aspects of meaning in memory. In Bower's model, emotions are represented as specific nodes or units in memory that collect together many different aspects of the emotion. Emotions thus play an important organizational role in memory. The aspects that collect around emotion nodes include autonomic reactions, standard roles, and expressive behaviors, and descriptions of standard evocative situations that lead to the particular emotion. According to Bower, each emotion node is also linked with propositions describing events from one's life during which the emotion was aroused.

These emotion nodes can be activated through the activation of any of the units in memory that are linked to the emotion node. For example, the activation of a specific episodic memory associated with a specific emotion can activate that emotion. Similarly, the activation of a particular expressive behavior linked to a specific emotion node can activate that emotion. The activation of any one particular unit in memory that is linked to a specific emotion node may not necessarily activate that specific emotion node, but may raise the threshold of that particular node, so that it will be more easily activated by another unit in memory that is linked to that emotion node.

Schema Models

Although the schema concept can be traced as far back as Bartlett (1932), it has more recently acquired a new prominence in cognitive psychology. While specific definitions of the schema construct vary from theorist to theorist, in general there is agreement that schemata can be thought of as cognitive structures in memory that organize information abstracted from prior experience and guide both the processing of new information and the retrieval of stored information. As evidence continues to accumulate about the central role of unconscious processing in human functioning, many researchers are turning to the concept of schematic processing in an attempt to clarify the fashion in which the automatic encoding of fundamental information takes place (Hasher and Zacks 1984).

As Fiske and Linville (1980) argue, the schema construct, while not without its problems, nevertheless appears to have some theoretical merit when evaluated against specific criteria of good scientific theory. Research has demonstrated that the schema construct does have some predictive utility, has been profitable in terms of generating productive research, and appears to have generalizability to a large number of domains of interest (e.g., memory, attention, social psychology, and clinical psychology). As we see it, the issue of generalizability is an important one because many of the constructs in cognitive psychology may be formulated at a level of analysis that is appropriate to the intensive investigation of specific processes at a molecular level of interest to cognitive psychologists, but may not be sufficiently molar to constitute an appropriate level for analysis for social and clinical psychologists.

Leventhal (1984) employed the schema construct as a way of understanding the relationship between emotion and other cognitive processes. He hypothesized that emotional experiences are included in memory in schematic structures consisting of a number of constituent components, which combine as a whole to create the experience of emotion. These constituent schematic elements include episodic memories for specific events associated with a specific emotional experience, autonomic patterns associated with these experiences of specific emotions, and images and expressive motor behaviors associated with specific emotions. Leventhal (1982) theorizes that these schematic structures are coded in memory at a preattentive level. According to him, when one component of a specific emotion schema is activated, it increases the potential for activating the entire schematic structure, resulting in the subjective experience of the emotion associated with that schematic structure.

This notion of schematic structures associated with emotions is compatible with Lang's (1983) theorizing about the role of emotion prototypes. According to Lang, emotion prototypes are structures in memory that are quite similar to the type of structures about which Leventhal wrote, and that consist of similar constituent elements. Lang also agrees that the activation of one element of an emotion prototype, or the right combination of critical elements, will activate the entire prototype and result in the subjective experience of the associated emotion.

INTEGRATIVE THEORY

It appears that schema and associative network constructs have a number of similarities. Specifically, they both specify that different events or features associated either temporally, semantically, or conceptually are linked in memory in one fashion or another. Furthermore, both constructs stipulate that information can be coded and linked in memory at a preattentive level, out of awareness. Finally, they both stipulate that the activation of one unit in memory can lead to the activation of associated units in memory, and that this activation can all take place at the *preattentive* or *unconscious* level.

There are undoubtedly specific differences in terms of the predictions that can be derived from schema theory and associative network theory, and it will be important in the future to specify exactly what are the similarities and differences in predictions. It may be the case that both concepts are required in order to adequately describe and explain the phenomena of interest. It may be, for example, that schema theory is useful for talking about the domain of processing external information, whereas associative network theory is more useful for making specific predictions about the processing of internal information. While these types of issues remain to be clarified, it nevertheless appears that the notions of schema, associative network, and *unconscious* or *preattentive processing* may be of some theoretical utility.

Bearing in mind these developments in information-processing theory, as well as the metatheoretical concerns discussed earlier, we will now outline some of the basic themes in our thinking about the relationships among emotion, cognition, and action. Our intention here is not so much to outline a comprehensive, integrative model of emotional processing, as it is to outline theoretical guidelines that we believe are useful in guiding our thinking about the relationships among emotion, cognition, and behavior in the therapeutic context.

The Adaptive Role of Emotion in Human Functioning

We take as a basic starting point the assumption that emotion plays an adaptive role in human functioning. This postulate can be accommodated within the ecological metatheoretical perspective and has dramatic implications for our thinking about the relationships among emotion, cognition, and action in the psychotherapy process. It is thus truly a basic epistemological assumption that shapes the very way in which we think about the phenomenon of interest. We also believe that this is a necessary assumption to allow us to think productively about affective phenomena in therapy in all their complexity (Greenberg and Safran 1984b, 1986a, Safran and Greenberg 1982a,b).

Along with other theorists (e.g., Arnold 1960, Izard 1977, Leventhal 1982, Plutchik 1980, Tomkins 1980), we postulate that emotional processing has evolved in the human species through a process of natural selection. Emotional processes thus play an adaptive role in human functioning. This is not to say that a specific emotion is necessarily adaptive in a specific context, but rather that, in general, emotional processes play an adaptive role in human functioning.

In what way do emotions play an adaptive role in human functioning? We hypothesize that emotions provide us with information about ourselves as organisms in interaction with the environment. Emotions function to motivate adaptive action in the world. In the words of Michotte (1950), emotions are functional connections between the individual and the environment. They thus constitute a bridge through which people are linked to their ecological niche. This bridge has evolved through a process of natural selection. Emotions are not epiphenomena or exclusively the product of the cognitive interpretation of nonspecific arousal, as Schachter and Singer (1962) theorize. The basic structure for emotions is hardwired into the human animal (e.g., Izard 1977, Leventhal 1982, Tomkins 1980).

Emotions function as action dispositions. Different classes of action are inherent in different emotions. Anger, for example, will lead to aggressive, self-protective behavior if carried through into action. Fear will lead to self-protective behavior through flight if carried forward into action. Loneliness can lead to affiliative action. Affiliative behaviors play a strong role in terms of the survival of the species. Love can lead to affiliation and to procreation.

Emotion and Nonverbal Behavior

It is commonly observed that there appears to be some kind of integral relationship between emotion and nonverbal behavior. This of course has tremendously important implications for the practice of psychotherapy. We essentially "read" other people or infer what is going on for them intrapsychically on the basis of nonverbal cues (Kiesler 1982b). Elsewhere (Greenberg and Safran 1986a) we have reviewed the growing body of evidence demonstrating that there are both cross-individual and cross-cultural similarities in terms of the specific nonverbal behaviors and configurations of nonverbal behavior that are associated with specific emotions. Research of this type has been seen by some (e.g., Izard 1977, Tomkins 1980) as corroborating the hypothesis that the basic structure for specific emotions is hardwired into the human species.

Moreover, because the majority if not all of this research has focused on the relationship between facial expression and emotion, some theorists have concluded that facial feedback and/or facial feedforward plays a central role in the production of emotional experience (e.g., Izard 1977, Leventhal 1982, Tomkins 1980). We hypothesize that the relationship between emotion and nonverbal behavior is not necessarily restricted to the facial region. However, we believe that the relative ease with which the relationship between emotions and facial expression can be detected is accounted for by the fact that facial expression plays a significant role in nonverbal communication. We thus hypothesize that facial expression has evolved into the most visible, nonverbal marker of emotional change, but that it is not necessarily the only anatomical cue pattern in which nonverbal specificity is associated with emotional change (Greenberg and Safran 1986a).

As stated previously, different emotions appear to have different action tendencies inherent in them. Emotions are thus not purely a subjective experience. They are inherently behavioral in nature. The experience of fear, for example, consists of nonverbal behavior as well as a subjective experience (Lang 1983). These nonverbal behaviors may consist of specific and recognizable facial expressions as well as particular patterns of muscular movement or tension in the upper or lower torso. Muscular tension in the upper and lower torso can potentially lead to fight or flight behavior if further elaborated. These nonverbal behaviors are thus part of an action disposition. If actualized, they will lead to more extensive actions in the world that are either directly instrumental in nature or have a communicative function. They are thus a biological link to the ecological niche.

Emotion and Perceptual-Motor Processing

As Turvey (1977) argues, there is an integral link between perception, action, and knowledge of the world. We argue further that there is an integral link between perception, action, knowledge of the world, and *knowledge of the self.* This fourth dimension, that is, knowledge of self, is brought into play through the cognitive representation of our own expressive/motor experience. There is something fundamental and basic about the perceptual motor system. As Piaget (1954) pointed out, a child's initial response to the world is perceptual-motor in nature. In acquiring knowledge of the world, a child constructs sensory motor schemata long before he or she can construct more abstract representations of the world. These sensory motor schemata are essentially representations of the child's actions upon the world. A child thus comes to know the world initially through a combination of his or her perception of objects in the world and through manipulation of these objects. As ecological theorists point out (Gibson 1979), perception and action are thus integrally related. Acquiring knowledge of the world through our actions upon it does not occur only in infants. As Polanyi (1966) argues, action upon the world lies at the heart of knowledge acquisition. Adults are able to operate upon the world through complex, abstract symbolic processes, but these abstract processes always remain ultimately tied to action and perception.

Emotions and Meaning

Gibson's (1979) concept of affordances is useful here for clarifying the relationships among emotion, perception, and meaning. According to Gibson (1979), objects in the world have an inherent meaning for human beings and this meaning is grasped in terms of what the objects *afford* to the person or what their functional value is. A flat surface affords a surface for walking. A small, hard object affords a potential missile for throwing. We thus perceive (and it is important to remember that for Gibson *perceiving* and *knowing* are synonymous) objects and events in terms of their *affordances*. The addition of emotions to Gibson's ecological analysis adds another dimension to the equation. We know objects not only in terms of what they afford us but also in terms of the way in which they impact upon us as biological organisms. This later information is gleaned through the action tendencies that different objects pull from us. As ecologically oriented theorists maintain, meaning is inherent in the act of perception. This meaning emerges out of perceiving not only objects and events, but also the implications of these objects and events for us as biological organisms. The meaning of an object or event for us as biological organisms is essentially the action disposition that it evokes in us. And this in turn is the root of emotional experience.

The Emotional Synthesis Process

Emotion theorists, who are oriented by a biological/evolutionary perspective, provide us with a view on some of the possible primary emotions and their functions. Izard (1977), for example, recognizes the existence of ten fundamental emotions: interest, joy, surprise, distress, anger, disgust, contempt, fear, shame, and guilt. Other theorists such as Tomkins (1980) and Plutchik (1980) have their own overlapping variations.

Although there is some disagreement among theorists as to what emotions are primary and what emotions are more complex derivations of these primary emotions, there is agreement among all theorists assuming a biological/evolutionary perspective on emotion that the structure for certain primary core emotions is wired into the human organism. Again, consistent with theorists such as Arnold (1960) and Leventhal (1979, 1982), we hypothesize that the neurological substrate for emotional experience that is wired .in includes a code for specific configurations of expressive motor behavior that correspond to specific primary emotions. We are in no sense, however, claiming that emotional experience in the adult human being is in any sense restricted to these simple, primary emotions and associated expressive motor configurations.

How is it that the basic neurological template for emotional experience becomes elaborated in the human being into the infinitely subtle blends of emotional experience that are character-istic of human functioning? How is it that expressive motor behav-iors or action dispositions become integrated with perceptual activity and higher-level abstract, conceptual processing to produce the subtle, complex cognitive-affective experiences that we have? At this point the information-processing concepts discussed in the previous section can be useful. We hypothesize that, as Leventhal (1979, 1982, 1984) suggests, a type of unconscious information-processing activity takes place that synthesizes information gener-ated through perception of the environment, neural impulses associated with expressive motor behaviors, and higher-level con-ceptual processing.

The human organism responds to the environment in an immediate, reflexive fashion. A moment's reflection will confirm for the reader that action in the world is often an automatic rather than a deliberate process. One perceives and acts in the same moment. One does not stop to think about putting one foot in front of the other before this takes place. Instead, perception and action are integrated perceptual-motor activities that occur simultaneously. We hypothesize that this process is the same in the realm of emotional experience. One engages in an immediate perceptual-motor ap-praisal of environmental events, which becomes synthesized into subjective emotional experience. This perceptual motor appraisal, or what Arnold (1960) refers to as the primary appraisal, does not depend upon a prior stage of conceptual appraisal. At the same time that it is taking place, however, the primary appraisal is being conceptually appraised. This conceptual appraisal is referred to by Arnold (1960) as the secondary appraisal. Thus, a complex, multi-directional type of information-processing activity at an unconscious level is constantly taking place. This activity integrates information generated from both inside and outside of the organism, and results in the conscious experience of emotion. In addition to generating emotional experience on a moment-to-moment basis, the information generated by this synthetic process becomes stored in memory. Thus, from the moment of birth, a child accumulates memory stores consisting of episodic memories and images of eliciting environmental events, evoked expressive motor responses, associated autonomic arousal, and associated conceptual appraisal.

These memories become progressively elaborated and refined over time and are central to emotional experience. The memory structures can be conceptualized either as schema-type structures (Lang 1983, Leventhal 1979, 1982) or as semantic networks (Bower 1981). As previously discussed, the specific differences in predictions that these theoretical constructs make will need to be tested before decisions can be made as to which is the more useful of the two concepts. The common theme to both of these concepts, however, is that emotional experience becomes coded in memory structures that incorporate a number of subsidiary components. When an individual either attends to information or generates information internally that matches one of the subsidiary components, the probability of other associated components becoming activated increases. As Fiske and Linville (1980) suggest, the theoretical and empirical refinement of schema theory will depend on our ability to find the answers to questions such as "When are schemata retrieved as a whole and when are they partially retrieved?" "Are exceptions stored within schemata?" and "To what extent do people unpack their schemata into component parts?"

Without the answers to these questions, however, we can still hypothesize that the information generated by the activation of a cognitive-affective schema or a semantic-emotion network is integrated at a preattentive level with the perception of the eliciting stimulus and with the conceptual appraisal of both external and internal information. The integration of information from all these sources results in the conscious experience of emotion. In this fashion, emotions, cognition, and action are fused through a type of preattentive information-processing activity that is constantly combining information from both external and internal sources. Emotional experience is thus in no way restricted to the simple, basic categories that constitute the underlying substrate for emotional experience. Complex and subtle blends or derivatives of the more basic emotion substructures are established through the development of the complex cognitive-affective structures in memory that store the individual's unique experiences in life, and his or her idiosyncratic responses to them.

Some of the major themes we have discussed so far can be summarized as follows:

1. Emotion, cognition, and behavior are fused.
2. The cognitive-affective system is adapted to the ecological niche.
3. Emotion has an adaptive function.
4. Emotional experience involves the synthesis of information from sources both external and internal to the organism.
5. The conscious experience of emotion is thus the product of a preattentive synthesis of subsidiary components.
6. Emotional experience tells us what events mean to us as biological organisms.
7. Emotion is a form of tacit meaning.

EMOTION AND PSYCHOTHERAPY

Our perspective on emotion can be thought of as a compromise between an information-processing and an ecological perspective. We believe that a number of assumptions more consistent with an ecological than an information-processing metatheory are necessary if we wish to understand clearly the relationships among cognition, emotion, and action. These include the recognition that (1) expressive motor responses are biologically in-wired action tendencies, (2) the organism is adapted to its ecological niche, (3) perception and action are interdependent, and (4) meaning is inherent in emotion and in the process of perception. Certain concepts derived from the information-processing metatheory are, however, also useful for purposes of fully understanding the relationships among emotion, cognition, and action. In particular, the information-processing tradition provides us with theoretical concepts that are useful in understanding the way in which emotional experience is synthesized from various subsidiary components, stored in memory, and activated under certain conditions.

The type of cognitive-affective system we have postulated, in which primary emotion prototypes interact with higher-level cortical processes, has some distinct advantages from an evolutionary perspective. While the wired-in nature of the emotional system allows the opportunity for immediate, adaptive, reflexive responses to environmental events, there is not an inflexible link between environment and behavior. The conceptual aspect of the emotional synthesis process creates a break in the environment–behavior chain. The emotional synthesis process thus generates *action disposition information*, which is subjected to further processing, and which can ultimately lead to action.

As we have argued previously (Greenberg and Safran 1984b, 1986a), a theoretical understanding of the relationships among emotion, cognition, and action can be extremely useful for purposes of understanding the development of emotional problems as well as clarifying our understanding of the process of change in psychotherapy. An understanding of the function of emotion and the way in which the cognitive-affective system functions under optimal conditions provides us with clues as to the way in which this system can break down when people have emotional problems. It can also provide us with clues as to how to restore the organism to healthy functioning.

Adaptive Affect as a Motivator of Change

If we begin to think of emotion from the vantage point that we have outlined, it becomes apparent that any theory of human change that overlooks the adaptive role of emotion in human functioning cannot be fully adequate. We thus believe that the refinement of cognitive-behavioral theory in a fashion that incorporates this perspective will have important theoretical and practical benefits.

Moreover, the importance of articulating a systematic theory of emotion that incorporates this functional perspective extends beyond the refinement of cognitive-behavioral theory. As Greenberg and Safran (1986a) have argued, traditionally psychoanalytic theory has never really had an adequate, systematic, general theory of emotion. And, while experientially oriented therapists such as Rogers (1951) and Perls (1973) have had a perspective on the adaptive role of emotion in human functioning, their view has not been embedded in the context of a systematic theory about the relationships among cognition, affect, and behavior. Moreover, many practitioners of experientially oriented therapies are guilty of advocating that clients "fully experience their emotions" without having either a framework for discriminating when this should occur or a systematic rationale as to how this is therapeutic. The variety of human potential and therapeutic encounter movements that proliferated during the 1960s and 1970s unfortunately contributed to the misconception that the full experiencing and expression of emotion is an end unto itself, regardless of the client's specific situation and state. This has increased the confusion as to the exact function of the experience and expression of emotions in psychotherapy.

A central tenet of the perspective outlined above is that primary emotions generate important information about the meaning of events for us as biological organisms and motivate behavior in a potentially adaptive fashion. It is important to recognize that affect is *information*. As Leventhal (1982) maintains, emotions play a role in providing us with information about the readiness of our biological machinery to interact with specific events in the environment, and in integrating abstract cortical functions with perceptual motor reflexes, so that we can sense, think, act, and feel in an integrated fashion. Emotions "can be regarded as a form of meaning. They have significance for the person experiencing and expressing them. Their meaning has two aspects: they 'say' something about our organismic state (i.e., they meter its moment-to-moment readiness) and they 'say' something about the environment" (Leventhal 1982, p. 122).

It follows that individuals who, for whatever reasons, are not able to fully use or do not have complete access to this information will function in a less than optimal fashion. Consistent with this, a common clinical problem, in our observation, occurs when clients fail to fully synthesize certain adaptive emotional experiences. Because of past experiences they may learn that it is inappropriate or dangerous to have certain types of emotional experience, and as a result they may restrict the expression of certain emotions or may even fail to completely synthesize certain types of emotions. We hypothesize that both intensity and degree of redundancy of specific classes of learning conditions play roles in determining to what extent an individual will have difficulty in synthesizing associated emotions. In more extreme maladaptive learning situations the individual may fail to develop in memory any elaborated representations of the relevant emotions and thus actually may have difficulty in completely synthesizing the relevant emotional experience. When the maladaptive learning is less extreme, the individual may be able to partially synthesize the relevant emotion, but may have difficulty in fully experiencing and expressing it. Common areas of emotional deficit are inability to synthesize experiences of weakness or vulnerability and experiences of anger (Greenberg and Safran 1986a, Safran and Greenberg 1982a). Deficits in emotional processing are, however, by no means restricted to these areas.

A brief clinical illustration may help provide an example of the type of deficit in emotional synthesis about which we are speaking. A 32-year-old woman was admitted for treatment. She had a five-year history of depression and a diagnosis of major depressive disorder with melancholia. The most distinctive feature of her clinical picture was her complete anhedonia and the nonreactivity of her mood state to any environmental events. This lack of emotional reactivity was one of the major clinical features leading to the diagnosis of an endogenous depression. Over the five-year period, she had been treated with a host of psychotropic medications, both conventional and experimental, without result.

She was finally placed on a trial of cognitive therapy in an attempt to help her. In therapy it emerged that her lack of emotional reactivity was very closely linked with tacit rules or dysfunctional beliefs she had about the importance of always being in control of her feelings and the potential dangerousness of expressing or even experiencing feelings of anger, love, and vulnerability. It is important to emphasize here that the emotional deficit was not restricted to the realm of expression. According to her retrospective report, prior to the commencement of therapy she literally did not experience these emotions. Failure to adequately synthesize and express these emotions helped to keep her trapped in an unsatisfactory life situation wherein she was not getting many of her basic needs for love, support, and gratification met either in her marital relationship or in any of the other major social relationships in her life. Therapy with this woman consisted of helping her to gradually learn to synthesize the constricted emotions. There were two major components of the intervention: (1) modifying her cognitions concerning emotion and (2) bringing automatic expressive motor-schematic processing into awareness.

The first component consisted of helping her become aware of her tendency to become self-critical whenever she began to experience emotion and to abstract and gradually challenge the underlying dysfunctional attitudes that guided this self-critical activity. Examples of such dysfunctional attitudes were "I must always be in control of my feelings in order to be a worthwhile person; I must always be strong in order to be worthwhile" and "A strong person never expresses feelings of anger or weakness." Further exploration revealed fears that she would be rejected if she ever expressed either weakness or anger. We view this type of intervention, in which dysfunctional attitudes about the experience and expression of emotions are brought to awareness and challenged, to be similar to Gestalt therapy methods of becoming aware of and identifying with or taking responsibility for resistances (Perls 1973). These methods originate in turn from Reich's (1949) notion of interpretation of resistances and defenses, which is an intervention advocated by many current psychodynamic theorists (e.g., Horowitz et al. 1984, Schafer 1983). It is important to note that in advocating an intervention similar in some ways to the interpretation of defenses, we are in no way endorsing the drive metapsychology of psycho-analysis. See Safran and Greenberg (this volume, Chapter 7) for a more detailed discussion of this point.

This emphasis on exploring and challenging self-critical activity and dysfunctional attitudes regarding certain kinds of emotional experience is not completely inconsistent technically with the practice of cognitive therapy (Beck et al. 1979). Important differences, however, are the nature of the cognitive activity that is targeted for intervention, as well as important metapsychological assumptions about the fundamental nature of emotion. From a conceptual perspective, the important addition to cognitive therapy suggested here is that emotions play a potentially adaptive role in human functioning, and that emotional problems can result from a failure to synthesize adaptive emotions. The failure results, at least in part, from a blocking of the integrative process at the conceptual level. It is this cognitive activity blocking emotional synthesis that often requires modification.

In addition to modifying the processing of affective information by challenging dysfunctional processing rules, the second component of intervention suggested by the theoretical considerations described in the previous sections consists of directing clients' attention to component expressive motor behaviors and underlying emotional schemata that are not being synthesized fully into complete emotional experiences. We hypothesize that there is a direct pathway between neural impulses and subjective emotional experience, and although we do not believe that emotional experience is necessarily dependent upon somatic feedback, we do hypothesize that somatic feedback can cue emotional experience in therapy (Greenberg and Safran 1986a). We are thus suggesting that in a therapeutic context people can learn to infer their internal states through a process of monitoring their own expressive motor behavior. In addition, we hypothesize that emotional experience, while not necessarily dependent upon somatic feedback, can, and often does, play a secondary or supportive role in the synthesis of emotional experience (cf. Leventhal 1984).

Elsewhere, we have reviewed the literature demonstrating that a number of therapeutic traditions ranging from focusing (Gendlin 1978) to Gestalt therapy (Perls 1973) to bioenergetics (Lowen 1967) employ techniques consisting of drawing clients' attention to their own somatic experiences in one fashion or another (Greenberg and Safran 1986a). Although it is possible that various processes such as hypnosis and suggestibility play a role in the efficacy of these procedures when they do work, the theoretical considerations described above suggest that the utility of interventions that direct attention to somatic changes may at least in part be accounted for by the intrinsically expressive-motor nature of emotional processing.

Our clinical experience is that interventions consisting of directing clients' attention to their own nonverbal behavior and somatic changes can be a useful and sometimes necessary adjunct in the process of helping clients become aware of potentially adaptive emotions. Simply teaching clients on a conscious, rational level that it is all right to experience feelings such as anger or vulnerability may not change the quality of the conscious emotional experience, because they may be lacking a perceptual motor skill rather than an exclusively conceptual skill. As Zajonc (1980) argues, the memory code for emotional experience may be more similar to the memory code for muscular action than it is to other memory codes.

Finally, the schema model of emotional memory also suggests that imagery plays an important role in emotional experience (cf. Leventhal 1979) and that encouraging clients to attend to fleeting images of which they are only marginally aware may activate cognitive-affective schemata that were previously not activated. This in turn may result in a more comprehensive processing of an emotional experience, or in classes of emotional experience that were previously not fully synthesized. We hope that future research will answer questions such as "What is the relationship between conceptual processing and the activation of specific cognitive affective schemata," but it is clear at a clinical level that imagery is an excellent method of evoking emotional memory. One cannot easily access underlying emotional schemata by simply talking with clients about their experience. It is often more effective to instruct the person to imagine a certain person or situation and to then instruct them to attend to their emotional responses to the image. A major task, therefore, in synthesizing new affect is one of bringing automatic processing into awareness by evoking previously unavailable schemata and attending to previously unattended-to expressive motor behaviors.

Challenging Maladaptive Cognitions

Although a variety of different procedures are used in different cognitive behavioral approaches, two commonly employed procedures are (1) accessing and exploring maladaptive cognitive processes, and (2) challenging maladaptive thoughts and beliefs. With respect to the second procedure, different approaches are used to challenge maladaptive thoughts or beliefs. Beck (1976), for example, suggests that clients learn to challenge their automatic thoughts by examining their distorted beliefs from a logical perspective, and by carefully examining the evidence relevant to the automatic thought. Other cognitive-behavior therapists such as Meichenbaum (1977) suggest that maladaptive thoughts can be challenged using positive self-statements or coping thoughts.

We have found that maladaptive thoughts can also be challenged effectively by confronting them with contrary affective experience (Greenberg and Safran 1986a). Using appropriate therapeutic procedures, the therapist can facilitate a process through which clients challenge their own maladaptive cognitive processes through affective information that is generated internally. The two-chair intervention in Gestalt therapy (Greenberg 1979, 1984a, Perls 1973) is a good example of a procedure that can be employed to evoke adaptive emotional responses, which can then be used to challenge maladaptive, self-critical cognitive activity. The therapist, using skillful timing, shifts the client back and forth between the chair in which he or she behaves in a self-critical fashion and the chair in which he or she responds to that self-criticism. Unlike the situation in a more standard type of cognitive-behavioral intervention, the client in this chair is not instructed to respond to self-criticisms in a rational fashion. Instead the client is instructed to respond in a fashion consistent with the way he or she is feeling at that moment

(Greenberg 1979). The process of relegating two different aspects of the person (i.e., the critical and the experiencing sides) to two different spatial locations initially serves to intensify the self-criticism. As the self-criticism becomes more concrete, more specific, and more intense, the client goes through a process of reacting to the criticisms. Often the initial reaction is one of defeat. As the conflict is intensified, however, and the client pays attention to underlying expressive motor and schematic level processing, he or she begins to experience adaptive emotions that challenge the self-criticism (Greenberg 1984a). The experience of these emotions can be facilitated through procedures described above such as directing the client's attention to nonverbal behaviors that are not initially in awareness. This process leads to clients becoming less self-critical and more self-compassionate. In this dialogue clients are more able to fully experience biologically adaptive emotions such as sadness or anger. These feelings supply the appropriate action tendency, and these new action dispositions form the base for challenging the negative cognitions. Clients in the experiencing chair often respond to their own self-criticisms with anger or self-assertion. Negative self-statements such as "You're no good, too weak, selfish," are challenged by clients themselves from an internally experienced sense of confidence and validity. Here arousal of angry feelings expressed assertively in statements such as "Stop doing this to me" or "I want to do what I am doing" challenges the self-criticism from the other chair and causes it to soften. Alternatively, an authentically experienced feeling of sadness or vulnerability in one chair can lead to a softening of self-criticism from the other chair, as the client becomes more self-compassionate. This process has been shown to be related to positive therapeutic outcome (Greenberg 1984a).

In summary, using procedures of the type we have described, the therapist can facilitate a process through which the client synthesizes internal information that can be used effectively to challenge self-critical activity. Challenging maladaptive cognitive processes through internally generated affective information can be particularly effective in situations wherein the client responds to logical or reality-testing interventions with statements such as "I know that it's illogical but that's the way I feel" or "I know that there is no evidence that I'm failing but that's the way I feel." As Rachman (1983) suggests, there are limits to the extent that undesirable emotional responses can be modified using rational therapeutic procedures. We recommend the type of affectively oriented procedure described above as a useful supplement to more standard cognitive behavioral procedures. Internally generated information, if attended to and fully synthesized, has a compelling quality about it that allows it to be a powerful agent in the modification and reorganization of cognitive structures.

Goldfried and Robins (1983) took the concept of self-schema from the social-cognition literature and applied it in a thoughtful analysis of the nature of the change process in cognitive behavior therapy. Consistent with available experimental research, they hypothesize that negative self-schemata bias the processing of information in a fashion that prevents people from attending to information that is inconsistent with their negative self-schemata. Following this analysis, Goldfried and Robins (1983) outlined a number of technical suggestions for ways in which therapists can help clients process self-schema information that will help change their negative self-schemata.

Maladaptive self-schemata bias not only the processing of external information. They can also bias the processing of internal information (Safran 1984a,b). Thus, for example, individuals who construe themselves as always being strong and in control of their feelings may have difficulty fully synthesizing feelings of hurt and vulnerability even when appropriate and acting adaptively in response to them. Allocating attention to components of emotional experience that are previously not fully synthesized can thus provide a client with irrevocable new information about who he or she is and can bring about a modification in the person's self-schema.

Assessing Mood-Congruent or Hot Cognitions

Another important therapeutic implication of the theoretical considerations we have outlined above is that biased or maladaptive information-processing activities may be most readily accessible when the client is in a problematic affective state (Greenberg and Safran 1984b, 1986a, Safran and Greenberg 1982a,b). As Bower (1981) and Teasdale and Taylor (1981) have demonstrated, negative memories and thoughts are most easily accessible when people are in a sad or depressed mood. These findings can be accounted for by both the semantic network and the schema models described above. Emotion plays an important organizational role in memory (Bower 1981). It should come as no surprise to cognitive therapists that clients have difficulty accessing automatic thoughts in therapy when they are not feeling particularly depressed or anxious at that moment. In fact, one might speculate that the fact that cognitive therapy procedures have been slower to develop with anxiety disorders than with depression may at least in part result from the fact that anxious emotional states are often more situationally bound than depressed emotional states. Because the therapeutic situation may not readily replicate the environmental contingencies that evoke the problematic anxiety reaction, clients with situation- ally bound anxiety may have more difficulty accessing automatic thoughts than the average depressed client, who is depressed even while in the therapy session. Our repeated observation has been that important automatic thoughts are more readily accessible in therapy when the client is experiencing the relevant emotional state. A variety of procedures ranging from using role plays, to focusing upon imagery, to in vivo procedures, to working with whatever thoughts and feelings are emerging in context of the present relationship between the client and the therapist can be useful for accessing emotions and associated automatic thoughts. To summa- rize the relevant principle concisely, the key is to work with clients in an emotionally vivid, real, and immediate fashion. There are an infinite number of choice points in terms of what particular situation or issue a therapist will explore with his or her client in a given session. In our opinion, one of the major deciding criteria should be "what is emotionally most alive for a client at any given point in time." It is not unusual for this guideline to lead the therapist in a different direction than he or she would go if he or she were to follow the agenda-determined approach of Beck's cognitive therapy (Beck et al. 1979). We argue that, for the reasons described above, a predetermined agenda should not take precedence over the criterion of emotional vividness.

Restructuring Maladaptive Schemata

A final principle of intervention suggested by the theoretical considerations outlined above can be thought of in some ways as an extension of the previous principle (i.e., accessing mood-congruent cognitions). This principle can be stated as follows. Habitual, maladaptive emotional reactions are most easily modified when the client is in the relevant emotional state. How does our previous theoretical discussion lead to this hypothesis? Although an important emphasis of this article has been the potentially adaptive role that emotions play in human functioning, we in no way wish to imply that all emotional experiences are necessarily adaptive. We hypothesize that through unfortunate learning experiences, an individual can develop maladaptive cognitive-affective schemata. For example, as a result of consistently negative experiences with significant figures in the past, a client may develop maladaptive cognitive-affective schemata that become automatically activated in response to cues associated with intimacy and that, when processed, generate anxiety and avoidance behavior.

In order to change and modify this dysfunctional emotional response pattern, it may be necessary to restructure or reorganize the relevant cognitive-affective schema. We hypothesize that this type of schematic restructuring may take place most readily when the relevant schema is fully activated (Greenberg and Safran 1986a). As Lang (1983) suggests, a cognitive-affective schema, or what he refers to as an emotional prototype, may be thought of as a subroutine in a computer program. In order to modify the program it is first necessary to access the relevant subroutine. The distinction between this point and our previous hypothesis about accessing mood-congruent cognitions may not be immediately apparent, so we will elaborate further. What we are suggesting here is that it may be important to work with clients while they are in affectively aroused states, not only because relevant cognitions are more readily accessible in these states, but also because the affective schemata themselves will be most amenable to restructuring in these states. Once the schema becomes activated, it is possible to subject it to further processing in conscious, focal awareness and to restructure it through this processing.

Further processing may take various forms. It may, for example, result from a schematic accommodation in response to the information provided by the evidence that there is no reason to be anxious in the present situation. Or it may take the form of elaborating at a conceptual level the implicit meaning of a specific emotional schema and then challenging certain implications that emerge from this type of elaboration. In any event, we are suggesting that "emotional learning" or learning in the domain of "hot cognitions" will be preferable to new learning in the domain of "cold cognitions." While this hypothesis is generated on the basis of theory, there is some preliminary empirical evidence that is corroborative in nature. Orenstein and Carr (1975), for example, found that there was a substantial positive correlation between physiological indexes of anxiety during treatment with implosive therapy and a decrease in self-recorded fear during a subsequent behavioral avoidance test. Lang (1977) has also found that subjects who were treated with desensitization showed greater improvement if there was increased heart rate response during therapy. In addition, Borkevec and Sides (1979) found that evidence of increased anxiety in subjects during treatment may be positively related to therapeutic outcome.

The critical reader at this point may ask what the advantage is of the type of schematic model of maladaptive emotional responding we are postulating over a simple classical conditioning model. For one thing a classical conditioning model would predict the opposite of the above results, that is, that an anxiety response is most readily unlearned when the client is engaged in an incompatible response such as relaxation. Moreover, a classical conditioning model conceptualizes problematic emotions as learned responses. The information-processing perspective we have outlined conceptualizes problematic emotions as more than learned responses.

They are also information with meaning. It is only when conceptualized from this perspective that we can begin to speak about accessing a maladaptive cognitive-affective schema so that we can begin to restructure it through a variety of procedures. These procedures may include but are not limited to exposure treatment. Accessing a schema allows one to, in a sense, unpack it and elaborate the meaning of an event for oneself in more explicit terms. This in turn can lead to the uncovering of negative appraisals or self-statements that can be challenged with more standard cognitive behavioral methods or through the activation of adaptive emotional responses in the fashion described earlier.

Another advantage of both the semantic network and schema models over the classical conditioning model is that the classical conditioning model would predict that events become associated with one another on the basis of simple contiguity in time. Both associative network and schema models predict that events become linked together, not only on the basis of temporal continuity but also on the basis of different forms of meaning similarity. In fact, research conducted by Bower and Mayer (1986) suggests that emotions and memories become associatively linked only when they are appraised as causally related at the time of initial encoding. Both semantic network and schema models thus suggest that simple exposure treatment may be inadequate to break the linkage between different nodes in memory that are linked together. It may be necessary to clarify the nature of the link between different nodes in memory by examining the meaning of the relevant nodes as well as the nature of the linkage between them. We hypothesize that this process of clarification is best accomplished when the individual is in the relevant affective state. It is only then that the client can subject the relevant emotional experience to further conceptual processing and extract the meaning implicit in it. As previously discussed, emotion functions as a type of tacit meaning. Our position is that whether or not a particular emotion is adaptive in a specific context, it still constitutes a type of tacit meaning that can provide the individual with information about the impact of an event upon him or her. Once this meaning is made explicit, the individual can either act adaptively in response to it or, if appropriate, question some of the assumptions inherent in his or her perception.

CONCLUSIONS

In this chapter we have outlined a number of theoretical considerations that we consider relevant to understanding the relationships among emotion, cognition, perception, and action in the process of psychotherapy. It has not been our intention to present a definitive theoretical model. Rather, our objective has been to elaborate upon some of the implications of different metatheories and different theoretical constructs and to evaluate what different metatheories and different theoretical constructs contribute to our understanding of the relevant processes. One of the major points of comparison has been between two substantially different metatheoretical or epistemological perspectives: the information-processing perspective and the ecological perspective. We conclude that both metatheoretical perspectives can contribute to our understanding of relevant processes and that neither is completely adequate for our purposes in and of itself. We thus suggest a rapprochement between the two perspectives.

This integrative position makes some specific assumptions about the functional significance of emotion in human functioning and also allows us to speculate about various avenues of intervention that may be promising. Our major assumptions are that emotional experience plays an adaptive role in human functioning and that emotions can be thought of as a type of tacit meaning that provides the individual with information about the impact of events upon himself or herself as a biological organism. The common denominator to the therapeutic avenues we have explored is that facilitating the experience of emotions in therapy and working with "hot cognitions" can be useful for a variety of reasons.

As we have argued previously, however (Greenberg and Safran 1984b, 1986a), it is important not to impose a uniformity myth upon affective phenomena in psychotherapy. Different affective processes will be therapeutic in different contexts. It is thus important to adopt a differentiated perspective with respect to our consideration of both affective processes and therapeutic contexts. At a more molar level we can formulate empirically testable hypotheses about individual-difference variables that interact with specific affective processes. For example, it may be that interventions designed to intensify affective experiences for the purpose of accessing mood-congruent cognitions are more important for clients with emotionally overcontrolled styles than they are for clients with emotionally undercontrolled styles.

At a more molecular level there is a need to formulate empirically researchable hypotheses about the interaction between specific therapy process contexts and specific affective phenomena. What specific discernible markers in therapy process inform the clinician that a specific affectively oriented intervention will be effective (Rice and Greenberg 1984)? Future theory, research, and practice will benefit from a careful consideration and exploration of a variety of different kinds of affective-change processes associated with different types of therapeutic events. We have outlined a few of these events in this chapter in an attempt to show that an integrative perspective can lead to a differentiated view of the role of emotion, cognition, and action in the process of psychotherapeutic change.

7

Affect and the Unconscious: A Cognitive Perspective

Jeremy D. Safran and Leslie S. Greenberg

Our objective in this chapter is to examine the concept of the "unconscious" from the perspective of a cognitive metapsychology. As Meichenbaum and Gilmore (1984) point out, "No other concept so clearly divides the traditional behavioral from the psychodynamic camps" (p. 273). The increasing interest in the theoretical integration of different therapeutic approaches has, however, stimulated an attempt by some cognitive behaviorists to analyze the concept of the unconscious from a cognitive perspective (e.g., Mahoney 1982, Meichenbaum and Gilmore 1984).

These authors, while agreeing that some form of unconscious processing takes place, are quick to point out that this does not necessarily constitute an acceptance of the psychoanalytic concept of the "unconscious." Meichenbaum and Gilmore (1984), for example, state that ". . . in a cognitive behavioral model, there is no commitment to an 'energy model' of psychodynamic conflict or to a particular mental or motivational model of the mind (i.e. id, ego, super ego processes). Instead there is an attempt to develop a taxonomy of cognitive events, processes, and structures and to develop a testable theoretical model of how these processes interact with each other as well as with feelings, behaviors, and environmental consequences" (p. 291).

Mahoney (1982), in his discussion of the unconscious, makes reference to Hayek's (1978) notion of the primacy of the abstract, and conceptualizes the unconscious as consisting of tacit, higher-level organizing principles that shape conscious cognitive processes and behavior. This notion appears to be reasonably convergent with the concept of "core organizing principles," which Meichenbaum and Gilmore (1984) conceptualize as unconscious structures that determine conscious cognitive processes and behavior.

A fundamentally important difference between *these* cognitive formulations of the unconscious and the Freudian psychoanalytic concept of the unconscious is that while the Freudian concept of the unconscious is inextricably linked to consideration as regarding the role of affect in the psychic economy, the cognitive formulations are essentially affect-free. The fact that contemporary cognitive-behavior therapists would conceptualize the unconscious without reference to emotional or motivational considerations is consistent with the general trend in experimental psychology to ignore the role of emotion and motivation in human functioning (cf. Greenberg and Safran 1986a). Dawes (1976), for example, has termed the social psychologist's traditional interest in the role of affective and motivational processes in influencing human behavior as "deep" psychology, and contrasts it with the increasing tendency in contemporary experimental psychology to account for human behavior in information-processing terms. He characterizes this contemporary trend as a "shallow" psychology. The cognitive-behavioral concept of the unconscious articulated by Mahoney (1982) and Meichenbaum and Gilmore (1984) is consistent with the information-processing model of man that views maladaptive behavior as resulting from dysfunctional rules and heuristics rather than from nonrational, affective processes.

For Freud, the unconscious and affect were central in understanding pathology (Nemiah 1984). Freud believed that under normal circumstances events activate both ideas and associated affect. Typically, the associated affect is spontaneously discharged, thus allowing the idea to move into the background and to cease to play an important role in the individual's functioning. However, when the associated affect is too threatening for the individual, it is warded off and becomes separated from the idea, before the normal process of discharge can take place, thereby creating dysfunction. In the cognitive-behavioral conceptualization of the unconscious articulated by Mahoney (1982) and Meichenbaum and Gilmore (1984), the pathogenic element is not the warding-off of affective processes, but rather dysfunctional rules that operate at an unconscious level. There is thus a fundamental difference between psychoanalytic and cognitive-behavioral formulations of the role of unconscious factors in psychopathology.

Freud's understanding of the role of unconscious emotional processes in psychopathology is linked to his drive metapsychology. We can distinguish, however, between some of Freud's basic insights about the relationship between emotion, the unconscious, and psychopathology, on one hand, and the drive metapsychology within which they are embedded, on the other. We will argue that Freud's essential intuition—namely that the role of the unconscious in psychopathology and psychotherapy is best understood in conjunction with its relationship to emotional processes—is an important one, and that this perspective is lacking in contemporary cognitive-behavioral formulations, which have been influenced by experimental psychology. We will argue that a major class of psychological dysfunction arises from the failure to fully process internally generated information that is consistent with the conscious experience of emotion. This internally generated information can be thought of as action/disposition information, which under normal conditions constitutes a vital component in the construction of emotional experience (Greenberg and Safran 1984b). This perspective, which will be elaborated upon later, integrates shallow and deep psychology by dealing with information processing, affect, and motivation in the same model.

We will begin by comparing some of the metapsychological assumptions upon which the psychoanalytic model of the unconscious is based, with the metapsychological assumptions guiding both theory and research in contemporary cognitive psychology. As we shall see, this task will be somewhat complicated by the fact that "cognitive theory" is not a single coherent set of ideas, but rather a number of different approaches to the study of cognition that are typically classified together under the rubric of cognitive theory (Neisser 1980).

We will then review some research evidence and associated theory emerging from experimental cognitive psychology, which is relevant to the topic of the unconscious. Our review will be a selective one. We will not, for example, review the extensive literature on subliminal perception or the literature on perceptual defense, both of which are relevant to the topic. We will instead focus primarily upon research and theory in the area of selective attention. Our objective in doing so is twofold. First, it is to provide the reader with a historical perspective on the fashion in which the investigation of unconscious processes has gradually come to assume legitimate status among experimental cognitive psychologists. Second, it is to provide some idea of the picture of unconscious processes, as well as the relationship between unconscious and conscious processes that is emerging from this research.

THE DRIVE METAPSYCHOLOGY

Freud's fundamental vision of the human condition is embodied in the drive model or psychic-energy model. As Greenberg and Mitchell (1983) articulate, the fundamental principles underlying the drive metapsychology are as follows:

1. The unit of analysis is the individual as a discrete individual. Man is not viewed as an intrinsically social animal. Society is imposed upon individuals who are already complete within themselves. People accept the protection of society at the cost of renunciation of many of their most personal goals. It is possible to speak about the individual outside an interpersonal context.

2. Because it *is* possible to speak of the individual divorced

from an interpersonal context, it is also possible to speak about a "constancy principle," which deals with the regulation and distribution of psychic energy within the organism. The constancy principle, in stipulating that the purpose of the psychic apparatus is to keep the level of stimulation within the individual as close to zero as possible, is thus the fundamental motivational postulate of drive theory.

3. The origin of all human activity can thus be ultimately traced to the demands of instinctual drive. The origin of this drive is not influenced by social context. It is inherited biologically.

4. There is no inherent object, no preordained tie to the human environment.

Embedded as it is within the drive metapsychology, Freud's view of the unconscious is as a "seething cauldron" of primitive impulses, which ultimately must be tamed or renounced in order to allow the individual to live within society (Eagle 1984). It is readily apparent that this concept of the unconscious has little in common with the cognitive-behavioral models we have discussed.

In his earlier writings, Freud considered the failure to make conscious and to discharge affect as being the central pathogenic process (Breuer and Freud 1895). While later psychoanalytic writings deemphasized the importance of catharsis as a critical ingredient of psychoanalysis, Freud never abandoned the view that the fundamental psychic danger facing the organism is excessive excitation (Eagle 1984). This notion is conceptually dependent upon the drive metapsychology, which views the regulation of psychic energy as the fundamental motivational principle.

Although subsequent interpreters of Freud have different opinions about the true nature of psychic energy, and whether it should be thought of as a real entity or a metaphorical concept, it is at least implicit in much of Freud's writing, as well as in psychoanalytic writing in general, that psychic energy or drive can be thought of as a quasi-physiological entity, which exercises force upon the mind and the body in a mechanistic fashion. Critics of the drive metapsychology from within the psychoanalytic community (e.g.,

Gill 1976, Holt 1976, Klein 1976, Schafer 1976) argue that it is impossible to link a psychology built on concepts of energy and structure with a psychology of meaning, and that for this reason the drive metapsychology constitutes an inadequate metapsychology for understanding human beings. Gill (1976), for example, argues that Freud clearly intended the drive metapsychology to be taken in biological and mechanistic terms, and that this biological/mechanistic metapsychology constitutes an inadequate psychology, because it is in a different universe of discourse from that of meaning.

The second major criticism of the drive metapsychology has been that Freud fails to take into account the inherently interpersonal nature of people (Eagle 1984, Fairbairn 1952, Sullivan 1953). In constructing the drive model, Freud drew upon the biological metaphors that were available in the intellectual climate of late-nineteenth-century Vienna. It is thus based on neurological conceptions and hydraulic metaphors that are now outmoded. Freud's drive theory is founded on the Darwinian assumption that all behavior must be understood in terms of its survival function. This is the same assumption that is central to contemporary ethologists (e.g., Bowlby 1969, Lorenz 1977). Freud, however, equates survival or adaptation with the avoidance of the danger of excessive excitation, resulting from a failure to discharge affect (Eagle 1984). For Freud, establishing psychoanalysis as a biological science and incorporating biological considerations into psychoanalytic theory meant that man is fundamentally a biological organism and only secondarily an interpersonal creature. Biology and the environment are viewed as two independent and often opposing forces.

THE COGNITIVE METAPSYCHOLOGY

As Neisser (1980) has pointed out, there is no one cognitive psychology. The metatheoretical perspective that has dominated the field of cognitive psychology since its inception, however, can best be characterized as the information-processing approach. This approach draws heavily upon the brain–computer analogy. Proponents of this approach have applied concepts stimulated by advances in the field of computer sciences to construct models that can clarify with a high degree of specificity the way in which information is encoded, represented, stored, and retrieved from memory. According to Neisser (1967), "The term 'cognition' refers to all processes by which the sensory input is transformed, reduced, elaborated, stored, recovered and used. It is concerned with these processes even when they operate in the absence of relevant stimulation, as in images and hallucinations. Such terms as sensation, perception, imagery, retention, recall, problem solving and thinking, among many others, refer to hypothetical stages or aspects of cognition" (p. 4).

The brain–computer analogy has played an important role in the emergence of the developing cognitive science. As Shaw and Bransford (1977) point out, it has been instrumental in liberating theorists and researchers from the excessive restrictions imposed upon them by behavioral psychology. Computer technology has stimulated the development of modeling techniques and experimental procedures that allow cognitive scientists to develop and test fine-tuned predictions about internal processes not directly observable. This has been an important aspect of the development of cognitive psychology as an empirically based science.

Information-processing theories are explicitly concerned with the fashion in which incoming stimulus information is processed in order to extract meaning from it. In theory, then, they should be less vulnerable to the previously articulated criticisms of drive theory, which state that it is incompatible with a psychology of meaning. As we shall see, however, when we discuss the ecological approach to cognitive psychology, this is not completely so.

A major criticism of the information-processing approach is that people are conceptualized as disembodied computing machines, rather than as active organisms that interact with their environment in an adaptive fashion. In the information-processing model, cognition is considered independent of emotion and action. Critics of the information-processing approach, however, question whether it is possible to truly understand the nature of human cognitive processes if we consider them out of context of action and emotion. Shaw and Bransford (1977), for example, make the following comments:

> It is wise to remember that computer scientists' systems are artificially contrived while ours are naturally evolved; their systems are passive while ours are active; their system are purposeless (except in a second-hand way) while ours pursue primary goals of self-survival and adaptation; their systems, as complex as they are, are still astronomically simpler than those psychologists must understand. And what of the role of emotional, personality, and social factors in determining the questions appropriate to humans but as yet undefined for artificial systems? [p. 3]

The major metatheoretical alternative to the information-processing approach in cognitive psychology is the ecological approach to perception, initially advanced by Gibson (1966, 1979). In contrast to the information-processing approach, the ecological perspective emphasizes the role of biological/evolutionary factors in human functioning. It thus shares the biological orientation of drive metapsychology. However, unlike drive theory, which equates survival and adaptation with the avoidance of excessive psychic excitation, the ecological perspective understands the survival of the species in terms of the adaptation of the organism to its ecological niche. One of the major objections that ecological theorists have to the information-processing metaphor is that once we begin hypothesizing about stages of information-processing activity that are necessary for transforming information into meaningful form, we end up in a process of infinite regress. Thus, if we theorize that the organism transforms sensory information into a usable form through a series of information-processing stages, the question then becomes: Who is the agent who uses this information in the final stage? From an ecological perspective, it is therefore seen as more parsimonious to assume that evolution, by designing perceptual systems that are adapted to extract meaning directly from the environment, has rendered a complex process of information processing unnecessary. As Shaw and Bransford (1977) state:

Hence, when asked where the buck of knowledge ceases to be passed, or where the epistemic regress ends, the ecological psychologist responds: At the beginning of the process; it starts with perception, the process upon which the intrinsic meaning of man's relationship to his world is founded. It is the perceiver who knows and the knower who perceives, just as it is the world that is both perceived and known. Neither memory, nor inference, nor any other epistemic process other than perception intervenes between the knowing agent and the world it knows, for knowing is a direct rather than an indirect process. [p. 10]

Ecological theorists thus question whether an epistemology based on the person–computer analogy can provide us with a theory of meaning.

Proponents of the ecological perspective also criticize the information-processing perspective because of its failure to conceptualize the human being as an organism that is adapted to its ecological niche. They argue that there is no way in which we can begin to understand human psychological functioning without a detailed understanding of the environment in which this functioning takes place. In the ecological approach, then, the emphasis is much more on the interface between people and their environment than on the information-processing stages that are hypothesized to be taking place inside the individual's head. Traditionally, the focus of investigation in ecological psychology (as in information-processing psychology) has been on object perception rather than person perception. An attempt has thus been made to characterize the geometric structure underlying the more important physical properties of the world (e.g., rigidity, nonrigidity, shape, size) and to understand the perceptual process in this context (e.g., Gibson 1966). The extension of an ecological perspective to the realm of "social knowing" suggests, then, that we cannot fully understand the nature of human functioning without a detailed understanding of the interpersonal context in which it takes place. Viewed from this perspective, it becomes apparent that the information-processing metatheory is no less guilty of failing to conceptualize people as fundamentally interpersonal creatures than is drive metapsychology.

In discussing the conceptualization of the relationship between cognition and action that emerges from the traditional information-processing perspective, Weimer (1977) makes the following comment:

> Common to these positions is an implicit notion that cognition is to be understood "from the outside inward," that it is a matter of the structuring and restructuring of sensory information by intrinsically sensory systems and that the product of cognition has to somehow subsequently be married (in a peculiar sort of shotgun wedding) to action. Thus cognition has a puzzling, dualistic character for sensory theorists. [p. 270]

In contrast, the conceptualization of the relationship between cognition and action that emerges from an ecological perspective is that cognition is essentially a skilled action. As Weimer (1977) explains: "The mind is intrinsically a motor system and the sensory order by which we are acquainted with external objects as well as ourselves, the higher mental processes which construct our common sense and scientific knowledge, indeed everything mental, is a product of what are, correctly interpreted, constructive motor skills" (p. 272). The processes underlying human knowledge are thus conceptualized as skilled actions. This is consistent with Piaget's (1954) position that the child initially comes to know the world, not through passive observation, but through the observation and internalization of his or her actions upon objects.

While our comparison of information-processing and ecological metatheories has been brief, it has, we hope, been sufficiently detailed to highlight some of the conceptual strengths and weaknesses of the two approaches. As we have argued elsewhere, the concerns that the ecological perspective attempts to address can add a useful corrective influence to the information-processing perspective (Safran and Greenberg 1986). We advocate a combined information-processing/ecological perspective, which holds that while it is useful to develop and empirically test models describing the fashion in which information is processed, it is vital not to overdraw the brain–computer analogy. Any approach that attempts to understand cognitive processes by temporarily bracketing them off from emotion, action, and the ecological niche in which they operate is in danger of yielding a distorted picture of the phenomenon of interest. This holds true in the case of conscious as well as unconscious cognitive processes.

In the next section we will provide a historical review of the developments in the area of selective attention that have led to a preliminary conceptualization of the distinction between conscious and unconscious processes from a cognitive perspective. Research and theory development in this area have been primarily influenced by the information-processing metatheory. Following this we will briefly review some theoretical and empirical developments in cognitive psychology, which we believe are more in line with the type of information-processing/ecological perspective we are advocating. We believe that the incorporation of these developments into our understanding of the nature of unconscious processes provides a more complete and clinically useful understanding of human psychological processes.

SELECTIVE ATTENTION

The study of attentional processes was a central topic of investigation in early academic psychology. Titchener (1908), for example, stated that "the doctrine of attention is the nerve of the whole psychological system, and that as men judge of it, so shall they be judged before the general tribunal of psychology" (p. 173). Similarly, William James (1890) considered attention to be the central organizing principle in human experience, as reflected in his statement: "My experience is what I agree to attend to. Only those items which I notice shape my mind—without selective interest my experience is utter chaos" (p. 402). While James considered attentional processes to be a suitable topic for investigation in scientific psychology, he warned that "The unconscious is the sovereign means of believing whatever one likes in psychology and of turning what might become a science into a tumbling ground for whimsies" (p. 163).

With the ascendance of the behavioral tradition in experimental psychology, the study of conscious psychological processes became as unacceptable as the study of unconscious psychological processes, and the topic of attention lost its legitimate status in the scientific community. As Kahneman (1973) points out, Osgood (1953) published an important text that covered the entire field of experimental psychology without mentioning the topic of attention more than once. That same year, a study was published by Cherry, which heralded the relegitimization of the topic of attention among experimental psychologists, as well as the emergence of the new cognitive psychology.

Cherry (1953) employed a dichotic listening task in order to investigate the nature of selective attention. In this procedure, subjects are presented with two messages to different ears, using earphones, and asked to monitor one of the two channels. The researcher can then investigate the way in which information that is not in focal awareness is processed, by assessing recognition or memory for characteristics of the unattended message. Cherry found that while subjects were aware of the presence of the unintended message, they could recall virtually nothing about it when subsequently questioned, with the exception of gross characteristics such as sex of the speaker. Subjects were thus unable to identify considerations more relevant to the meaning of the unattended-to stimulus.

This finding led Broadbent (1958) to propose his initial filter theory of selective attention. Broadbent theorized that incoming information is processed through a single channel. He hypothesized that selective attention operates by setting a filter in this channel to select a certain class of stimuli and to reject all others. According to Broadbent, this filtering process takes place early in the process of perception. He also theorized that the criteria for message selection are exclusively of a physical nature (e.g., message intensity, pitch, or location in space). In his model, any analysis of a message for meaning takes place only subsequent to the initial filtering process.

While Broadbent's model is commonly acknowledged as having played an important role in repopularizing the investigation of attentional processes, it was quickly realized that there are certain phenomena that it simply cannot account for. For example, the "cocktail party phenomenon" described by Cherry (1953), in which one suddenly becomes aware of a previously unattended-to conversation upon overhearing one's name, suggests that information that is not in focal awareness is nevertheless being analyzed on more than the basis of simple physical characteristics. This selective attention for one's name was demonstrated using a dichotic listening task, by Moray (1959), who found that subjects responded to their name spoken in the unattended ear while shadowing or repeating the message delivered to the other ear.

A simple study by Gray and Wedderburn (1960) also demonstrated the inadequacy of Broadbent's filter model. They found that when words were divided into syllables that were presented simultaneously to two different ears, subjects attended to both ears to extract meaning, rather than selecting one physical channel, thereby processing the information as meaningless syllables. This evidence suggests that subjects must be initially processing the unattended channel for meaning rather than for simple physical characteristics.

Evidence of this type led Treisman (1960, 1969) to propose her attenuation theory of selective attention. Treisman essentially suggested that the filtering process that takes place is not an all-or-nothing process and that the rejected meaning is really only attenuated. She hypothesized that the attenuated signal is matched against "dictionary units" in memory. These units have different thresholds of activation. If a specific attenuated signal exceeds the threshold of activation for the relevant unit or analyzer in memory, the unit becomes activated and the signal becomes conscious. While Treisman maintained the concept of a filter or "bottleneck" that exists early in the process of perception, she departed significantly from Broadbent by postulating that a signal can be processed by many analyzers simultaneously. This is a departure from the single-channel processing assumption of Broadbent's (1958) model and, as we shall see, anticipated subsequent theorizing about the multi-channeled nature of preattentive processing.

Deutsch and Deutsch (1963) proposed an important alternative to Treisman's filter/attenuation model, as a way of accounting for the fact that the criteria for message selection are not limited exclusively to physical characteristics. According to them, all incoming information is subjected to a complex, higher-level analysis, on the basis of which only a subset of the information is selected for processing in focal awareness. Also according to Deutsch and Deutsch (1963), information is multichanneled in nature until much later in the process than Broadbent's (1958) model suggests.

Neisser (1967) was perhaps the first theorist in the area of selective attention to reject the notion of a filter altogether. He described perception as a process of analysis by synthesis. He maintained that one understands spoken messages by covertly reproducing them, and that visual perception takes place by an analogous synthetic process. He thus saw perception as a constructive set. This notion of analysis by synthesis anticipated subsequent conceptualizations of the relationship between perception and action advanced by theorists writing within the ecological tradition (e.g., Turvey 1977, Weimer 1977). According to Neisser (1967), unattended-to information is not "filtered out." It is simply not selected for further perceptual synthesis. He maintained that all conscious awareness is preceded by a preliminary, preattentive process that organizes the perceptual field into coherent units, thus separating the stimuli into figure and ground. This preattentive processing is simultaneous and holistic in nature, in contrast to focal attentional processing, which is logical and sequential in nature. Although he theorized that preattentive processes perform a preliminary sorting and organization of sensory data, Neisser identified detailed perceptual analysis with focal attention, and focal attention with awareness.

A classic and often-cited study conducted by Corteen and Wood (1972) provided evidence that challenged this position. They demonstrated that subjects who received shocks during a dichotic listening task subsequently demonstrated a significant galvanic skin response in reaction to words (which had never been presented before) that were semantically related to shock-associated words that had been presented to the unattended ear. It is to be noted that this emotional conditioning to semantically associated words took place despite the fact that the words or stimuli that were conditioned were at first not perceived consciously. The study thus suggests that emotional reactions can take place in response to a sophisticated semantic analysis that takes place outside conscious awareness.

Informed by this and similar evidence, Kahneman (1973) developed a model of attention that was similar to Neisser's (1967), insofar as he conceptualized attention as an active process of elaboration, rather than a filtering or selecting-out process. Kahneman, however, hypothesized that more detailed meaning analyses can take place outside awareness. According to him, the critical factor that determines whether information is processed in focal awareness is the amount of attentional capacity that is focused upon it. Awareness or consciousness is thus identified with information that is allocated greater amounts of attentional capacity. Detailed meaning analyses, however, are not restricted to conscious processing. Kahneman (1973) also saw preattentive processing as multi-channeled in nature, rather than single-channeled or sequential. Norman and Bobrow (1975) articulated a model of selective attention that is similar in many ways to Kahneman's.

UNCONSCIOUS VERSUS CONSCIOUS PROCESSING

Research continues to demonstrate that complex, semantic processing takes place outside awareness, and that preconscious processing is qualitatively different from conscious information processing. The Corteen and Wood study (1972) was successfully replicated by Corteen and Dunn (1974) and Von Wright and colleagues (1975). More recently Dawson and Schell (1982) replicated the Corteen and Wood (1972) findings, using even more stringent experimental controls.

Underwood (1977) found that subjects in a dichotic listening task who were required to shadow words in one ear showed a reduced latency in shadowing time if semantically related words had previously been presented to the unattended ear. This suggests that words that are not *consciously* processed are nevertheless able to activate a perceptual set for semantically related words. Spence (1980) demonstrated that response latencies for discrimination between words and nonwords were significantly reduced by a subliminal stimulus which, while too brief to permit conscious representation, was nevertheless able to activate a perceptual set that facilitated the recognition of a target word.

On the basis of her research, Conrad (1974) concluded that in unconscious processing, all possible meanings of a perceived input are activated and processed in parallel. In one condition, she presented subjects with potentially ambiguous words that were disambiguated by the sentences in which they were embedded. In the second condition, she presented words embedded in sentences that did not disambiguate them in the manner described above. Subsequently, she found that the ambiguous word interfered with the process of naming a visually presented word, as long as this word was semantically related to any of the possible meanings of the ambiguous word. This was true even in the condition in which the ambiguous word had been disambiguated by a sentence. These results suggest (1) that multiple meanings of the ambiguous word were indeed activated for subjects, even if only one meaning of the word was conscious for the individual when the word was disambiguated by the sentence; and (2) that processing of information and perception of information are integrally tied to responding. Similar findings have emerged from studies conducted by Neely (1977) and Marcel (1980).

According to Posner and Snyder (1975a,b), sensory input automatically activates a variety of different pathways in the nervous system. As long as this information is not processed at the conscious level, minimal demands are made upon attentional capacity. From a survival perspective this can be seen as benefiting the organism because a wide array of information is constantly being processed, in parallel, in a variety of different ways. Because conscious processing is serial in nature rather than parallel, however, the admission of one stimulus, or one aspect of a stimulus, to consciousness automatically prevents other signals from becoming conscious. Conscious processing thus plays an inhibiting or restricting role with respect to signals that are not currently in conscious awareness.

Posner and Snyder (1975a) argue that unconscious processes operate not only at the level of perception but also at the level of preparation of responses in memory. The Stroop test, for example, provides a classic illustration of this observation. When the name of a specific color (e.g., blue) is printed in ink of a different color (e.g., red) the individual shows an increased response latency when asked to name the color of the ink. The semantic information provided by the written word thus appears to interfere with the person's performance on the task despite the fact that he or she attempts to ignore this information. Posner and Snyder (1975a) suggest that this phenomenon demonstrates that (1) a stimulus automatically activates multiple meanings, despite the fact that only one meaning may be conscious at a given point in time, (2) those meanings that are not conscious may nevertheless affect performance; and (3) the presentation of a stimulus (in this case the name of the color) automatically activates a pathway that includes not only semantic components but also a motor program associated with the output (in this case the naming of the color).

As the foregoing review suggests, the evidence acquired from research has gradually shifted the focus of theory away from an exclusive preoccupation with the question of how information is selectively admitted to awareness, to a more broad-scope attempt to understand the difference between the principles that characterize unconscious and conscious processing, as well as the nature of the interplay between the two. As Van Den Bergh and Eelen (1984) suggest, the reintroduction of consciousness into the framework of experimental psychology has functioned like the Trojan Horse, carrying unconscious cognitive processes in its belly.

Dixon (1981) argues that a biological frame of reference can be useful, if not absolutely necessary, for purposes of understanding the nature of, and relationship between, conscious and unconscious processes. Both types of processing activity can be understood in terms of their survival function. They can be conceptualized as complementary processing activities with different but equally im-portant survival features. Conscious processing is more restrictive than unconscious processing, with respect to the amount of sensory inflow that can be registered at one time. It has the advantage, however, of being more flexible in nature, allowing for sophisticated learning and for the formulation of action plans in response to sophisticated problem-solving activity. According to LaBerge (1981), the research evidence suggests that several properties are associated with unconscious processing. These include an unlimited attentional capacity; a lack of awareness, or absence of intentionality; a high degree of efficiency; and a resistance to change. Unconscious processing, because of its large capacity in contrast to conscious processing (cf. Kahneman 1973, Shiffrin and Schneider 1977), allows for the processing of multiple channels of information at the same moment. This allows the organism to register a large amount of information that may be important for purposes of survival. It also allows for rapid and immediate responses to a variety of stimuli in situations that are potentially threatening to the organisms of survival.

UNCONSCIOUS PROCESSING, ACTION, AND EMOTION

The experimental evidence emerging from research on selective attention and related areas is making it increasingly evident that any conceptualization of conscious cognitive processes is necessarily inadequate without an understanding of the nature of unconscious cognitive processing. As Shevrin and Dickman (1980) conclude, following their review of a number of relevant experimental studies, there is evidence both that information processing does take place at an unconscious level and that conscious and unconscious processing are characterized by different organizational features.

An important finding is the evidence that the unconscious processing of information is in some way integrally tied to responding, or at least to action disposition (e.g., Conrad 1974, Posner and Snyder 1975a,b). This evidence is consistent with Trevarthen's (1968) observation that "visual perception and the plans for voluntary action are so intimately bound together that they may be considered products of one cerebral function" (p. 391). It is also consistent with the ecological metatheoretical perspective, which views cognition and action as inextricably linked (Turvey 1977, Weimer 1977).

In an attempt to recognize the essentially motoric nature of cognition, a number of theorists from within the cognitive tradition have postulated the existence of structures in memory that represent, in a common locus, autonomic arousal, expressive motor behaviors, and memories or images of events that have elicited expressive motor behaviors (Bower 1981, Lang 1983, Leventhal 1982). Although there are differences in the specific details of these various models, which we will not go into here (for example, some theorists conceptualize these structures as semantic networks, whereas others conceptualize them as a schemalike structures), a hypothesis common to all is that these memory structures operate at an unconscious or a preattentive level, and that the activation of one element in the memory structure (e.g., a specific image) has the potential for activating other elements in that memory structure (e.g., a particular configuration of autonomic responses and expressive motor behaviors). It is thus hypothesized that a particular pattern of expressive motor behaviors and autonomic responses can automatically be activated without conscious awareness. Although at first glance it may appear that this conceptualization is little different from a classical conditioning account of automatic response activation, the characteristics of the proposed memory structures, as we have argued elsewhere (Safran and Greenberg 1986), are specified in a fashion that accounts for relationships of meaning between concepts. The model thus goes beyond a simple associative one.

Some theorists (e.g., Bower 1981) stipulate that the memory structures also contain nodes for specific emotions, and that in this fashion emotion becomes tied to ideas and expressive motor behaviors in memory and plays an organizational function. We believe that this type of formulation begs the question as to what "emotion" is. Our position, which has been influenced by Leventhal (1979, 1982), is that the subjective experience of emotion is the result of the processing of action–disposition information that emerges when expressive motor, autonomic, and imagery codings from these schematic structures are accessed and combined with information processed from the environment (Greenberg and Safran 1984a,b). Again, we wish to emphasize that this information is synthesized at a *preattentive* or *unconscious* level.

Elsewhere we reviewed the evidence consistent with the hypothesis that the expressive motor behavior accompanying specific basic emotional experiences is constant across developmental ages, across cultures, and is wired into the main organism (Greenberg and Safran 1986b). Following evolutionary theorists such as Izard (1977) and Tomkins (1980), we hypothesize that this wired-in expressive motor substrate for emotional experience has evolved through a process of natural selection and that it has survival value. Thus, for example, the expressive motor configuration associated with anger is hypothesized to be compatible with a self-protective fight response. The expressive motor configuration associated with fear is hypothesized to be compatible with a flight response.

The act of processing this type of information at an unconscious level provides the individual with action–disposition information, which he or she can then process at a conscious level and elaborate into an action plan, if he or she so chooses. The preattentive synthesis of emotional information thus takes advantage of the multichanneled nature of unconscious processing, in order to provide the individual with a multitude of information, potentially relevant for a survival, in the form of an efficient and economical emotional signal. The type of cognitive-affective-behavioral system we are describing (Greenberg and Safran this volume, Chapter 7) is thus seen as having the following characteristics:

1. The conscious experience of emotion is the product of an unconscious or preattentive synthesis of subsidiary components.
2. Emotional experience involves a synthesis of information from sources both external and internal to the organism.
3. The cognitive-affective system is adapted to the ecological niche.
4. Emotion has an adaptive function.
5. Emotional experience tells us what events mean to us as biological organisms.

With regard to this final point, Leventhal (1982) argues that emotions ". . . can be regarded as a form of meaning. They have significance for the person experiencing and expressing them. Their meaning has two aspects: they 'say' something about our organismic state (i.e., they meter its moment-to-moment readiness), and they 'say' something about the environment" (p. 122).

The model we have been discussing is consistent with an information-processing metatheory in that it specifies definite cognitive operations through which information is processed and combined with other information to provide information that is utilizable by the organism. At the same time, however, it is also consistent with an ecological metatheory in that (1) it conceptualizes people as biological organisms rather than as disembodied computing machines; (2) an attempt is made to understand psychological functioning from an evolutionary perspective: emotional and cognitive processes are viewed as having evolved to meet the demands of a particular ecological niche; and (3) cognition, emotion, and action are viewed as fused, or as different aspects of the same process, rather than as independent processes.

We will conclude this section by articulating two themes that have been implicit, if not explicit, in our discussion so far. The first is that by expanding the cognitive conceptualization of the unconscious to include concerns of ecological relevance, we are offering a cognitive alternative to a drive theory of *motivation*. Cognitive psychologists have, for the most part, conscientiously stayed away from dealing with motivational issues. However, there is no intrinsic reason for cognitive psychologists to avoid dealing with motivational issues. If we wish to have a truly adequate understanding of both conscious and unconscious psychological processes, it is necessary that we look at them in relationship to emotion and action. As Weimer (1977) asserts: "We must acknowledge that motivation is intrinsic to the operation of the CNS [central nervous system] and that the extrinsic sources of motivation that can be retained from classic motivation theory have their 'source' in the intrinsic motivation of nervous systems; that is, cognitive psychology must develop a 'motor theory' of motivation" (p. 295).

The second theme is that the conceptualization of emotional processing along the lines we have articulated will ultimately permit us to develop a model of human functioning that is truly compatible with a psychology of meaning. We view our analysis of emotional processing as consistent with, and extending, Gibson's (1979) concept of affordances. According to Gibson, people perceive objects and events in the world in terms of what they *afford* to them as organisms. A flat surface is thus perceived in terms of its walk-on-ability. A stick is perceived in terms of its grasp-ability. We, on the other hand, argue that we know objects and events in the world in terms of their *meaning* for us as biological organisms. This meaning is apprehended through the action dispositions that they evoke in us, and these action dispositions are the core of emotional experience. We thus conceptualize these action tendencies as a form of tacit knowledge, which is made explicit when the action-tendency information is synthesized and elaborated consciously.

As we have detailed elsewhere (Greenberg and Safran 1984b, 1986a, Safran and Greenberg 1986), the model we have articulated has some important clinical implications. Perhaps one of the most important ones is that psychological problems can result from a failure to fully synthesize potentially adaptive action–disposition information. For example, the person who fails to synthesize action–disposition information consistent with anger may fail to protect himself or herself from a destructive interpersonal situation. The person who fails to synthesize action–disposition information consistent with loneliness may fail to engage in intimacy-seeking behaviors that could lead to the establishment of an adaptive interpersonal relationship.

The model also facilitates the generation of hypotheses regarding the specific information-processing deficits from which this failure to synthesize adaptive action–disposition information results, as well as therapeutic interventions that can potentially remedy these deficits. We hypothesize that deficits of this type can result from a failure to *attend* to action–disposition information or expressive motor behaviors consistent with a specific emotion. As Underwood (1978) states, attention may be viewed as the "major control process in the passage of information into and out of the memory system and indeed through the human information-processing system as a whole" (p. 325). In this respect, the conceptualization emerging from the perspective we have outlined is closer to Sullivan's (1953) notion of selective inattention than it is to Freud's notion of regression.

Also consistent with Sullivan (1953), we hypothesize that anxiety-provoking interpersonal encounters can obstruct the processing of information both around and within the individual (Safran 1984a,b). This can result in a failure to develop elaborated schematic structures appropriate to certain classes of emotional experience that have been associated with anxiety-fraught interpersonal encounters. This, in turn, can result in what is essentially a structural inability to synthesize certain classes of emotional experience in any kind of refined or mature fashion. And consistent with Eagle (1984), we hypothesize that, in some cases, the failure to develop mature schematic structures associated with specific classes of emotions can result in accessing very primitive, explosive, and age-inappropriate emotions when they *are* synthesized. This can have the secondary complication of increasing the amount of fear an individual has in experiencing certain classes of emotion, thus making it all the more difficult to access those emotions.

CONCLUSIONS

The view of the unconscious that arises from the cognitive perspective we have outlined can ultimately be contrasted with the Freudian conception of the unconscious in the following fashion. Whereas Freud saw the unconscious as a "seething cauldron" of instinctual drives, which must be controlled or renounced in order to adapt to reality, the current perspective views the unconscious as providing action–disposition information that has not been synthesized and elaborated in focal awareness. In this respect, the concept of the unconscious derived from a cognitive perspective is much closer in nature to the more recent psychoanalytic developments articulated by theorists such as George Klein (1976), Schafer (1976, 1983), and Eagle (1984) than it is to the traditional psychoanalytic conception. In both the more recent psychoanalytic perspective and the cognitive perspective we have outlined, the goal of psychotherapy is one of owning disclaimed action tendencies, rather than one of acknowledging, and then taming or renouncing chaotic instinctual drives.

The cognitive perspective presented here augments current psychoanalytic thinking by elaborating upon the mechanisms through which actions can be disclaimed, as well as by articulating, in information-processing terms, what it means to acknowledge a disclaimed action. We believe that this results in more than a mere translation of concepts from one language to another. Understanding the processes of owning and disowning action tendencies in information-processing terms can provide us with insights as to how to facilitate the synthesis of adaptive emotional processes when this synthesis is not taking place. A variety of examples can be found in Greenberg and Safran (1986a) and Safran and Greenberg (1986).

The cognitive framework we have outlined shifts our understanding of the unconscious from a clinical/descriptive level to the level of theory that is strongly grounded in, and linked to, experimental research. It shifts the level of analysis from a descriptive level to an explanatory one. As Toulmin (1972) and Weimer (1979) point out, explanation is at the core of science. In this respect, both the topographic and structural models of the mind that Freud initially developed were, because of their explanatory nature, important attempts to frame the phenomenon of the unconscious in a scientific context. Drive theory is to be faulted, not on the basis of its attempt to explain, but rather on the basis of the inadequacy of the explanation. This failure may result, at least in part, from the fact that Freud attempted to establish psychoanalysis as a biological science, by using concepts that were prominent in the scientific climate of his time, but are now outdated.

More recent psychoanalytic developments (e.g., Eagle 1984, Klein 1976, Schafer 1976) have, in our opinion, provided a descriptive analysis with a greater degree of verisimilitude than Freud's metapsychology. However, these developments lack the explanatory power that is an essential part of a true scientific theory. We believe that casting the unconscious within a cognitive framework is an important step in this direction. Information-processing theory is an explanatory theory with the scientific merit of having important aspects of the nomological net grounded in observables. This enables us to modify theory in response to new evidence yielded by scientific investigation.

Along with critics of Freud from within the psychoanalytic community (e.g., Eagle 1984, Klein 1976), we are critical of certain aspects of Freud's drive metapsychology. We are, however, sympathetic to his attempt to understand humankind from a biological perspective and to view both conscious and unconscious processes in relationship to human passions. In contrast, the picture of the unconscious emerging from a purely information-processing approach is a sterile one and provides an incomplete picture of human functioning. A metatheory completely devoid of biological considerations is ultimately no more satisfactory than a metatheory that incorporates biology in a mechanistic fashion. As we have emphasized, however, there is no intrinsic reason for cognitive psychologists to continue to study cognition out of context of emotion, action, and environment. Our hope is that the information-processing/ ecological perspective we have offered (Greenberg and Safran 1984b, 1986a, Safran and Greenberg 1986) will provide cognitive psychologists with a way to talk about emotions and the unconscious, and psychoanalytic theorists with a way to talk to cognitive psychologists.

8

Emotion in Cognitive-Behavioral Theory and Treatment

BACKGROUND AND CURRENT STATE OF THE ART

Prior to the 1980s, emotion was treated by the cognitive-behavioral tradition primarily as a post-cognitive phenomenon. It was assumed that undesirable emotions were produced by faulty thinking processes and that the focus of intervention should consist of reducing these emotions through modifying dysfunctional cognitive processes or through behavioral interventions. The role of more positive emotions in human functioning was for the most part neglected, and the general emphasis was on controlling emotions rather than facilitating their experience. Another commonly accepted assumption was that rationality is the hallmark of mental health and that change is brought about either by thinking about things in a more rational way or by using hypothesis-testing procedures.

Two developments in the field of general experimental psychology set the stage for reconsidering the standard assumptions about the relationship between emotion and cognition. First, Zajonc's (1980) provocative article in *American Psychologist* led to a lively debate about whether it is reasonable to assume that cognition precedes emotion. Then, Bower's (1981) research on mood and memory pointed to the potential importance of evoking specific emotions in therapy in order to access underlying cognitions.

Mahoney (1980) was probably one of the first to draw cognitive therapists' attention to the fact that they were subscribing to an overly restrictive conceptualization of the role of emotion in human functioning. Les Greenberg and I (Greenberg and Safran 1984b, 1986b, 1987, Safran and Greenberg 1982a, 1986, 1991) followed Mahoney in arguing for the importance of broadening our conceptualization of the role of emotion in the change process. Influenced by the experiential approaches (Gestalt therapy and client-centered therapy), we argued that clients are often all too good at coming up with rational reevaluations of their experience and that the therapeutic task is often one of accessing hidden appraisals that are occurring at a more affective level.

We also attempted to integrate theory and research in the area of emotion theory with cognitive information-processing theory in order to articulate a framework for dealing with emotion in a more comprehensive fashion. Bower's (1981) research on mood and memory and Zajonc's (1980) review of research on the primacy of emotion were used to provide theoretical justification for the clinical practice of accessing automatic thoughts in an emotionally lively way, or accessing "hot cognitions"—a term borrowed from Ableson (1963). Additional theoretical scaffolding was provided by Leventhal's (1979) concept of the emotion schema.

Over the last decade or so my impression has been that the importance of accessing "hot cognitions" has gained a reasonably large acceptance among cognitive-behavioral therapists. A second set of principles, however, has been slower to be absorbed into cognitive-behavioral theory and practice. These involve the recognition of the adaptive role of emotion in human functioning and the potential value of interventions that access emotional experience because of its adaptive nature. Here we based our thinking on the work of a number of different theorists, including Arnold

(1960), Ekman and Friesen (1975), Leventhal (1979), Izard (1977), and Tompkins (1980). These ideas, while grounded in contemporary emotion theory, were anticipated by early analytic theorists such as Rank (1936) and Reich (1942) and by experiential therapists (Perls 1973, Rogers 1961). It is interesting to speculate about the reasons why these principles and related interventions have been slower to catch on with cognitive therapists.

One reason may be that the modification of the theory to accommodate this broader conceptualization of the role of human functioning necessitates some fundamental revision of metatheoretical assumptions. An important distinction between cognitive-behavioral theory and experiential theory is that cognitive-behavioral interventions are grounded within a metatheoretical framework that sees change as resulting from a willful attempt to modify the self (self-control). In contrast, experiential interventions are grounded within a paradoxical world view that holds that change takes place when one stops trying to change. The emphasis is thus on accepting or "letting go" rather than on self-control. A second related issue is that the ability to work with interventions that evoke intense emotions requires therapists to develop a certain acceptance of emotional experience that can only arise out of having gone through and witnessed related therapeutic processes themselves.

A third reason is that many affectively oriented interventions are difficult to implement properly without extensive training. The recent development of a manual on experiential approaches by Greenberg and colleagues (1994) may somewhat remedy the situation, but it is still the case that many of these interventions are difficult to acquire without proper training at an experiential level.

There are a number of recent developments that may create a more receptive climate among cognitive therapists to interventions that recognize the adaptive role of emotions in human functioning. First, some mainstream cognitive therapists have recently advocated shifting toward a more paradoxical view of human change that emphasizes the role of acceptance (Jacobson 1994, Linehan 1993). Second, many cognitive therapists are becoming interested in exploring the potential contributions of other therapeutic traditions to cognitive therapy (e.g., Goldfried and Davison 1994). Third,

research evidence has accumulated regarding the efficacy of certain
interventions derived from the experiential tradition (Greenberg et
al. 1994).

I will now summarize some of the central assumptions about
emotion in human functioning that are common to a variety of
contemporary theories of emotion (e.g., Izard 1977, Leventhal
1979, Plutchik 1980, Tomkins 1980) and I will outline some of the
implications for psychotherapy.

Emotions Play an Adaptive Role in Human Functioning

Emotions are wired into the human organism through an evolutionary process because of their adaptive nature. In order to have a full
understanding of how to work with emotional experience therapeutically, it is important to have an understanding of the role that
emotions play in healthy human functioning.

Emotions safeguard the various goals and the subgoals of the
biological organism. Some of these goals are innate and some of
them are learned. Fundamental goals are wired into the biological
system (e.g., self-protection, attachment, procreation). Other goals
are derivatives of more basic goals, and they develop as a result of
learning. For example, the specific beliefs one develops about the
way one needs to be in order to maintain relatedness or maintain
proximity to the attachment figure are learned.

Emotions provide action–disposition information. They provide information about the readiness of the biological system to act
in certain ways. Cognition provides information about the environment, but emotion provides information about the self in interaction with the environment. For example, anger provides information
regarding the readiness of the system to protect itself in an
aggressive fashion. Love provides information regarding the readiness of the systems to act in an affiliative fashion.

Psychological problems often arise from a failure to fully process adaptive emotional experience. Emotion can provide people
with the conviction that a certain course of action is right for them
and with the motivation to pursue that course of action. For

example, a person in an abusive relationship may begin the process of ending it when she accesses her feelings of anger. Socially isolated individuals may begin to face their anxiety and make social contact when they fully process and experience their sadness and pain.

Emotions Organize Systemic Priorities through Their Salience

Because emotions play a role in safeguarding important systemic goals, they have a compelling quality about them that can override the entire system and move it in a certain direction. For example, anger may override a rational decision to act in a more cautious fashion. Attraction may override a rational evaluation regarding the risks of becoming emotionally involved. This compelling quality is important to survival. For example, if one is in a life-threatening situation (for example, being attacked by a predator), it is adaptive for the mobilization of the system toward flight to take precedence over other goals such as eating. For this reason, emotions are activated and continue to color one's perception of the situation until they are processed and dealt with in some way. For example, feeling angry at someone will predispose one to look at that person critically even if one is not fully aware of the anger. Therapeutic interventions designed to rationally reevaluate situations may not always be effective.

Affective Responses Are Mediated by the Perception of Interpersonal Consequences

A person's ability to experience a particular emotion is shaped both by the history of his or her interpersonal learning experiences and by his or her anticipation and perception of current interpersonal consequences. For example, an individual who has learned that the experience of sadness will alienate other people will have difficulty fully experiencing and expressing such feelings. Learning experiences of this type tend to shape the perception of current interpersonal situations.

In therapy, an important part of helping clients to access emotional experience consists of exploring and challenging dysfunctional beliefs regarding the experience of various emotions. Moreover, the therapist's spontaneous response to a client's emotional experience will mediate his or her ability to access it. For example, a therapist who fears the client's sadness will have difficulty helping the client access it.

Emotions Have a Somatic Component

Different emotions are associated with different somatic experiences. For example, the emotion of love is associated with somatic correlates of softness and vulnerability (decreased muscular tension). Anger is associated with muscular tension and somatic correlates of aggression.

This has important significance from a therapeutic perspective. An emotional experience that people have not fully articulated to themselves may nevertheless be implicit as a bodily felt sense (Gendlin 1962). Thus an important intervention consists of directing clients' attention to their bodily felt sense experience in order to promote the construction of emotional experience.

Emotion Is a Primary Communication System

Emotion plays a primary role in human communication. Human beings are biologically wired to make sense of and respond to the emotional expressions of others. From a therapeutic perspective this has important implications. People may be communicating things to other people without being fully aware that they are doing so. For example, somebody may communicate hostility toward others through his or her voice tone, body posture, or facial gesture without being fully aware of this anger. Providing clients with feedback about the emotions they evoke in others can be an important form of therapeutic feedback (Kiesler 1988, Safran and Segal 1990).

Emotion Is a Form of Tacit Meaning

Because emotions provide us with information regarding how well we are progressing toward the goals and subgoals of the overall system, they also implicitly provide us with information about what these goals and subgoals are. For example, the fact that a child becomes frightened when the attachment figure leaves reflects the fact that maintaining proximity to the attachment figure is an important goal of the system. Many of the goals we develop through learning are tacit rather than explicit. Because much of this learning takes place at an early, preverbal stage of development, many of these attitudes are implicit in the functioning of the system rather than verbally explicit. For this reason, attending to the nuances of one's emotional experiences can provide one with important information about one's goals.

AFFECTIVE ASSESSMENT

A question that often comes up for cognitive therapists who are learning to work in a more emotion-focused fashion is when to deepen the intensity of the client's emotional experience and when not to. Here it is important to differentiate between different types of emotional experience. Les Greenberg and I (Greenberg and Safran 1987) have articulated a clinical heuristic that distinguishes among three types of emotional expression: primary emotion, secondary emotion, and instrumental emotion. *Primary emotion* consists of the individual's initial affective appraisal of the situation prior to more complex conceptual activity. This is a biologically adaptive signal that provides information about the individual's action dispositions, motivates adaptive behavior, and provides implicit information about the meaning of events for the individual. The therapist may wish to help the client to access primary emotions as an end toward a number of therapeutic goals such as motivating adaptive behavior or obtaining information about the individual's tacit values.

A *secondary emotion* consists of the emotional expression that results from the individual's secondary internal response to the primary emotional appraisal. For example, an individual feels angry and then begins to feel self-critical because of his or her anger. This leads to feelings of sadness and hopelessness. Another example is the individual who begins to feel needy and vulnerable and then responds with anger because of his or her anticipation of being abandoned. In this situation the anger is a secondary emotional reaction to an underlying feeling of vulnerability. The therapist's task here is to help the client ultimately access the underlying primary emotion rather than the secondary emotion. For example, a client tended to react to others in an angry, defensive, and self-protective fashion whenever he felt vulnerable. This alienated others and made it difficult for them to respond to his needs in a nurturing fashion. By helping the client to access underlying feelings of vulnerability, the therapist was able to help him function in a more adaptive fashion. Rather than lash out at people when he was angry, he was able to acknowledge his vulnerability in a way that brought people closer to him.

Instrumental emotions are emotional patterns that people have learned in order to influence others. For example, the individual cries in order to evoke sympathy or expresses anger as a way of controlling people. As with secondary emotions, it would be a mistake for the therapist to attempt to deepen the client's experience of instrumental emotions. Instead the task is to illuminate the nature of the underlying emotional experience. Distinguishing between these different types of emotional experience, while critical, is a complex clinical task that requires experience. Many of the cues are subtle and difficult to articulate. A key source of information consists of the therapist's own emotional reaction to the client. If the client is expressing a primary emotion, the therapist is more likely to feel attuned to and empathically connected to him or her than if the client is expressing a secondary or instrumental emotion. To the extent that clients are in contact with and expressing their own primary emotional experience, the clinician is more likely to feel affectively engaged.

If the clinician does not feel engaged with the client's emotional experience, it can be a cue that the client is alienated from his or her primary emotion. Of course the therapist must always seriously consider the possibility that the lack of engagement may be attributable to a lack of empathy resulting from his or her own issues.

Another source of information can emerge from putting one's self in the client's shoes and imagining how one would feel in the situation and then contrasting the client's expressed emotional experience with one's own anticipated feelings. For example, a client was describing a situation in which her boyfriend was mistreating her and then burst into tears. The therapist, through an act of identification with the client, experienced anger rather than sadness. This discrepancy in reactions alerted him to the possibility that the sadness might be a secondary emotion. When the situation was explored more carefully, it emerged that the client had a habitual style of responding to her own feelings of anger with self-criticism, fears of abandonment, and helplessness. By becoming aware of this process, she was able to experience her anger more fully and ultimately was motivated to leave the situation.

The therapist has no choice ultimately but to rely on his or her own emotional experience during therapy as an important therapeutic tool. This notion can be distressing to those who see psychotherapy as more of a science than an art or who are mistrustful of emotion as an important source of information. There is always an affective component to our appraisals, however, even if we are unaware of it, and the best safeguard against making therapeutic mistakes involves becoming fully aware of our emotional experience rather than trying to ignore it. There is an inevitable element of subjectivity to our perceptions, and it is safer to make use of and acknowledge this subjectivity than to delude ourselves into believing that our judgments are made on purely rational grounds.

AFFECTIVE PROCESSING DYSFUNCTIONS

In this final section I will describe a number of specific dysfunctions in emotional processing and briefly outline some of the relevant interventions.

Anxiety as a Secondary Response to Primary Emotion

In this situation the client presents clinically with anxiety-related problems. This anxiety is a secondary response to an underlying primary feeling that the individual anticipates will be threatening to interpersonal relatedness. For example, a client who has difficulty fully processing and experiencing anger because she perceives it as threatening to interpersonal relatedness presents with diffuse anxiety symptoms. The therapeutic task is to work with the client to help her attend more fully to a bodily felt sense associated with anger that is currently not being fully processed. An important piece of the work may involve exploring and challenging automatic thoughts and dysfunctional beliefs related to the prohibition of anger.

Multiple Anxiety Concerns Secondary to Avoidance

In this syndrome the focus of the client's attention shifts from one anxiety concern to another in rapid succession. A presentation of this type can be rather overwhelming to the therapist who has not yet begun to get a grasp of one problem before the client moves on to another. In addition, the client's feeling of being overwhelmed is communicated to the therapist. Multiple anxiety-related concerns of this sort can often be the reflection of a client's difficulty in experiencing one particular situation and the painful feelings associated with it more fully. An important therapeutic intervention here consists of directing the client's attention to avoided feelings more fully and helping him or her to become aware of ways in which those feelings are avoided.

Depression Resulting from Deactivation of Behavioral Systems

In this syndrome the client experiences a sense of hopelessness and depression because his or her primary emotions are not being attended to. As Bowlby (1980) suggests, depression is an organismic response constellation that in one way or another involves a deactivation of behavioral systems. When an individual feels that exertion of further effort is futile or dangerous, the normal link between emotional processing and actions can be broken through a failure to fully attend to and synthesize relevant emotional information. For example, a depressed client who experiences a pervasive sense of numbness may in fact be failing to fully attend to underlying feelings of sadness. This blockage may result from a belief that he or she may be abandoned if he or she expresses this sadness or that nobody will be there. In a situation of this type, therapeutic interventions aimed at helping the client to fully experience the underlying sadness can be a powerful experience that helps him or her regain contact both with the self and with the rest of the world. Feelings of numbness and deadness can be replaced with yearning and a desire for nurturance and can lead to interpersonal contact and support, if expressed.

Cognitive Disconnection of Response from Situation

This form of dysfunctional affective information processing, also identified by Bowlby (1980), involves a failure to make the connection between a particular emotion and the environmental stimulus that elicits it. For example, rather than feeling anger in response to a particular person in a specific situation, the individual walks around with a diffuse sense of anger and bitterness that is not attached to anything and that cannot be worked with. This affective information processing dysfunction serves a defensive or avoidance function in that it helps the individual to avoid exploring and expressing feelings in a particular interpersonal situation that may seem too dangerous or threatening. An important therapeutic intervention here consists of working with the client to help him to continue to attend to a relevant interpersonal situation that evokes a response rather than to experience things in a more diffuse fashion. In this respect, it is useful to focus on the here and now of the therapeutic relationship as an interpersonal laboratory in which emotions are constantly evoked and to help the client become aware of the way he or she may avoid experiencing certain feelings in the relationship.

Unresolved Grief or Incomplete Mourning

The normal grieving or mourning process is one that has been observed and described by a number of theorists and researchers. An important part of the grieving process typically involves the experience of intrusive thoughts about the person being grieved for and alternations between feelings of sadness, pain, and anger.

Although it is not fully understood how the normal process of mourning operates, one commonly accepted hypothesis is that the intrusive images of the loved one permit the individual to gradually change his internal representation of the interpersonal world in order to accommodate to the new reality. In this process both sadness and anger are natural responses to the loss of a loved one. The sadness motivates the individual to attempt to recover the loved one while the anger is associated with the severing of the connection to the loved one when one's goal of recovery cannot be attained. Both emotions can be extremely painful and defensively avoided. In the natural grieving process, however, the oscillation back and forth between periods of sadness and anger in response to the intrusive images ultimately functions to sever emotional connection to the loved one and to modify the individual's cognitive representations of the interpersonal world (Horowitz 1979).

CONCLUSIONS

There has been an explosion of interest among academic psychologists in the topic of emotion since the early 1980s. Cognitive therapists have been influenced in certain respects by these developments, but their potential impact on the field has yet to be fully realized. In this chapter I have summarized a number of theoretical and technical principles relevant to the adoption of a broader range of approaches toward affective experience. It is probably more accurate to think of these principles as generic in nature rather than specific to cognitive therapy. As cognitive therapists become more familiar with these principles, however, the possibility of a distinctive cognitive-behavioral approach to emotion emerges.

Part III

Ruptures in the Therapeutic Alliance

9

The Therapeutic Alliance Rupture as a Therapy Event for Empirical Investigation

Jeremy D. Safran, Peter Crocker,
Shelly McMain, and Paul Murray

An *alliance rupture* consists of an impairment or fluctuation in the quality of the alliance between the therapist and client. Alliance ruptures vary in intensity, duration, and frequency, depending on the particular therapist–client dyad. In more extreme cases, the client may overtly indicate negative sentiments to the therapist or even terminate therapy prematurely. At the other end of the continuum are minor fluctuations in the quality of the therapeutic alliance that may be extremely difficult for the outside observer or for even the skilled therapist to detect.

While the features of alliance ruptures vary from case to case, most therapy cases, even the more successful ones, are characterized by at least one or more ruptures in the therapeutic alliance over the course of therapy. While much of our discussion will ring true to the reader, our intention is to "unpack" familiar concepts such as the therapeutic alliance in a fashion that leads to more differentiated understanding and research.

WHY IS THE ALLIANCE RUPTURE AN IMPORTANT PHENOMENON TO INVESTIGATE?

The concept of the therapeutic alliance has received a considerable amount of attention by psychotherapy researchers. Although the concept originated early in the psychoanalytic literature (Bibring 1937, Sterba 1934), it was Bordin's (1979) integrative conceptualization of the alliance that gave impetus to the current flurry of research interest. Bordin (1979) views the therapeutic alliance as a common change factor in all forms of psychotherapy, which consists of three interdependent components: the relational bond between the client and the therapist; the tasks of psychotherapy (i.e., the specific action in which the client is required to engage); and the goals of psychotherapy (i.e., the general outcome that is sought). According to Bordin, the quality of the therapeutic alliance is a function of the degree of agreement between therapist and client about the goals and tasks of psychotherapy. This in turn is mediated by the quality of the relational bond between therapist and client, which is affected by the degree of agreement about goals and tasks. This conceptualization of the alliance thus eliminates the rigid distinction between general relationship factors and specific technical factors and combines them within an overarching theoretical framework (Greenberg and Pinsof 1986).

There is now a large body of empirical evidence that demonstrates that the therapeutic alliance, as rated from client, therapist, and third-party perspectives, is the best predictor of psychotherapy outcome (Alexander and Luborsky 1986, Horvath and Greenberg 1986, Marmar et al. 1986, Suh et al. 1986). Given the importance of the therapeutic alliance to therapy outcome, it would seem important to clarify those factors involved in repairing ruptures in the therapeutic alliance.

A preliminary study by Foreman and Marmar (1985) attempted to identify therapist actions capable of enhancing initially poor alliances. They examined the sessions of six clients who were rated as having poor therapeutic alliances in the early phases of treatment. At termination, three had sustained poor alliances and poor outcomes, and three had improved alliances and good outcomes.

Foreman and Marmar (1985) found that in each of the improved outcome cases, the client's problematic feelings toward the therapist were directly addressed and linked to the defenses used to ward them off (e.g., "When you begin to feel angry with me, you withdraw and fall silent"). In the unimproved alliance cases, either this link was not made, or problematic feelings toward the therapist were avoided or ignored by the therapist.

While this study provides an important starting point, it is limited by the small sample size and by the fact that the analysis is at a very general descriptive level. In order to capture the subtlety of the processes involved in healing alliance ruptures, it will be necessary to investigate them in a more intensive fashion. A first step toward this type of investigation involves the examination of the relevant phenomenon from a conceptual perspective. This will set the stage for subsequent empirical analysis.

A CONCEPTUAL FRAMEWORK

The growing evidence of the importance of the alliance in therapy might lead some to conclude that therapy technique is less important than the relationship aspects of therapy. However, as Bordin's (1979) conceptualization of the alliance suggests, technical and relationship factors are interdependent aspects of the same process. The traditional distinction between technical and relationship factors assumes that treatment through psychotherapy is analogous to treatment through medication (Parloff 1986, Strupp 1986, Wilkins 1985). The effect of medication, however, is theoretically distinguishable from the psychological meaning of the treatment. In contrast, the action of psychotherapeutic techniques is intrinsically linked to the interpersonal context in which they occur (Butler and Strupp 1986, Luborsky 1984, Safran 1990a,b). Thus as Butler and Strupp (1986) argue: "The complexity and subtlety of psychotherapeutic processes cannot be reduced to a set of disembodied techniques because techniques gain their meaning and, in turn, their effectiveness from the particular interaction of individuals involved" (p. 33).

The impact of the therapist's behavior on the client must ultimately be understood in terms of the client's perception of that behavior, and this perception is ultimately determined by the client's unique learning history. The same therapeutic intervention may thus be interpreted very differently by two different clients. While one client may construe it in a fashion that promotes the therapeutic alliance, another may construe it in a manner that impedes it. For this reason, it seems vital to have an understanding of the factors shaping a client's perception of the meaning of therapeutic interventions.

A number of theorists suggest that a client's perception of the meaning of other people's actions is organized by core cognitive structures or schemata (Arnkoff 1980, Guidano and Liotti 1983, Horowitz 1988, Mahoney 1982, Meichenbaum and Gilmore 1984, Safran et al. 1986). These core cognitive structures can be thought of as generalized expectations about self–other interactions or interpersonal schemata that are based on past experiences (Safran 1990a, Safran et al. 1990). When these core cognitive structures are dysfunctional, they activate maladaptive cognitive-interpersonal cycles in which the client's expectations lead to behavior on his or her part that elicits predictable interpersonal consequences that confirm their dysfunctional expectations (Carson 1969, 1982, Kiesler 1982, 1986, Luborsky 1984, Safran 1984a,b, 1990a,b, Safran and Segal 1990, Strupp and Binder 1984, Wachtel 1977). For example, one individual anticipates others will abandon him and thus behaves in a clinging, dependent fashion that ultimately alienates people and confirms his expectations. Another person anticipates that others will be critical of her and thus acts in an excessively self-justifying fashion that irritates people and ultimately elicits the type of criticism that she expects.

When the therapist acts in a fashion that is consistent with the client's dysfunctional interpersonal schema, he or she perpetuates an existing dysfunctional cognitive-interpersonal cycle. For example, the therapist who responds to the client's hostility with counterhostility may confirm his belief that the world is a hostile place that should be met with hostility. Conversely, if the therapist is able to refrain from participating in the client's cognitive-interpersonal cycle, the client encounters an important experiential challenge to his dysfunctional beliefs.

An important related concept has been articulated by Weiss and colleagues (1987), who maintain that people's problems result from pathogenic beliefs about interpersonal relationships that have developed as a result of interactions with significant others. They theorize that the process of disconfirming the client's pathogenic beliefs is a central mechanism of change in psychotherapy, and that clients unconsciously submit their therapists to transference tests in an attempt to disconfirm their pathogenic beliefs. In an extensive series of studies, they have demonstrated both that pathogenic beliefs can be measured reliably, and that the disconfirmation of pathogenic beliefs is related to both the immediate (i.e., in-session) and ultimate outcome (Weiss et al. 1987).

The above theory and research suggest that therapist interventions that disconfirm the client's dysfunctional beliefs about self–other interactions will be construed in a fashion that permits collaboration on the task and goal components of the alliance. Conversely, interventions that confirm the client's dysfunctional beliefs perpetuate a maladaptive cognitive-interpersonal cycle and make collaboration on a particular task or toward a particular goal difficult.

For example, the client who anticipates that others will attempt to dominate him or her will have difficulty establishing a therapeutic alliance with a domineering therapist. The client who anticipates that others will be emotionally unavailable will have difficulty establishing an adequate therapeutic alliance with a withdrawn therapist. For this reason, particular types of therapy are at risk for particular types of alliance ruptures (Safran and Segal 1990). Cognitive therapy, for example, with its active techniques for challenging cognitions, is at risk for alliance ruptures in which the client feels criticized or invalidated. Forms of psychodynamic therapy in which the therapist plays a less active role are at risk for ruptures in which the client feels that the therapist is emotionally unavailable to him or her. Thus, as Bordin (1979) suggests, different clients will find it easier to meet the alliance demands of different forms of psychotherapy, depending on the particular demands of the relevant therapeutic tasks.

Because alliance ruptures are likely to occur at junctures where the therapist's actions confirm a client's dysfunctional interpersonal schemata, they are ideal points for phenomenological exploration. The existence of an alliance rupture provides the therapist with a unique opportunity to explore expectations, beliefs, emotions, and appraisal processes that play a central role in the client's dysfunctional cognitive-interpersonal cycle (Safran and Segal 1990). For example, a therapist becomes aware that a client responds to intervention by withdrawing in a sullen fashion. By exploring the client's experience at this point, she discovers that the client feels patronized but has been reluctant to say anything for fear that the therapist will be angry. Further exploration reveals that this theme cuts across a variety of interpersonal situations.

The successful resolution of an alliance rupture can be a powerful means of disconfirming the client's dysfunctional interpersonal schema. While failure to adequately resolve an alliance rupture is likely to lead to poor outcome in psychotherapy, the successful resolution of an alliance rupture can be one of the more potent means of inducing change. In the above illustration, for example, metacommunication about the alliance rupture can potentially help the client to clarify whether she really has been patronized and to challenge her belief that it is too risky to discuss this experience with others.

The current perspective suggests that empathic failures take place when the therapist fails to adequately understand the nature of the client's dysfunctional beliefs about self–other interactions and thus inadvertently confirms them. The resulting alliance rupture, however, provides an important opportunity. First, it allows the therapist to refine his or her understanding of the problematic cognitive structure, by activating it and bringing the relevant construal processes to the surface. Second, once the relevant cognitive structure has been activated, the possibility of a corrective interpersonal experience emerges.

A converging perspective is offered by Kohut (1984), who pinpoints the client's negative response to the therapist's empathic failure as a critical juncture for intervention. According to him, the therapist's ability to deal empathically with the client's response to these inevitable lapses in empathy plays a vital role in activating the change process in psychoanalysis. While the focus on the therapist's empathic failure is a central emphasis in self psychology, the current perspective attempts to cast the event within a more general theoretical framework.

An illuminating developmental perspective on the significance of alliance ruptures in therapy can be found in the research on affective miscoordination and repair (Tronick 1989). In healthy mother–infant dyads, the interaction frequently moves back and forth between periods in which the affective communication is coordinated and periods when it breaks down. When the infant's affective experience (e.g., sadness) is misinterpreted by the mother, the infant reacts with a secondary affect (e.g., anger). In healthy mother–infant dyads, the mother responds to the secondary affect empathically, and the affective communication becomes coordinated once again.

In dysfunctional mother–infant dyads, the mother fails to become attuned to the secondary affective response as well as to the initial affective response. A state of affective miscoordination between mother and infant thus continues. Tronick and Cohn (1989) hypothesize that in healthy mother–infant dyads the continuous oscillation between affective miscoordination and interactive repair helps the infant to develop expectations that disruptions in the relationship are remediable and that negative affective experience will be transformed into positive affective experience. They thus develop a representation of themselves as interpersonally effective and of the caretaker as trustworthy. They are thus able to maintain interpersonal engagement in the face of stress.

Infants in dysfunctional dyads are not able to develop this type of adaptive representation of self in interaction with others and thus have difficulties maintaining interpersonal engagement in less-than-optimal situations. Moreover, because of consistent misattunement by the caretaker to both the primary and the secondary affect, they may have problems in learning to process and express both types of affective experience.

Safran and Segal (1990) hypothesize that developmental experiences of this type can have implications for alliance ruptures that emerge in therapy. For example, a client who has consistently had the emotion of sadness misattuned to as a child may have difficulty expressing that emotion when appropriate in therapy and may respond in anger when the therapist fails to become attuned to the underlying sadness. There will thus be a rupture in the therapeutic alliance. If the therapist is able to adequately empathize with the anger, the alliance will be strengthened and the client may, over time, be better able to access and express both the anger and the underlying sadness that was misattuned to. It is then critical to empathize with the underlying sadness as well. In this fashion the client may gradually be able to develop a new representation of herself as capable of maintaining interpersonal contact in the face of disruption, and of others as being emotionally available.

ALLIANCE RUPTURE MARKERS

The alliance rupture is a potentially fruitful domain for empirical investigation. As a recurring, circumscribed, and operationalizable occurrence in therapy, the resolution of an alliance rupture qualifies as the type of change event amenable to investigation through the new "events paradigm" in psychotherapy research (Elliot 1984, Rice and Greenberg 1984, Safran, Greenberg et al. 1988).

In a preliminary effort to map out the domain of the alliance rupture for empirical investigation, we selected a number of therapy segments in which ruptures had been identified for intensive observation. These segments were selected from psychotherapy sessions of clients being treated for depression or anxiety disorders with an integrated cognitive-interpersonal approach (Safran 1984a,b, 1990a,b, Safran and Segal 1990). Using postsession questionnaires, we selected a number of sessions in which both therapists and clients had identified problems in the therapeutic alliance. By listening repeatedly to audiotapes of these sessions, we attempted to identify consistent themes.

Below, seven different themes are featured because of their

recurrent emergence in the sample of alliance ruptures studied. It is not our intention to imply that this list is exhaustive or that the rupture types are mutually exclusive. Each theme, however, can potentially be thought of as what Rice and Greenberg (1984) have referred to as a process *marker*, that is, a distinctive type of client verbalization and/or behavior indicating the presence of a distinctive underlying psychological process, and a potential readiness for a particular type of intervention. Although the current list of rupture markers is framed in terms of client indicators, it should be borne in mind that all ruptures in the therapeutic alliance are conceptualized as involving both client and therapist. The precise contribution of each will vary, depending on the particular rupture.

1. *Overt expression of negative sentiments.* A commonly observed sign of a disruption in the therapeutic alliance is a client's expression of negative sentiments toward the therapist. For example, the client directly attacks the therapist's competence or accuses the therapist of being cold or heartless.

2. *Indirect communication of negative sentiments or hostility.* While some clients communicate negative sentiments directly, these feelings are most often communicated indirectly through sarcasm, nonverbal behavior, or passive-aggressive behavior. For example, one client became withdrawn and subtly derisive when she perceived the therapist as moving from an intimate discussion of concrete events and feelings to a more abstract and impersonal level. When this behavioral pattern was explored, she acknowledged that she felt as though the therapist was playing the "psychologist" in a "clichéd manner" at these points in the session, and thus she didn't feel comfortable revealing herself to him.

   One frequently observed example of an indirect expression of negative sentiments involves the client's allusion to negative sentiments or concerns about the therapeutic relationship through a thematically linked discussion of out-of-session events, or an allusion to the transference (Gill and Hoffman 1982). For example, one client, who in an earlier session felt rejected by his female therapist and dissatisfied by her evasive responses to his questions, initiated the session by discussing feelings of frustration and humiliation associated with a recent interaction with another woman who he felt had rejected and humiliated him. Only after sensitive and empathic exploration by the therapist was he able to acknowledge similar feelings toward her.

3. *Disagreement about the goals or tasks of therapy.* Another commonly observed marker involves the client questioning or rejecting the goals or tasks of therapy. This observation is consistent with Bordin's (1979) suggestion that the strength of the therapeutic alliance is mediated by the degree of agreement between therapist and client about goals and tasks. While in some cases there may be fundamental incompatibilities between the goals and tasks of a particular therapeutic approach and the client's worldview, in other cases this disagreement may be the surface manifestation of other underlying themes. For example, one client consistently asked the therapist to provide her with strategies and advice of a more concrete and tangible nature. This client had a core belief that others were never available to provide the kind of nurturance that she needed. The development of this belief had been influenced by her relationship with an alcoholic and emotionally unavailable father. Because of her desire for nurturance she consistently pulled for support and advice from others. At the same time, however, she resented others giving her directions because she perceived them as dominating her.

   During her sessions, she repeatedly urged the therapist to provide her with tangible techniques and specific advice. However, when he did comply by becoming more directive, she became resentful and angry. In this instance the disagreement about the tasks of therapy reflected an underlying cognitive interpersonal cycle that was problematic for the client.

4. *Compliance.* Client compliance with the therapist is also a common marker of problems in the therapeutic alliance. In this type of situation, rather than risk threatening the

relationship with the therapist, the client acquiesces. In one case, for example, the client who initially indicated a reluctance to try a particular exercise, eventually responded to the therapist's coaxing and agreed to comply with the task. The therapist, however, detecting a begrudging quality in her voice, began to explore the experience associated with the act of compliance for her. This led to an exploration of some central beliefs, related to the need to submerge her own needs in order to avoid rejection, and to an eventual improvement in the alliance. Another common indicator of compliance involves a hasty agreement with the therapist, with no further elaboration.

5. *Avoidance maneuvers.* Clients also engage in avoidance maneuvers to reduce the anxiety associated with a rupture in the alliance. The client may, for example, protect himself from a sense of threat by becoming unresponsive to the therapist's interventions or by skipping from topic to topic in a fashion that prevents the therapist from exploring issues in depth. In some situations the client may become unclear or confused by a therapist's interventions or may completely ignore a therapist's remarks. Other more extreme reactions include the client arriving late, cancelling the appointment, or failing to attend a session.

6. *Self-esteem-enhancing operations.* Client behavior during the process of a rupture is sometimes characterized by self-justifying or self-aggrandizing communications. A client may attempt to justify or defend himself or herself as a means of regaining a deflated sense of self-worth. For example, one client in our sample tended to provide extended explanations as to how she had become the way she was, when the alliance appeared strained.

Other examples of self-esteem-enhancing operations include clients' attempts to boost their self-esteem by presenting positive images of themselves to their therapist. For example, one client tended to boast about his previous accomplishments when it appeared that he felt criticized by the therapist. Another client discussed the nature of his problem using highly theoretical terms, in what appeared to be an attempt to impress the therapist.

Clients may support their floundering self-esteem by attacking or deprecating the therapist. The client may belittle the therapist with overt remarks or by devaluing the therapist covertly through sarcasm. Both avoidance maneuvers and self-esteem-enhancing operations can be considered to be reflections of what Sullivan (1953) termed security operations, that is, operations that function to reduce or avoid anxiety resulting from a deflation of the individual's self-esteem. From an interpersonal perspective it is hypothesized that self-esteem is associated with a subjective sense of interpersonal relatedness and that an impairment in the therapeutic relationship will thus be associated with an increase in anxiety (Safran 1990a,b, Safran and Segal 1990).

7. *Nonresponsiveness to intervention.* A final alliance rupture marker can be designated as nonresponsiveness to intervention. This marker is characterized by a sequence of events in which the client fails to respond positively or make use of a particular therapeutic intervention. For example, the therapist offers an interpretation that is rejected by the client or attempts to challenge a cognitive distortion without success. Failed interventions of this type often (but not always) reflect preexisting problems in the alliance. Alternatively, a poorly timed or unempathic intervention can disrupt an alliance that has been satisfactory. In either case, further exploration can potentially lead to a better understanding of the client's interpersonal schema. It should be emphasized that the fact that a failed intervention can lead to a better understanding of the client's interpersonal schema does not mean that the client is responsible rather than the therapist. An alliance rupture is always an interactional phenomenon.

The above list provides a preliminary description of seven potential alliance rupture markers. Further investigation will be required to establish whether they can be reliably identified. Moreover, it will be important to clarify whether the underlying processes are sufficiently distinct to justify retaining the entire list or whether one or more marker subtypes should be collapsed.

RESOLVING ALLIANCE RUPTURES:
GENERAL PRINCIPLES

Resolving alliance ruptures involves a process of therapeutic meta-communication, that is, talking about what is currently transpiring in the therapeutic relationship. Therapeutic metacommunication is, of course, a central intervention in any interpersonal approach to therapy and is not restricted for use in the context of an alliance rupture. It is precisely in the context of an alliance rupture, however, that metacommunication becomes most critical. In this section we will emphasize those aspects of the metacommunication process that are hypothesized to be most important in the process of resolving an alliance rupture. Five general principles will be dis-cussed. Our discussion of this issue has been influenced by a number of different sources. Most directly influential, however, has been Kiesler's (1982a, 1986, 1988) operationalization of the prin-ciples of therapeutic metacommunication.

1. *Attending to ruptures in the alliance.* This step is critical because the process of resolution cannot begin until the rupture has been noted. Because clients are, however, often reluctant to communicate negative sentiments directly, this first step can be problematic. For this reason a perceptual readiness for the presence of alliance ruptures should be cultivated. The systematic identification of alliance rupture markers will hopefully facilitate this process.

2. *Being aware of one's own feelings.* This is a critical step for a number of reasons. First, the therapist's feelings provide a useful barometer regarding the quality of the relationship in a moment-by-moment fashion. If the client is feeling suffi-ciently safe to allow the therapist access to his inner world, the therapist should have a subjective feeling of true empa-thy with the client (Safran and Segal 1990). The absence of

this experience may indicate the presence of an alliance rupture. Second, the therapist's feelings provide important information that can be employed in the process of meta-communication (Kiesler 1982, 1986, 1988). Third, the accurate identification of one's own feelings is an important part of the process of accepting responsibility. Unless the therapist is able to accurately identify her own feelings, her actions will be biased by factors outside of awareness. For example, a therapist who is angry at her client, but not aware of that anger, may nevertheless communicate it in subtle ways. Thus, an intervention, which at one level is intended to help the client, may in fact be delivered in a punitive fashion.

3. *Accepting responsibility.* The preliminary model suggests that one of the more important components in resolving an alliance rupture consists of the therapist acknowledging his or her role in the interaction (Kiesler 1988). Gill (1982) has spoken particularly clearly about the importance of analysts being able to acknowledge their role in the transaction as part of the transference interpretation. The reason that this is so important is that often when there is a rupture in the therapeutic alliance, the client and the therapist become locked into interactional positions in which they are both trying to validate themselves.

   Consider the following example. A therapist and client are involved in a struggle over what their topic of focus will be. In an attempt to metacommunicate with the client about what is going on, the therapist says: "I feel like you are trying to control the interaction." The client who is involved in the current struggle in order to maintain his own self-esteem perceives this comment as blaming, and experiences an even greater need to control the interaction in order to maintain self-esteem. If the therapist includes himself in the description of the interaction and acknowledges his own role, it is easier for the client to view the process of exploration as a collaborative activity. The situation begins to shift from one in which there is a sense of "me against you" to one in which there is a sense of "we-ness." By speaking about the rupture as "our problem," rather than "your problem" a sense of connectedness begins to develop.

A more effective response in the above example would be for the therapist to state: "I feel like I'm involved in a struggle with you and I'm not sure what's going on. Does this connect with your experience in any way?" With this response, the client no longer feels blamed or invalidated to the same extent and is thus freed up to begin trying to discover in collaboration with the therapist exactly what is going on in the situation. Thus, an important transition takes place when the therapist shifts from a stance of blaming the client for what is going on in the interaction to accepting responsibility for his or her own role in the interaction.

In some situations, even when the therapist acknowledges his or her own role in the interaction and then comments on the client's role, the client may still continue to feel criticized or blamed and thus may have difficulty letting go of her self-protective stance. In these instances it can be important for the therapist to stop short of commenting on the client's contribution to the interaction. Simply accepting responsibility for his or her part of the interaction may help free the client up to begin to explore his or her role in the interaction.

Another reason that it is important for therapists to begin intervening by acknowledging their role in the interaction is that often clients in situations of this type feel particularly threatened because they are not quite sure where reality lies. Their own responses to the situation may seem irrational or disproportionate to them and they may thus have an even greater need to defend their position. They may thus have difficulty truly acknowledging their own feelings either to themselves or to the therapist. This can make it particularly difficult for the client to begin to understand his or her role in the interaction. If, however, the therapist is able to honestly clarify his or her own role in the interaction, the client may begin to understand the context of their own reactions and thus begin to feel somewhat more comfortable in accepting his own feelings and reactions. This makes it easier for the client to begin exploring his or her contribution to the interaction.

For example, a therapist who perceived that her client was angry with her reacted in a defensive fashion. When she asked the client whether she was angry, she denied such feelings. However, when the therapist became aware that she had been critical of her client and acknowledged this, the client's own responses became more understandable to her, and she found it easier to acknowledge her feelings of anger at the therapist. The therapist's acceptance of responsibility for her contribution to the interaction in this situation thus made it easier for the client to begin the process of self-exploration which eventually led to the resolution of the alliance rupture.

4. *Empathizing with the client's experience.* In addition to acknowledging his or her contributions to the interaction, it can be useful for the therapist to convey an empathic understanding of the client's experience to him or her. In the above situation, for example, it might have been useful for the therapist to indicate that if she were the client, she imagined she would be feeling angry. If the therapist is able to accurately empathize with the client's experience during an alliance rupture and convey this understanding, the client may feel understood and find it easier to begin exploring what is going on in the interaction. In addition to feeling understood, an accurate empathic response in this situation may help the client to acknowledge feelings that he or she is not fully aware of.

Attempts at therapeutic metacommunication can be fruitless unless they are grounded in an accurate empathic understanding of the nature of the client's struggle. There is often an observable "shift point" in the interaction when the therapist finally develops and is able to communicate a true empathic understanding. For example, one therapist who felt distanced by his client's intellectualized attempts to talk about the therapeutic relationship communicated this feedback in various forms, without a positive therapeutic impact. When, however, he was able to truly empathize with the client's intense and painful experience of struggling in vain to improve this and other relationships, the client's stance changed from one of self-protection to self-disclosure and exploration.

Although conveying an empathic understanding of the client's experience often facilitates the process of resolution, in some instances it can also impede the process of resolution. Our observation has been that this tends to happen when the client appears to feel patronized by the therapist's empathic response—as if the therapist's empathic response implies that the problem is the client's rather than a shared problem.

5. *Maintaining the stance of the participant-observer.* Once the therapist has begun the process of metacommunication, it is vital for him or her to maintain the stance of the participant-observer, to use Sullivan's (1953) term. A common error observed is for therapists to become hooked into a dysfunctional interpersonal cycle at a new level once the process of metacommunication has begun. For example, in one case the client tended to be rather closed and reluctant to share his inner experience with the therapist. The more the therapist attempted to explore the client's experience the more closed the client became. Moreover, in response to the therapist's attempt to metacommunicate about the process, the client continued to be closed. After the failure of this metacommunication the therapist appeared to intensify his efforts to get the client to open up, and this appeared to intensify the client's withdrawal. In this situation the process of metacommunication was a recapitulation of the already existing dysfunctional interpersonal cycle at a new level. It thus appears to be important for the therapist to

avoid the pitfall of maintaining the status quo of the current interactional dynamic, through his or her metacommunication.

A PRELIMINARY MODEL

The next phase in the research process involves moving beyond the articulation of the general therapeutic principles outlined in the previous section toward a finer-grained empirical examination of the therapist–client interactional patterns through which alliance ruptures are best resolved. Following Rice and Greenberg's (1984) task analysis approach to psychotherapy research, it is important to generate a preliminary model that can guide the intensive observation of the actual change process. This model should be refined continuously in response to new information as it is compared with the phenomenon of interest (Greenberg 1986, Safran, Greenberg et al. 1988).

First, the model is used informally to facilitate an evaluation of the degree of fit between the model and the actual change process observed. Once a certain degree of refinement of the model has taken place, however, it can be used to generate specific hypotheses that are empirically testable—about the nature of the interaction between client and therapist—when the alliance rupture is resolved.

The preliminary model to be articulated here has been developed through a combination of intensive observation of successfully resolved alliance ruptures in our sample and through available psychotherapy theory. Our impression is that this particular model is most applicable to ruptures that are marked by a pattern of avoidance of direct confrontation on the client's part (e.g., indirect communication of negative sentiments, compliance, avoidance maneuvers). The model, which consists of an eight-stage sequence of client–therapist interactions, is diagrammed in Figure 9–1.

Stage 1—Client Avoids Confrontation Marker. This stage is marked by an apparent avoidance of confrontation on the client's part. The client may indicate negative sentiments indirectly (e.g., through

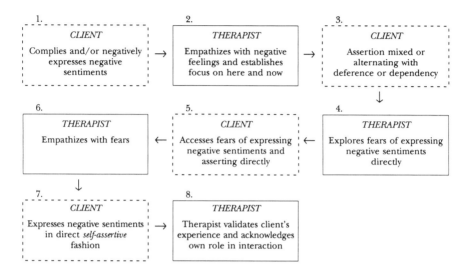

Figure 9–1. Preliminary model of resolution process.

sarcasm, or through an allusion to the transference). Alternatively, she may comply or defer to the therapist. When this happens there is often a somewhat begrudging quality, suggesting that the response is compliance rather than true agreement. Alternatively, the client may appear to agree with the therapist too hastily or readily, without taking the time to integrate things or elaborate on her own perspective.

Stage 2—Therapist Empathizes with Negative Feelings and Establishes a Focus on the Here and Now. In this stage it is important for the therapist to empathize with any negative feelings the client is expressing. When the client is expressing negative feelings indirectly (e.g., through sarcasm), it is helpful for the therapist to use self-disclosure in order to convey the impact of the client's behavior at a personal level (e.g., "I feel criticized"). If the client is speaking about negative feelings in general terms and the therapist has reason to suspect that these feelings are relevant to the current transaction, it is important for the therapist to explore the relevance of these feelings to the present interaction. This exploration should be conducted in a noncontrolling fashion, which respects any decision on the client's part not to discuss negative feelings toward the therapist in the present context. This is particularly important with clients who tend to be compliant, because to push for an exploration of something the client is not ready to explore will invite more compliance.

Stage 3—Client Engages in Assertive Behavior, Alternating with Deference or Dependency. In this stage the client begins to express his or her concern about the therapeutic relationship more directly. This assertive expression, however, is mixed with compliance or dependency. For example, the client begins to express negative feelings toward the therapist, but then withdraws or softens the statement (e.g., "I guess I'm feeling somewhat dissatisfied . . . I don't know . . . maybe I'm expecting too much").

Stage 4—Therapist Explores the Client's Fears of Expressing Negative Sentiments Directly. In this stage the therapist questions the client regarding expectations or beliefs that would make it difficult to express negative feelings directly. For example: "What would be the risk of telling me about your dissatisfaction?" "What is your concern about disagreeing with me?"

Stage 5—Client Accesses Fears of Expressing Negative Sentiments and Self-Assertion. In response to the therapist's probing, the client begins to explore attitudes, beliefs, and expectations that prohibit self-assertion or the direct expression of negative sentiments. It is important for the client to explore these fears and beliefs in an experientially real way, rather than in an intellectualized fashion. A common deflection from productive therapeutic process here involves denying or invalidating one's own fears (e.g., "Well, I guess there's not really any risk. You're not going to throw me out of therapy"). This type of self-invalidation appears to prevent the client from gaining a perspective on the way in which his or her own fears and beliefs block self-assertion.

Stage 6—Therapist Empathizes with Client's Fears. By empathizing and accepting the client's fears, the therapist facilitates the process of self-exploration. In addition, it appears that there is something about the therapist being empathic with this process rather than dismissing the client's fears that provides the client with experiential evidence that it is safe to reveal vulnerability to the therapist, thus strengthening the therapeutic alliance.

Stage 7—Client Expresses Negative Sentiments in Direct Self-Assertive Fashion. At this point the client expresses a negative feeling in a direct fashion, without lapsing into compliance or dependency. This stage is often marked by an energetic and lively quality in the client's voice, which has not been there before. It is important to note that the negative sentiments expressed are not always angry or hostile in nature. The client may, for example, talk with the therapist about feelings of hurt or vulnerability that he or she has been afraid to discuss previously (e.g., "When you gave me that feedback before it really hurt"). Both angry and vulnerable sentiments in this context are considered a form of self-assertion because they involve an honest communication of the client's feelings that is not possible when the client is deferring or complying in order to protect the relationship with the therapist.

Stage 8—Therapist Validates Client's Experience and Acknowledges His or Her Own Role in Interaction. It is crucial that the therapist respond to the client's self-assertion in a validating and nondefensive manner. In situations where the client has accurately identified a therapist behavior that contributed to the rupture, it is vital for the therapist to acknowledge his or her contribution. For example, the client indicates that he or she felt criticized by the therapist's statement, and the therapist acknowledges that he was feeling critical at the time that he said it.

Future Directions

The current preliminary model lends itself well to investigation and empirical refinement with the type of task analysis approach advocated by Rice and Greenberg (1984) or the type of stage process design employed by Cashdan (1973), McCullough (1984a,b), and Hudgins and Kiesler (1987). Given the importance of this type of change event to psychotherapy process, we would encourage researchers in this direction. It will be important to clarify which features of this preliminary model generalize across different rupture markers and which features are unique to ruptures that involve an avoidance of confrontation on the client's part.

There are also a number of definitional and conceptual issues that will need to be clarified. How intense must the strain in the alliance be before it is considered a rupture? Should the term be reserved for fairly serious disruptions in the therapeutic alliance that become the focus of therapeutic metacommunication or should it be applied to the momentary and subtle fluctuations in the quality of therapist–client contact as well? Is it important to distinguish between situations in which a rupture takes place in the context of an already established alliance and those in which an adequate working alliance has never been established? Should a distinction be made between situations in which an apparent rupture is a sign of therapeutic progress (e.g., the client has begun to feel safe enough in the relationship to express his anger), and those in which the rupture indicates a reversal of therapeutic progress (e.g., the rupture results from a clear therapeutic error)? These are complex definitional and conceptual issues, the resolution of which will depend partially on the individual investigator's theoretical assumptions, and partially on the stance that is likely to be most theoretically and empirically generative.

IMPLICATIONS FOR TRAINING

Finally, we would like to comment on the implications of this type of research for the training of psychotherapists. Over the course of observing psychotherapy sessions with an eye toward clarifying our understanding of the nature and structure of alliance ruptures and the processes leading to their resolution, we have found that we have become more sensitized to the occurrence of alliance ruptures and better able to detect them in situations where they may have previously eluded observation. This has been particularly useful in the training of clinical interns on our research team. The research process has sharpened their perceptual abilities.

Commenting on his failure to locate even a "single instance in which a difficult client's hostility and negativism were successfully confronted or resolved," Strupp (1980) noted that a major deterrent to the formation of good working alliance was "the therapist's personal reaction" (pp. 953–954). This observation was applicable to our own sample of alliance ruptures where therapists often avoided or "sealed over" rifts in the alliance without addressing the rupture, despite having a general understanding of the importance of this type of exploration.

Directly addressing alliance ruptures with a client can be an uncomfortable and threatening experience for the therapist—one that activates concerns around competency as a therapist. Because ruptures may entail failures in empathy and therapist errors, there is a natural tendency to avoid addressing them with clients, and to respond defensively, especially among relatively inexperienced therapists. Focusing on the alliance rupture as a potential change event, however, and studying the processes involved in resolution, reframes the meaning of the phenomenon and fosters an enthusiasm for detecting and addressing alliance ruptures.

10

The Therapeutic Alliance Rupture as a Transtheoretical Phenomenon: Definitional and Conceptual Issues

INTRODUCTION

The objective of this chapter is to further refine our understanding of therapeutic alliance ruptures by examining a number of conceptual and definitional issues. My hope is to stimulate the interest of theorists and researchers from diverse theoretical orientations in the investigation of a therapeutic event that, I believe, has the potential of yielding conceptually rich bounty for our understanding of both common and specific principles of therapeutic change. A therapeutic alliance rupture can be defined as a negative shift in the quality of the therapeutic alliance or an ongoing problem in establishing one (Safran 1993, Safran, Crocker et al. 1990, 1994). These ruptures vary in intensity and duration from subtle, momentary miscommunications between client and therapist, to major barriers to the establishment of the alliance which, if unresolved, result in treatment failures and dropouts.

A number of different terms can be used to designate this

phenomenon (e.g., therapeutic alliance breach, miscommunication, misunderstanding, misattunement, tear in the alliance, misencounter). In my discussions with people, I have come to understand that the term *rupture* connotes a rather harsh or intense event for many, thereby failing to capture the subtleness with which problems in the alliance are often manifested in therapy. Our observation has been that therapists are often unaware of these more subtle fluctuations in relatedness, and that early attunement to them can be extremely important therapeutically. It may thus be that one of the above terms may ultimately be more useful.

I believe that Kohut is essentially referring to the same phenomenon with his concept of the *empathic failure*. He and others in the self-psychological tradition have certainly done more than anyone else in terms of highlighting its profound significance in the therapeutic process. One advantage of these other terms over the term empathic failure is that they underscore the interactional nature of the phenomenon.

The term *therapeutic resistance* is also commonly used to designate the same phenomenon. An important disadvantage of the concept of resistance, however, is that not only does it fail to recognize the interactional nature of the phenomenon, but it places the entire responsibility on the client's shoulders. From an interpersonal perspective, however, even resistant intrapsychic processes, such as disowning affective processes, are mediated by the interpersonal context in which they are taking place (Safran and Segal 1990). Unlike the concept of resistance, the concept of the therapeutic alliance rupture or breach avoids the potentially pernicious effects of blaming the client for therapeutic problems. It also opens the doorway to exploring some of the more subtle interpersonal processes through which therapeutic problems arise.

THE THERAPEUTIC ALLIANCE

The concept of the therapeutic alliance has come to assume a growing significance in the fields of psychotherapy theory and research. While originating in psychoanalytic theory (e.g., Greenson

1967, Sterba 1934, Zetzel 1956), the transtheoretical implications of the concept are becoming increasingly apparent. One impetus for this development has been Bordin's (1979) conceptualization of the alliance in terms of bond, goal, and task components. According to him, different forms of therapy involve different characteristic tasks and different characteristic goals. For example, a characteristic task in cognitive therapy is self-monitoring automatic thoughts between sessions, and a characteristic goal is the remission of specific symptoms. A characteristic task in psychoanalysis consists of the exploration of developmental memories, and a characteristic goal is character restructuring. According to Bordin, the quality of the alliance is a function of the degree of agreement between therapist and client regarding the tasks and goals of therapy. This agreement is mediated by, and in turn mediates, the quality of the bond (i.e., the nature of the personal affective engagement) between therapist and client.

As this conceptualization suggests, while the quality of the alliance should be critical in diverse therapeutic approaches, the specific variables mediating this quality will vary as a function of a complex, interdependent, and fluctuating matrix of therapist, client, and approach-specific features. The therapeutic alliance is thus an extremely rich and deceptively simple concept that highlights the fundamental interdependence of therapy specific and nonspecific factors (Safran and Segal 1990).

In recent years, empirical investigation has demonstrated that the quality of the therapeutic alliance, as measured in the early phases of therapy, is a good predictor of outcome in diverse therapeutic approaches (Alexander and Luborsky 1986, Horvath and Greenberg 1989, Horvath and Symonds 1991, Marmar et al. 1989, Orlisky and Howard 1986, Suh et al. 1989). Now that the predictive validity of a variety of alliance measures has been well established, questions regarding predictive validity need to be augmented with more differentiated conceptual and methodological questions regarding the construct of the therapeutic alliance. The investigation of therapeutic alliance ruptures constitutes a rich focus for further investigation (Bordin 1994, Forman and Marmar

1985, Kivlighan and Schmitz 1992, Safran 1993, Safran, Crocker et al. 1990, 1994).

THERAPEUTIC SIGNIFICANCE

Alliance ruptures are important therapeutic junctures because the resolution of such ruptures would seem to be a critical factor in helping clients at risk for poor outcome. As Strupp (1980) observed, a major factor distinguishing between good-outcome and poor-outcome cases in the Vanderbilt I study was a tendency for therapists to become locked into negative interactional cycles with their clients. There are both good conceptual grounds and empirical evidence to suspect that this pattern of negative client–therapist complementarity is associated with poor therapeutic alliances and treatment failure (Henry et al. 1986, 1990, Kiesler 1986, Kiesler and Watkins 1989).

A second reason that alliance ruptures are important junctures is that the exploration of factors underlying them can potentially provide important assessment information regarding core organizing principles mediating the client's perception of the meaning of the therapist's interventions (Safran, Crocker et al. 1990, Safran and Segal 1990). For example, a client who perceives the analyst's neutral stance as withholding may have an interpersonal schema that predisposes him or her to perceive others as emotionally unavailable. A client who perceives the more active interventions of the cognitive therapist as hindering may have an interpersonal schema that predisposes him or her to perceive others as domineering or manipulative.

A third reason is that the exploration and resolution of a therapeutic alliance rupture can provide an important corrective emotional experience for the client. As I have argued elsewhere, the experience of working through an alliance rupture can play an important role in helping the client to develop an interpersonal schema that represents the self as capable of attaining relatedness and others as potentially available emotionally, in the face of life's inevitable breaches in relatedness (Safran 1993, Safran and Segal 1990).

THERAPIST, CLIENT, AND APPROACH: SPECIFIC CONTRIBUTIONS

Different therapeutic approaches and tasks are at risk for inducing characteristic types of alliance ruptures. The more active, directive approaches (e.g., behavior therapy or Gestalt therapy) are more likely to induce ruptures stemming from the client's feeling of being controlled or manipulated. Experiential approaches, with a strong emphasis on the moment-by-moment tracking and exploration of client experience, are at risk for inducing feelings of being invaded. Interpretations can lead to the experience of feeling viewed reductionistically. The impact of any intervention will of course be mediated by the personal qualities of the therapist. Gestalt therapy in the hands of Fritz Perls would be a radically different approach in the hands of Carl Rogers. In a sense, then, it is more accurate to think of the therapist and the approach as an organic therapist-approach unit than as separate treatment variables.

There is a danger, in emphasizing the therapeutic alliance rupture's value as a window into the client's core organizing processes, that the contributions of the therapist-approach unit to the interaction will be ignored or underestimated. Therapeutic alliance ruptures always should be understood as a function of both therapist and approach contributions (Safran, Crocker et al. 1990). The relative contributions of these sources, however, will vary from case to case. To the extent that the client contributes a substantial amount to the rupture, the exploration of that rupture is likely to lead to a clarification of a core dysfunctional interpersonal schema.

For example, a therapist has difficulty forming a good therapeutic alliance with a client because of the client's generalized stance of mistrust. In this case, the exploration of the perceptions and expectations impeding the development of a good alliance can potentially play an important role in clarifying the client's core organizing principles.

In contrast, a client who feels patronized by the therapist, but not by others, is likely to be contributing less to the interaction than the therapist. In this case, the exploration of the client's experience of being patronized is less likely to clarify his or her core organizing principles. Nevertheless, the exploration of both parties' contributions to the interaction will be essential if therapy is ultimately going to be helpful to the client. To the extent, however, that the therapist-approach unit contributes more to the alliance rupture than the client, it may be more therapeutic to refer the client elsewhere.

IDENTIFICATION AND CLASSIFICATION OF ALLIANCE RUPTURE EVENTS

A critical task from a research perspective consists of developing reliable and valid methods for identifying and classifying alliance rupture events. Like any therapeutic event, an alliance rupture can be identified from three different perspectives: therapist, client, and third-party observer. For example, in a study conducted with Chris Muran and Lisa Wallner Samstag (Safran et al. 1994), we extracted six questions from the Working Alliance Inventory (WAI) (Horvath and Greenberg 1989). Two questions corresponded to each of the three dimensions of the therapeutic alliance, as conceptualized by Bordin (1979), that is, task, goal, and bond. The six questions were chosen on the basis of demonstrated ability in a previous data set (Safran and Wallner 1991) to predict outcome in short-term therapy across a range of dependent measures.

These six questions were then administered independently to clients and therapists after every session. Both therapists and clients were instructed to think of the therapy session as consisting of three parts (i.e., a beginning, a middle, and an end), and to rate each portion of the session separately on each of the questions. In this fashion, we were able to obtain subjective perceptions independently from both therapists and clients regarding fluctuations in the quality of the therapeutic alliance over the course of each session.

We reasoned that sessions in which both therapists and clients rated the quality of the alliance as significantly poorer in the middle phase than in both the beginning and end phases would have a reasonably high likelihood of providing events in which an alliance rupture had ensued within the course of the session, but had then been resolved. A fluctuation of at least 20 points (on a 100-point scale) was chosen as the criterion. In contrast, we reasoned that questionnaires on which both therapist and client rated the middle portion of the session as being at least 20 points lower on the therapeutic alliance items than the first portion, and as not showing substantial improvement in the final portion, could be taken as indications of sessions in which alliance ruptures had occurred and had not been resolved by the end of the session. On this basis, samples of resolution and nonresolution events were selected. Two trained independent raters were subsequently able to rate these events in terms of the degree of resolution achieved, with adequate reliability. The highest rated events corresponded to those that had been classified as resolution sessions on the basis of therapist and client ratings.

In this particular study, we selected resolution and nonresolution events on the basis of *converging* therapist, client, and third-party observer ratings. The history of psychotherapy process research, however, testifies to the fact that the three perspectives do not always agree. Whether one chooses to use converging perspectives or to favor one perspective over others depends upon one's ultimate objective. For example, rupture events that are identified by both therapists and clients are likely to have different characteristics than those identified by clients and not by therapists.

A related issue concerns the question of how intense a breach in the alliance needs to be before it is considered worth examining. Once again, the answer to this question depends upon the researcher's objectives. In our research we have been interested in clarifying the processes involved in resolving alliance ruptures. It has thus been important to use more stringent criteria (i.e., reasonably high ratings of intensity, and convergence from all three perspectives), in order to maximize the possibility of selecting sessions in which some attempt was made to work through the therapeutic impasse, thereby allowing us to study the resolution process. If, however, one is interested in exploring the subjective experience of one or both participants in events where the rupture is more subtle, less stringent criteria will be appropriate.

Identification procedures of the type described above provide the researcher with a rough indication of where to look for the rupture event in the session. They do not, however, indicate exactly where in the session the event begins. In the study described above, we identified the onset of rupture events by coding session transcripts with the Structural Analysis of Social Behavior (Benjamin 1974). For example, 2–5 (deferring and submitting), 2–6 (sulking and appeasing), and 2–8 (walling off and avoiding) codes were all taken as indications of rupture events in which the client withdrew rather than directly confronting the therapist. We are currently experimenting with the use of a rater consensus procedure, in which multiple raters are asked to indicate whenever they believe a rupture in the alliance has taken place, and those points in a session that are identified by a majority of raters (e.g., four out of six) are then subjected to further process analyses.

Another issue relates to the classification of rupture events into different types. Breaches in the alliance are likely to take place for a variety of different reasons and to involve different processes as a function of different rupture characteristics. Different processes are thus likely to be involved in healing or resolving different alliance rupture types. In a preliminary attempt to develop a classification system, Peter Crocker, Shelly McMain, Paul Murray, and I (Safran, Crocker et al. 1990) identified seven different rupture types: overt expression of negative sentiments, indirect communication of negative sentiments or hostility, disagreement about the goals of therapy, compliance, avoidance maneuvers, self-esteem enhancing operations, and nonresponsiveness to therapeutic interventions. These seven different types can be grouped into the two superordinate categories of: (1) confrontation ruptures (in which the client directly expresses negative sentiments toward the therapist), and (2) avoidance of confrontation ruptures (in which the client deals with the breach through withdrawal, distancing, or avoidance). Future research will need to clarify whether the processes underlying these different types are sufficiently distinct to justify retaining the entire list, and which ones should be grouped together on the basis of underlying similarities. In addition, reliability of rupture-type classification will need to be established.

PATTERNS UNDERLYING THE DEVELOPMENT
OF THERAPEUTIC ALLIANCE RUPTURES

In this section, I will describe three common patterns underlying the development of therapeutic alliance ruptures that we have observed in our attempts to investigate the processes leading to their resolution (Safran, Crocker et al. 1990, Safran, Muran et al. 1994). I hypothesize that these three patterns cut across different therapeutic orientations, although different patterns may be more commonly associated with specific approaches.

The client misperceives the meaning or intent of the therapist's actions in a schema-consistent fashion. In this type of rupture, the client construes an intervention that would be experienced as facilitative by most clients, in a fashion consistent with his or her maladaptive interpersonal schema. For example, the therapist makes a comment that most clients would experience as supportive. The client, however, experiences it as patronizing, and a strain or rupture in the alliance ensues. Or the therapist attempts to explore the client's feelings in a way that most clients would experience as facilitative, and the client experiences it as invasive. In situations of this type, the exploration of the meaning that the client attributes to the therapist's intervention will potentially yield important information about an important dysfunctional interpersonal schema.

The therapist participates in a dysfunctional cognitive-interpersonal cycle that is characteristic for the client. In this type of rupture the therapist unwittingly becomes hooked by the client's interpersonal pull, thereby reenacting a dysfunctional cognitive-interpersonal cycle that is characteristic for the client. For example, the client expresses hostility toward the therapist, thereby eliciting counter-hostility that confirms his or her expectations that others are hostile. This results in an alliance rupture. Or, a client who anticipates

rejection from others acts in a withdrawn and emotionally overcontrolled way. This distances the therapist, who as a result feels bored
and unengaged with the client. This confirms the client's dysfunctional beliefs and obstructs the development of a good therapeutic
alliance.

In situations of this type, the exploration of both parties'
contributions to the rupture will potentially yield important information both about dysfunctional cognitive-interpersonal cycles that
are characteristic for the client and about maladaptive interpersonal
schemata and construal processes that are associated with the
dysfunctional cognitive-interpersonal cycle. Moreover, the exploration of both parties' contributions to the alliance rupture will
potentially provide a therapeutic challenge to the client's dysfunctional interpersonal schema.

For example, a therapist who has unwittingly been acting in a
hostile fashion becomes aware that he or she has been reacting to a
subtle quality of sarcasm in the client's communications. The
therapist then metacommunicates with the client about their interaction, exploring both parties' contributions (Kiesler 1986, 1988,
Safran 1990a,b, Safran and Segal 1990). Through this process of
metacomunication, the client becomes aware of both the sarcastic
nature of his or her communications and the underlying feelings
and perceptions associated with them. This leads to the exploration
of a fundamental worldview in which others are perceived as hostile
and untrustworthy and the self is perceived as victimized. It also
leads to the exploration of a dysfunctional cognitive-interpersonal
cycle in which the client expresses anger indirectly because of a
belief that the consequences of expressing it directly are too
dangerous.

*The therapist refrains from participating in a dysfunctional cognitive-
interpersonal cycle that is characteristic for the client.* Here, the therapist,
through disengaging (either intentionally or unwittingly) from a
dysfunctional cognitive-interpersonal cycle, places a strain on the
therapeutic alliance. For example, the therapist becomes aware of
responding to a strong interpersonal pull for advice and reassurance. Suspecting that this pull may reflect a characteristic dysfunc-

tional interpersonal style for the client, the therapist intentionally refrains from being overly directive and reassuring, in the hope of providing a new, constructive interpersonal experience for the client. At this point, an alliance rupture ensues.

While the therapeutic relationship may have appeared harmonious prior to the emergence of the alliance rupture, this harmony may have been based upon the therapist's participation in a dysfunctional cognitive-interpersonal cycle. The therapist's stance may be nontherapeutic but, nevertheless, comfortable for the client because it supports the client's current self-definition. This type of situation may be thought of as a misalliance (Langs 1975). Failing to respond in a complementary fashion to someone with a rigid interpersonal style may engender intense anxiety, because it may constitute a threatening challenge to his or her self-definition (Kiesler 1986). It may thus be critical for the therapist to calibrate the extent to which he or she deviates from a complementary interpersonal stance in a manner that is sensitive to the client's anxiety level.

At the same time, exploring any rupture in the alliance precipitated by this deviation from complementarity can yield vital information about client construal processes associated with the client's interpersonal pull and reaction to the therapist's non-complementary response. Does the client experience the therapist's failure to be more directive or reassuring as emotional abandonment? Does the client believe that the therapist's attitude means that he or she does not appreciate the intensity of the client's distress? Are client perceptions of this sort related to prototypical ways of construing self–other interactions for him or her?

If the therapist and client are able to explore and metacommunicate about the themes that emerge in this context, and the therapist is able to understand and empathize with the client's experience, the client may gradually come to experience the therapist as emotionally available and trustworthy, even though the therapist is not providing the more tangible direction that was initially being pulled for.

ARE CLIENT EXPRESSIONS OF ANGER OR
NEGATIVE SENTIMENTS ALWAYS INDICATIVE
OF PROBLEMS IN THE ALLIANCE?

On one hand, client expressions of hostility toward the therapist are commonly recognized indications of problems in the alliance. Consider, for example, the following items from the California Psychotherapy Alliance Scale (Gaston and Marmar 1990): "Client acts in hostile, attacking and critical manner toward the therapist," "Client engages in power struggle, attempting to control the session." Or consider the following items from the Penn Helping Alliance Scales (Alexander and Luborsky 1986): "The client believes the therapist is not helping him or her," "The client feels not understood and not accepted by the therapist."

On the other hand, various theorists have made the point that the expression of hostile or negative feelings by the client can paradoxically be an important part of the change process. For example, Winnicott (1965) theorized that the client's expression of anger toward the therapist and the therapist's ability to survive the anger play an important role in helping the client to experience the therapist as an object that can be used in the growth process. Weiss and colleagues (1987) suggest that a client's expression of anger can be an important transference test that can challenge a pathogenic belief that feelings of anger are dangerous or unacceptable to others. Clearly, as both of these views point out, client expressions of anger or hostility are often associated with progress in therapy. The argument can thus be made that the expression of anger in this context is not indicative of an alliance rupture.

I think that it is safer, however, to regard the client's expression of hostility or discontent in this context as indicative of an alliance rupture. Whether the expression of anger results in therapeutic progress or a therapeutic setback will ultimately depend on how the therapist responds to the anger. Even in those cases when the expression of anger does play an important role in testing a client's dysfunctional interpersonal schema, it is likely that the expression of anger reflects or stems from the client's experience of being hurt or assaulted by the therapist in some way.

Viewing a client's expression of anger as a transference test can help therapists distance themselves from the emotional impact of the anger, thereby allowing them to respond therapeutically rather than with counterhostility. If the expression of anger is regarded merely as a transference test, however, there is a danger of paying insufficient attention to an underlying perception that fuels the anger. This can potentially result in a failure to adequately empathize with the client's experience and to understand his or her construal processes and interpersonal schema more fully.

ALLIANCES AND META-ALLIANCES

When a particular instance in which the client expresses negative sentiments toward the therapist results in therapeutic progress, it does not necessarily mean that it is not at the same time a rupture in the therapeutic alliance. It might be argued, however, that a particular client may only have been able to express negative sentiments toward the therapist because he or she was feeling sufficiently safe or trusting to do so. For example, a client who has a dysfunctional interpersonal schema representing the expression of negative sentiments as dangerous may, over the course of extended experience with the therapist, gradually come to feel sufficiently trusting to more directly express his or her negative sentiments.

On the other hand, an alliance rupture may emerge later in therapy for the first time, as the therapist becomes progressively hooked into the client's cognitive-interpersonal cycle over time. The cycle may intensify, ultimately resulting in an alliance rupture. For example, a therapist becomes hooked by a client's interpersonal pull for support and reassurance. This confirms the client's perception of his or her own sense of helplessness and of others as powerful and dominant. It also fuels a subtle feeling of resentment in the client because he or she feels dominated and diminished. Over time, the therapist begins to feel resentful toward the client both because no amount of reassurance and support seems adequate, and because the client's feelings of resentment are expressed in subtle ways. As the therapist's feelings of resentment intensify, they leak out or become expressed indirectly. At some level, the client perceives this hostility, thereby contributing to his or her own feelings of resentment and victimization. In this fashion, negative feelings on both sides intensify over time, ultimately erupting in a clear-cut alliance rupture.

While both of these events can be understood and empirically investigated as ruptures in the therapeutic alliance, it is important to distinguish between the immediate alliance rupture and the under-lying, more enduring relationship context in which it takes place. This underlying relationship context can be thought of as a kind of meta-alliance, that is, a kind of higher level or superordinate relationship context within which momentary fluctuations in the quality of the alliance must be understood.

Distinguishing between the alliance and the meta-alliance becomes particularly important if we are interested in studying the quality of the therapeutic alliance in a more molecular fashion over the course of therapy, rather than limiting ourselves to gauging the quality of alliance at one particular point for purposes of predicting outcome. Ultimately it is important to study the progression of the meta-alliance over the course of therapy at the same time that we are studying more momentary fluctuations in the quality of the alliance. Both forms of investigation are equally important and become truly meaningful only in context of one another.

In a related vein, Bordin (1994) has recently suggested that it is vital to distinguish between ruptures taking place in the context of an alliance that has already been established versus those taking place in the context of one that has not yet been established. He argues that this distinction is important, because the presence of an adequate preexisting alliance is necessary for the client to profitably explore his or her own contribution to the alliance rupture as a reflection of a self-defeating style. While I agree with Bordin in some respects, I believe that it is more useful to think of these two types of ruptures as two points along a continuum rather than as completely distinctive phenomena. At one end of the continuum, the quality of the meta-alliance is insufficient to allow collaboration on the task of self-reflection, and the critical task will consist of building trust through corrective emotional experiences. Note, however, that even this task will require an adequate meta-alliance to prevent the client from dropping out and to allow the client to take the risks necessary to test the therapist in a way that will facilitate the development of trust.

As this trust develops, the client may be able to shift to the task of reflecting on his or her own contribution to the rupture and its possible relationship to a self-defeating pattern. At any point in time, however, a new rupture may render self-reflection impossible for the client, and the task of testing the therapist may need to assume priority. Moreover, even while the client is reflecting on his or her contribution to the interaction, the client will be gauging the quality of the therapist's responsiveness, thereby continuing to engage in the task of building trust.

EARLY VERSUS LATE ALLIANCE RUPTURES

It may be the case that alliance ruptures taking place in the early versus the middle or later phases of therapy have a different significance. For example, Bordin (1994) has suggested that alliance ruptures taking place later in therapy are more likely to be related to the client's core themes than those taking place early in therapy. His thinking here, presumably, is that time is required in order for the transference to develop sufficiently for core conflictual relationship themes to emerge in the therapeutic relationship. On the other hand, one might hypothesize that a client with whom it is difficult to establish a therapeutic alliance from the outset is more likely to have a fundamental view of things (e.g., mistrust) that interferes with the establishment of an alliance.

Ultimately, it is difficult to make any absolute statements about the relative significance of alliance ruptures taking place at different points in therapy. As suggested above, the significance of any alliance rupture can only be determined by the meta-alliance context in which it takes place. When an alliance rupture emerges later in therapy in the context of a good meta-alliance (i.e., a good superordinate relationship context), it may be a sign of progress, reflecting the fact that the client has come to feel trusting enough to articulate concerns about the relationship that were too threat-ening to acknowledge at the outset. This does not necessarily mean that these concerns are any more or less related to the client's core themes than those articulated early on in therapy. It may simply be that a particular client requires a certain meta-alliance to be established in order for these relationship concerns to emerge.

Often alliance ruptures emerge at the outset of therapy and persist over an extended period of time. In this type of situation, it is necessary to have some way of distinguishing between those situations in which progress is taking place despite the consistent emergence of alliance ruptures, and those situations in which it is not. Tracking the way in which the rupture expresses itself over time is critical if we are going to evaluate whether the current alliance rupture is an indication of deterioration, stasis, or progress.

It may thus be necessary to have a case-specific formulation of the client's core themes in order to evaluate whether the quality of the meta-alliance has improved, despite the fact that alliance ruptures continue to emerge and no discernible sign of improve-ment on standard measures of the therapeutic alliance is evident. Alternatively, it may be possible to track shifts in the quality of the meta-alliance over time, if we have available generalizable stage process models (Greenberg 1984b, Hudgins and Kiesler 1987, McCullough and Carr 1987) describing the way in which therapeu-tic alliance ruptures become resolved. For example, Safran and Muran (1996) have reviewed evidence regarding the ability of a four-stage model to capture the process through which alliance ruptures, characterized by client avoidance of direct confrontation, are resolved.

In this model, the resolution process proceeds through the following sequential stages: (1) attending to the rupture marker, (2) partial or qualified exploration of avoided experience, (3) explora-tion of fear, expectations, and beliefs that block the expression of underlying needs and wishes, and (4) self-assertion and the expres-sion of underlying wishes.

Using this type of model, it may be possible to evaluate whether improvement in the meta-alliance has taken place over the course of therapy, despite the persistent evidence of problems in the alliance, by tracking whether there is a progression from lower-level to higher-level stages over the course of therapy.

CONCLUSIONS

In this chapter, I have highlighted and explored a number of definitional and conceptual issues relevant to our understanding of ruptures or strains in the therapeutic alliance. Because theoretical and empirical attention to this area is in the early phases, there are few established conventions to follow. The particular stance I have taken on these issues has been determined by what seems to me to be conceptually heuristic at this point in time, in full recognition that there is always an element of arbitrariness to enterprises of this sort. By cutting the conceptual pie in this particular fashion, however, my hope is to bring an important psychotherapy event into sharper focus and to stimulate both conceptual and empirical attention to this area.

Different types of therapeutic alliance ruptures are likely to occur in response to different treatment approach characteristics, and different change processes are likely to be important in the context of different types of ruptures. There is thus a need for theorists and researchers from different theoretical orientations to elucidate types of ruptures and associated resolution processes that commonly occur within their own therapeutic traditions. This type of parallel investigation of the same critical phenomenon can, I suggest, play a vital role in helping to assemble the proverbial elephant's parts into a whole.

11

Breaches in the Therapeutic Alliance: An Arena for Negotiating Authentic Relatedness

About a year after the separation of my parents broke up the home of my childhood in Vienna . . . I had been brought to the house in which my grandparents lived. It had a rectangular inner courtyard surrounded by a wooden balcony extending to the roof on which one could walk around the building at each floor. Here I stood once in my fourth year with a girl several years older, the daughter of a neighbor, to whose care my grandmother had entrusted me. We both leaned on the railing. I cannot remember that I spoke of my mother to my older comrade. But I hear still how the big girl said to me: "No, she will never come back." I know that I remained silent, but also that I cherished no doubt of the truth of the spoken words. It remained fixed in me; from year to year it cleaved ever more to my heart, but after more than ten years I had begun to perceive it as something that concerned not only me, but all men. Later I once made up the word *Vergegnung*—"mismeeting," or "mis-encounter"—to designate the failure of a real meeting between men. When after another twenty years I again saw my mother, who had come from a distance to visit me, my wife, and my children, I could not gaze into her still astonishingly beautiful eyes without hearing from somewhere the word *Vergegnung* as a word spoken to me. I suspect that all I have learned about genuine meeting in the course of my life had its first origin in that hour on the balcony.

Martin Buber 1973, pp. 17–18

BRIDGING BREACHES IN THE THERAPEUTIC ALLIANCE

Recent years have witnessed a clear shift in emphasis in psychotherapy theory and practice in the direction of an interpersonal perspective and toward the recognition of the importance of the therapeutic relationship as a therapeutic mechanism of fundamental significance. Greenberg and Mitchell (1983) and Eagle (1984) have done excellent jobs of charting the shift that has taken place in psychoanalytic theory toward more relationally oriented perspectives. In the cognitive-behavioral tradition, a growing number of authors are emphasizing the importance of integrating cognitive and interpersonal perspectives and of systematically incorporating the use of the therapeutic relationship as an instrument of change (Arnkoff 1983, Goldfried and Davison 1976, Jacobson 1989, Safran 1984a,b). The once tarnished concept of the corrective emotional experience (Alexander and French 1946) is being rehabilitated and given new life by a range of theorists from diverse traditions (Arkowitz and Hannah 1989, Jacobson 1989, Kohut 1984, Safran and Segal 1990, Strupp and Binder 1984, Weiss et al. 1987).

The consistent failure to find differences in the efficacy of different forms of psychotherapy and the finding that therapy-nonspecific factors account for a good proportion of the variance are leading a growing number of psychotherapy researchers to focus on the therapeutic relationship (Lambert 1983). In this context the therapeutic alliance has emerged as a concept of pivotal significance. While originating in psychoanalytic theory (Greenson 1967,

Sterba 1934, Zetzel 1956), the alliance has come to be conceptualized in transtheoretical terms as a prerequisite for change in all forms of therapy (Bordin 1979), and an impressive body of empirical research consistent with this conceptualization has accumulated (Alexander and Luborsky 1986, Horvath and Greenberg 1989, Horvath and Symonds 1991, Marmar et al. 1989, Orlinsky and Howard 1986, Suh et al. 1989).

In this chapter I will argue that: (1) the exploration and resolution of difficulties in establishing and/or maintaining a good therapeutic alliance can play a critical role in helping people change; (2) the clarification of in-session transactions involved in resolving problems in the therapeutic alliance is one of the most important practical challenges confronting therapists and psychotherapy researchers today; and (3) the clarification of the theoretical mechanisms through which resolving such problems can lead to change is a particularly important and potentially illuminating task. I will begin by exploring the value of focusing on alliance ruptures from the perspectives of therapeutic efficacy and theory development. I will then speculate on the processes through which healing such breaches or ruptures can lead to change.

In this discussion of underlying processes, I will argue that breaches in the alliance are particularly important junctures in therapy to explore, because they are paradigmatic of a fundamental dilemma of human existence, that is, the need to reconcile our innate desire for interpersonal relatedness and the reality of our separateness. I will illustrate various ways in which this theme recurs as a central issue in a wide range of psychological, philosophical, and spiritual traditions, and then attempt to clarify some of the ways in which the process of working through alliance ruptures can help to facilitate the reconciliation of this dilemma.

THERAPEUTIC EFFICACY

The consistent finding that the average client tends to benefit from psychotherapy, regardless of the particular approach employed (Luborsky et al. 1975, Shapiro 1985, Smith and Glass 1977), obscures the fact that in any treatment study, some specific clients improve while others either fail to improve or deteriorate (Bergin 1970). Who are the clients who fail to benefit from psychotherapy? The empirical evidence suggests that the quality of the therapeutic alliance is the best available predictor of therapy outcome. At a practical level, it would thus seem critical to develop ways of helping those clients who do not benefit from therapy as readily as the average client—those clients with whom it is difficult to establish or maintain a good therapeutic alliance.

Evidence is beginning to emerge that different therapists possess different abilities in this respect (Lambert 1989, Orlinsky and Howard 1986, Ricks 1974). Luborsky and colleagues (1985), for example, demonstrated that while clients responded equally well to three different treatment conditions, individual therapists (regardless of treatment condition) displayed different levels of effectiveness with their clients, and that a major variable mediating their effectiveness was their ability to establish good therapeutic alliances. In a follow-up to this study, Luborsky and colleagues (1986) reanalyzed the data from four major outcome studies and found that, in all studies, the contribution to outcome of the individual therapist variable overshadowed treatment modality effects.

In the first Vanderbilt psychotherapy study, Strupp (1980) observed that a major factor distinguishing poor outcome cases was the therapists' difficulty establishing good therapeutic alliances with their clients, because of a tendency to become caught in negative interactional cycles in which they responded to client hostility with their own counterhostility. This observation was subsequently supported in a more systematic fashion with data from the Vanderbilt II study, where it was demonstrated that a major factor distinguishing treatment failures from treatment successes was the tendency in failure cases for therapists to become locked into negative complementary cycles with their clients (Henry et al. 1986, 1990).

The importance of focusing our theoretical and research efforts on the topic of refining our understanding of the best way to work with problematic therapeutic alliances becomes highlighted when one stops to consider that the therapists in both of these studies were well trained and experienced. As Strupp (1980) remarked in the wake of the Vanderbilt I study:

> The plain fact is that any therapist—indeed any human being—cannot remain immune from negative (angry) reactions to the suppressed and repressed rage regularly encountered in patients with moderate to severe disturbances. As soon as one enters the inner world of such a person through a therapeutic relationship, one is faced with the inescapable necessity of dealing with one's own response to the patient's tendency to make the therapist a partner in his difficulties via the transference. In the Vanderbilt Project, therapists—even highly experienced ones and those who had undergone a personal analysis—tended to respond to such patients with counter-hostility that not uncommonly took the form of coldness, distancing, and other forms of rejection. [p. 953]

These observations become particularly trenchant in light of the fact that the therapists in the Vanderbilt II study were explicitly trained to work with the type of negative interactional cycles that had been observed in the Vanderbilt I study. The clarification of the processes involved in working therapeutically with these negative interactional cycles and in resolving ruptures in the therapeutic alliance would thus seem to be an important direction for future psychotherapy research and theory development (cf. Foreman and Marmar 1985, Safran, Crocker et al. 1990, Safran and Segal 1990). I have described our research program in this area elsewhere (Safran 1993, Safran, Crocker et al. 1990, 1994, Safran and Muran 1996), so I will focus here exclusively on theoretical issues.

THE ALLIANCE RUPTURE AS A WINDOW
INTO CORE THEMES

While a breach or rupture in the therapeutic alliance can be a serious barrier to therapeutic progress, it can also provide the therapist with indispensable information. The impact of any therapist action is always mediated by the client's construal of that action. A problem in the alliance thus provides an important opportunity for clarifying construal patterns that may be characteristic for the client (Safran 1993, Safran, Crocker et al. 1990, Safran and Segal 1990). From an interpersonal perspective, any strain in the therapeutic alliance reflects both client and therapist contributions. The relative importance of these two contributions will vary from case to case. In some cases the therapist may intervene in a fashion that the average client will experience as helpful, but which is experienced as critical, invalidating, or withholding by a particular client. In such cases, the exploration of the way in which the client is construing the therapist's actions can potentially lead to the clarification of core organizing principles that shape the meaning of interpersonal events for the client. For example, a client who experiences a therapist's silence as hindering may have a general tendency to perceive others as withholding or emotionally unavailable. A client who experiences a therapist's more active interventions as hindering may have a generalized tendency to perceive others as controlling or intrusive.

Thus, as interpersonally oriented theorists emphasize, it is always important for the therapist to clarify the contributions that both parties are making to the interaction (Gill 1982, Greenberg 1991, Hoffman 1991, Kiesler 1986, Stolorow 1988). In some cases a hindering intervention reflects either a technique or a therapist characteristic that will emerge with most clients. For example, a therapist who employs a particularly confrontative approach, either because of therapeutic orientation or because of aggressive interpersonal style (or both), may have difficulty establishing an alliance with many clients. In other cases therapists contribute to problems in the therapeutic alliance by unwittingly participating in vicious cycles not unlike those characteristic of the client's other interactions. For example, a therapist who responds to a hostile client with counterhostility confirms the client's view of others as hostile and obstructs the development of a good therapeutic alliance. A therapist who responds to a withdrawn client by pushing for self-disclosure confirms the client's view of others as intrusive, thereby perpetuating a vicious cycle in which others are seen as intrusive, and the client withdraws as a form of self-protection.

The idea that clients and therapists often enact the type of vicious cycles that are thematic of the client's other relationships has become a central theme in interpersonal/relationally oriented approaches to therapy. This theme, typically discussed under the general rubric of transference–countertransference dynamics, is understood in different terms by different theoretical traditions. Some theorists (e.g., Cashdan 1988, Ogden 1986, Racker 1968, Tansey and Burke 1989) invoke the concept of projective identification to explain the mechanism through which these vicious cycles become enacted. Others hypothesize that they result from self-fulfilling prophecies in which the client's dysfunctional expectations and maladaptive coping strategies lead them to behave in a way that ironically confirms their beliefs (e.g., Carson 1969, Kiesler 1986, Safran 1990a, Strupp and Binder 1984, Wachtel 1977).

Regardless of the particular theoretical perspective one takes on this issue, however, the implication is that the interactional dynamic that impedes the development of a good therapeutic alliance may provide information about what Luborsky (1984) terms core conflictual relationship themes in the client's life, and that the exploration of the way in which both therapist and client are contributing to the alliance breach can provide the therapist with critical data that would otherwise be unavailable. Another implication is that by resolving a breach in the alliance, rather than participating in a habitual dysfunctional cycle, the therapist can provide the client with a new, constructive interpersonal experience—a corrective emotional experience.

THE CORRECTIVE EMOTIONAL EXPERIENCE

The concept of the corrective emotional experience, while popularized by Alexander and French (1946), can be traced back to Ferenczi's work in the early days of psychoanalytic thinking (a theme we shall return to later). To speculate about the factors that led to the discrediting of this concept in psychoanalytic thinking for many years, as well as those responsible for the current resurgence of interest in it, is beyond the scope of this chapter. (But see Haynal [1988] for an interesting discussion of this theme.) The trend in this direction, however, is clearly evident (Bollas 1989, Kohut 1984, Mitchell 1988, Safran 1990b, Strupp and Binder 1984). It is also important to note the growing body of empirical evidence consistent with the hypothesis that the therapist's ability to disconfirm the client's dysfunctional beliefs about interpersonal relationships through the therapeutic relationship is an important mechanism of change (Weiss et al. 1987).

Kohut (1984) has been particularly influential in sensitizing clinicians to the therapeutic significance of resolving alliance breaches, or what he terms empathic failures, and has also made an important attempt to articulate the mechanisms through which healing such breaches can lead to change. According to Kohut (1984), therapeutic impasses typically reflect empathic failures on the therapist's part, and the process of working through these empathic failures provides an important corrective emotional experience for the client. He theorizes that this process takes place through what he refers to as a transmuting internalization.

This, according to him, consists of the establishment of new internal structures through (to use his terminology): (1) the withdrawal of narcissistic cathexis from selfobject images, and (2) a subsequent process of internalization in which the client takes over some of the selfobject functions the therapist has been assuming, such as maintenance of self-cohesiveness and regulation of self-esteem. This model, while appealing at one level, becomes problematic when one is pressed to operationalize certain core constructs. To quote Eagle (1984):

> Generally, the concept of internalization in the psychoanalytic literature is confused and confusing, and Kohut's concept is no exception. When one attempts to ascertain what Kohut means, specifically, by "transmuting internalizations," one reads, for example, that this involves the creation of internal psychic structures through the withdrawal of cathexes from object images. But what are psychic structures? And what does it mean

to withdraw cathexes from object images? Unless one's responses to these questions are reasonably clear and with empirical content and reference, the explanations of "transmuting internalizations" remain as vague as the term itself. Unfortunately, I believe one has to conclude that at this point, this key concept, employed by Kohut to describe and explain therapeutic change, has at best only approximiate or perhaps apparent meaning. [p. 70]

In what follows, I will attempt to elucidate some of the meaning contained within this concept. My intention is to tease out some of the ideas and assumptions that either explicitly underlie or are implicit in Kohut's formulation, and to advance some related ideas that are not. I will begin by exploring the potential significance that healing alliance ruptures may have in the growth process in fairly broad philosophical terms, and then move toward operationalizing some of the specific mechanisms that may be involved, in a later section of the chapter.

ALONE WITH OTHERS

In life we must all inevitably negotiate the paradox that by the very nature of our existence we are both alone and yet inescapably in the world with others. We are alone at a fundamental level. In the stark words of the eighth-century Buddhist philosopher, Shantideva: "At birth I was born alone and at death too I must die alone" (Batchelor 1979, p. 98). Although we are able to share many things with other people, many of our most important experiences will never be shared. At the same time, we are by the very nature of our existence inescapably tied to others. We are born in relationship with others (we emerge from our mother's womb) and attain a sense of self only in relation to others. Theorists as diverse as Kohut (1984), Lacan (1964), and Mead (1934) have used the metaphor of the mirror to express the role that the other plays in developing and maintaining one's sense of self. As current developmental research demonstrates, human beings are biologically programmed to seek relation-

ships with other people and to develop in context of relationships
with other people (Bowlby 1969, Stern 1985). Moreover, beginning
at a very early age, we appear to have a remarkable capacity for
intersubjectivity—for sharing in and empathizing with the subjective experiences of others (Murphy and Messer 1977, Trevarthan
and Hubley 1978).

Yet despite the intrinsically interpersonal nature of human
existence, we are ultimately encapsulated by our own skin and set
apart from others by virtue of our existence as independent
organisms. No matter how hard we try, we cannot, on a continuing
basis, achieve the type of union with others that permits us to escape
from our aloneness. As human beings we thus spend our lives
negotiating the paradox of our simultaneous aloneness and togetherness.

Balint (1935) spoke about what he termed the *basic fault* as
being the essence of the human condition. According to him, the
basic fault results from the fact that the environment fails to move in
complete harmony with our needs. One's first experience of this
type is typically with the mother, who inevitably will be either absent
when we need her or intrusive when we need to be left alone. As a
result of this inevitable mismatch, one has one's first experience of
the environment being off in some sense. We begin to have a sense
of being separate from our environment. This basic fault—the sense
of there being something fundamentally wrong, of having fallen
from a state of grace—is a universal theme in mythology, and the
attempt to heal this basic fault is a central concern in all spiritual
traditions.

In the Judeo-Christian tradition, this sense of having fallen
from a state of grace is reflected in the myth of the expulsion from
the Garden of Eden. Jewish culture is imbued with a sense of living
in exile, both as an historical and a cosmic principle. Both Jewish
and Christian traditions are concerned with healing our sense of
separateness through obtaining a sense of union with the divine and
with other human beings. This is particularly true of the Kabbalistic
and Hasidic traditions in Judaism and of the Gnostic traditions in
Christianity. The Hindu tradition sees the dilemma of the experience of human separateness as arising from the failure to recognize

that we are all part of one universal essence—Brahma, and the
recognition and experience of our fundamental being as part of this
universal essence, as the solution. Buddhism views the basic human
dilemma as arising from a mistaken conception of self as having a
permanent and substantial nature, and the recognition of the
nonduality of self and others as the solution. The pain and longing
of separation, and the ecstasy of gnostic union, are expressed
exquisitely in the poems of the thirteenth-century Sufi mystic, Rumi:

> *Burning with longing-fire,*
> *Wanting to sleep with my head on your doorsill,*
> *My living is composed only of this trying*
> *to be in your presence.*
> [Moyne and Barks 1986, p. 64]

> *He is in each of my atoms,*
> *Each of my raw nerves . . .*
> *I'm a harp leaning against Him*
> *This grief just a play of His*
> *fingers.*
> [Harvey 1988, p. 68]

Various psychological theorists have, in different terms, written
about the attempt to escape our isolation through union with others
and about the different ways in which this theme is played out in
everyday life and within the arena of psychotherapy (e.g., Mahler
1974, Rank 1929, Spitz 1965, Stone 1961). It is interesting to note
that from the early days of psychoanalytic theory, there were two
parallel strands of thought regarding the fundamental nature of
human motivation. At the same time that Freud was articulating his
drive metapsychology, which holds that the fundamental motivational principle consists of maintaining libidinal energy at a constant level, Ferenczi (1931) was emphasizing the importance of what
Balint (1935), his student, later came to term "primary love," that is,
the desire to "be loved always, everywhere, in every way, my whole
body, my whole being" (Balint 1935, p. 50).

Ferenczi believed that neurosis develops as a result of splitting off a part of the self in order to maintain a relationship with one's parents, and that therapy can provide what Balint (1935) later termed a "new beginning," in which the client learns to relate to the therapist without this type of split. According to Ferenczi, the therapeutic situation can be used to allow the client to abandon himself or herself to the phase of "passive object-love," i.e., that phase in which, like the child, the client's needs are responded to perfectly by the other. When the client inevitably experiences the reality of the therapeutic situation, and the limits of the analyst's responsiveness become apparent, a trauma will ensue that reenacts the trauma that initially took place when the infant was disillusioned about his or her own omnipotence in childhood.

Rank (1929), stimulated in part by his collaboration with Ferenczi, came to emphasize the birth trauma as being of fundamental etiological significance in all neuroses. Thus according to him, the major trauma involves the initial separation from the biologically symbiotic relationship with the mother, and all of life can be understood as an attempt to recover this symbiotic state. According to Rank (1945), the central problem for most persons seeking treatment is an inhibition in the ability to will. Willing is anxiety-provoking and guilt-producing for many clients because it involves self-assertion, which always involves a separation from the other. According to Rank, developmentally, one of the first expressions of will is in the form of negative will. The young child begins to differentiate himself from the parents by saying "no." If the parents are able to tolerate and validate these acts of self-assertion, it facilitates the development of a healthy and creative will and sense of agency in the child. If, however, the parents are threatened by this expression of will and enforce compliance, the child's will becomes paralyzed and he or she never develops the ability to will in a healthy and creative fashion.

DISILLUSIONMENT AND MATURATION

When the infant is born, he or she is completely dependent upon the mother, and she in turn is predisposed to be physically and emotionally attuned to the infant. Winnicott (1965) referred to this as a state of primary maternal preoccupation. Because of this pre-occupation, the infant begins, in a sense, with an absolute claim on his or her mother. Theorists such as Winnicott and Kohut believe that a phase in which the mother allows herself to be an object of the infant's needs plays an important role in helping the infant to acquire a fundamental sense of creativity. As Winnicott suggests, she participates in the creation of an illusion with the child. Through a type of playful activity the mother and child co-create the illusion that the child can, in a sense, create his or her own world, and this is instrumental in helping the child to develop a fundamental sense of his or her own agency, spontaneity, and creativity.

Gradually, however, as the mother moves out of her state of primary maternal preoccupation and becomes more attuned to her own needs and less responsive to the infant's needs, the infant begins to experience disillusionment. If the mothering takes place in an optimal fashion (what Winnicott referred to as good-enough mothering and Kohut referred to as optimal frustration), this process of disillusionment is always within the range of the infant's tolerance and is thus not experienced as traumatic. In a healthy developmental process, the individual, to some extent, comes to accept the independent existence of the other. One comes to accept the other's status as a subject rather than as an object of one's needs, without having to stifle one's own creativity and bodily felt needs in order to maintain contact with the other. If, however, the degree of disillusionment is traumatic, then the infant experiences an im-pingement on his or her own development and is required to adapt to the mother's need rather than gradually learning to develop a sense of self that synthesizes his or her own bodily felt needs.

While in some cases this disillusionment process—of coming to terms with the separate existence of the other—is less traumatic than in others, it never takes place completely smoothly. To varying degrees, then, individuals spend their lives struggling with this issue of aloneness versus togetherness—with maintaining a sense of self as a vital, alive, and real subject at the same time as maintaining a sense of others as real, independent subjects.

To varying degrees people continue to relate to others as

objects—as characters in their own dramas, rather than as independent subjects. People try to control and possess others by trying to
squeeze them into forms that fit their fantasies and needs. In Martin
Buber's terms, people relate to others as "its" rather than as
"Thou's."

The problem here is twofold. First, the world and people in it
stubbornly refuse to conform to the shapes that we try to assign to
them. There is thus a constant experience of frustration. Second, to
the extent that we do treat people as objects and fail to recognize
their status as subjects, we deprive them of the independent
existence necessary for them to be able to provide relief from our
experience of isolation (Hegel's master–slave dialectic). There is
thus a supreme irony here, in that to the extent we succeed in
obtaining our goal of possessing or controlling others (or at least
deceiving ourselves into believing that we do), we increase our sense
of aloneness.

In addition to attempting to manipulate others in an attempt to
meet their own needs, people manipulate themselves, in an attempt
to be some way that will help them maintain relatedness through
meeting the needs of others. No matter how hard we try to bend
ourselves into a particular form, however, we ultimately remain what
we really are, for everyone to see. This of course was one of the
brilliant insights that Wilhelm Reich had, when he pointed to the
fact that one's defenses are an integral part of one's character and
are manifested in every molecule of one's being. The photographer
Diane Arbus (1972) once said that her portraits were designed to
capture the discrepancy between intention and effect, that is, the
paradoxical way in which no matter what our illusions about
ourselves are, we are there with all of our flaws, including our
attempts to hide them, for everyone to see.

The pathological nature of this type of self-manipulation has
always been a central theme in humanistic psychotherapies (e.g.,
Perls et al. 1951, Rogers 1951). It was also recognized to some extent
in classical psychoanalytic formulations, which emphasized the role
of sexual repression in psychopathology and saw the relaxation of
the harshness of the superego as being an important part of the
curative process. And just as there has always been a strand of

psychoanalytic theory parallel to the mainstream that emphasizes the importance of desire for union in human experience and of the corrective emotional experience in therapy, there has always been a strand emphasizing the importance of liberating the organismically based self from the shackles of overconformity (Ferenczi 1931, Rank 1945, Reich 1942). Increasingly, however, with the development of more relationally oriented psychoanalytic theories (e.g., Balint 1935, Guntrip 1969, Horney 1945, Sullivan 1953, Winnicott 1965), the notion of the betrayal of the self through overconformity to society became a prominent theme.

Winnicott (1965) showed a particular concern with the problems caused by paralyzing one's spontaneous, organismically based self through overconformity. This is captured with elegant simplicity in his distinction between the true self and the false self. According to him, the mother, by providing what he termed the appropriate "holding environment," helps the infant to develop a sense of himself or herself as real. By recognizing the infant's spontaneous gestures, she helps the infant begin to synthesize his or her spontaneous experience as part of the self, and this is the fundamental basis of the experience of being real.

SEPARATION/INDIVIDUATION AND THE REPRESENTATION OF SELF–OTHER INTERACTIONS

According to Mahler (1974), the separation/individuation process is the most important developmental task facing the individual. She theorizes that the infant has a desire both for symbiotic union with the mother and a natural tendency to individuate. The infant's natural curiosity in the world leads him or her to explore, thereby facilitating individuation. It requires the presence of the mother and her emotional availability, however, to facilitate this exploration and movement into the world. Mahler (1974) refers to this as "safe anchorage." In a healthy developmental process the mother provides the optimal balance between emotional availability and the encouragement of autonomy. According to her, the development of emotional object constancy, that is, the ability to maintain a symbolic representation of the mother in her absence, plays a crucial role in consolidating the individuation process and allowing the infant to engage in exploratory behavior without her actual physical presence.

Bowlby (1969) also emphasizes the important role that the mother's emotional availability plays in providing the infant with what he refers to as a "secure base" from which to explore. He, however, understands the significance of the mother–infant tie in ethological terms. From his perspective, attachment behavior, that is, maintaining proximity to the attachment figure, is a biologically wired-in behavioral system that plays an adaptive role in the survival of the species. Bowlby's (1969) concept of the working model provides a particularly useful way of understanding the way in which the infant's cognitive-affective representation of interactions with attachment figures mediates development and subsequent interaction with others.

According to Bowlby, the infant's internal representation of interactions with attachment figures plays an important role in maintaining proximity, by allowing him or her to predict self–other interactional contingencies. For example, the infant who learns that the expression of sad or angry feelings will result in abandonment can hide such feelings in order to maintain relatedness. As I have argued elsewhere, the working model can be thought of as a type of interpersonal schema that functions as a program for maintaining interpersonal relatedness (Safran 1990a, Safran and Segal 1990). This concept is similar in certain respects to other models of internalization (e.g., Fairbairn 1952, Ogden 1986, Sandler and Sandler 1978). A critical distinction, however, is that it clearly specifies the way in which interpersonal events are internally represented, in terms consistent with contemporary memory theory (see Safran [1990a] and Stern [1985] for elaborations of this point). It thus has the advantage of the type of conceptual clarity that lends itself well to empirical investigation (e.g., Hill and Safran 1993, Main et al. 1985), and a growing number of theorists have been adopting it and elaborating upon it (Beebe 1985, Nelson and Greundel 1981, Safran 1990a, Stern 1985).

AFFECTIVE MISCOORDINATION AND REPAIR

Recent research on empathic communication in infant–mother interactions provides some intriguing suggestions regarding the role that emotional attunement and its absence may play in the development of adaptive and dysfunctional interpersonal schemata. As theory and research in the areas of emotion and infant development suggest, emotional experience plays a central role in providing the individual with information about his or her own action dispositions (Greenberg and Safran 1987, Lang 1983, Leventhal 1984). The extent to which an individual integrates and synthesizes affective information of various types thus determines the extent to which he or she ultimately develops a sense of a self that is grounded in his or her organismic, biologically rooted experience (Safran and Greenberg 1991, Safran and Segal 1990). Thus, as Stern (1985) points out, the process of affect attunement plays a central role in helping the child to articulate emotional experience. Through this process, the child develops a sense of self that is grounded in his or her own bodily felt experience and is communicable to the other.

A number of studies have demonstrated that there are consistent differences between the way in which healthy and dysfunctional mother–infant dyads deal with moments of affective attunement and misattunement (Tronick 1989). In both healthy and dysfunctional dyads there is an ongoing oscillation between periods where mother and infant are affectively attuned or coordinated and periods where they are miscoordinated. In healthy mother–infant dyads, moments of affective miscoordination are typically followed by a repair in the interaction. For example, a child begins to experience sadness or joy and the mother misattunes to this emotion. In response to this misattunement, the child experiences a secondary emotion (e.g., anger). The mother then attunes to the secondary emotion and the dyad becomes affectively coordinated once again.

In contrast, in dysfunctional mother–infant dyads, the mother fails to attune not only to the primary emotion but to the secondary emotion as well. Tronick (1989), using Bowlby's model of internalization, suggests that in healthy mother–infant dyads, the ongoing oscillation between periods of miscoordination and repair ultimately serves a useful function by helping the infant to develop an adaptive interpersonal schema—one that represents the other as potentially available and the self as capable of negotiating relatedness even in the face of interactional rupture.

In contrast, the infant in the dysfunctional dyad never develops this type of self–other representation and, as a result, is likely to give up the possibility of establishing authentic emotional contact. This infant does not develop faith in his or her ability to maintain authentic contact in the face of differences and, in a desperate attempt to maintain some type of interpersonal relatedness, will develop self-manipulative and other-manipulative strategies to maintain some type of interpersonal contact. As both Ferenczi (1931) and Winnicott (1965) suggested, the individual relates to others with a false self in order to buy time until the situation emerges where the possibility of real, authentic interpersonal contact exists.

Because of the emotional deprivation the individual has experienced, and because of the ongoing experience of failure to establish real contact, he or she seeks desperate solutions to either maintain or establish some semblance of contact, and to avoid the possibility of further rejection. The very solution that the individual attempts, however, ultimately impedes real relatedness (Safran and Segal 1990, Wachtel 1977).

The individual who, for example, because of consistent misattunement as a child, has difficulty fully experiencing and expressing sadness will continue to experience misattunement to such feelings from others. This will create a barrier to relatedness that may leave the person feeling deprived and angry. Others, in turn, may be alienated by and may fail to empathize with this anger. The situation can be further complicated if the individual, for fear of alienating others, expresses angry feelings in an indirect or passive-aggressive way. This can create yet another barrier that may make it difficult to establish rewarding relationships in everyday life and to establish or maintain an alliance in therapy. In treatment, the therapist's ability to attune to whatever secondary feelings of anger or hurt are there will be an important prerequisite to the emergence of whatever primary feelings are being submerged and misattuned to (Safran and Segal 1990). This, of course, is only one example of the infinite number of ways in which a client's dysfunctional schema can influence and be influenced by the development of a therapeutic alliance.

RUPTURE RESOLUTION AND SCHEMATIC CHANGE

In the same way that the process of oscillating back and forth between states of affective miscoordination and repair is hypothesized to play a role in helping the infant to develop an adaptive interpersonal schema, working through alliance ruptures may do so for the client in psychotherapy. It can provide a learning experience through which the client gradually comes to develop an interpersonal schema that represents the other as potentially available and the self as capable of negotiating relatedness even in the context of interactional ruptures (Safran 1990b, Safran and Segal 1990).

What does it mean for the client to (as Kohut would have it) modify the structure of the self by internalizing the therapist and taking over some of his selfobject functions? Again, as Eagle (1984) has pointed out, there is a tendency in self-psychological theory to reify the construct of the self—to write about concepts such as lack of self-cohesiveness, fragmented self, and self defects as if they were referring to actual cracks in a substantial structural entity. From an interpersonal perspective, the self is always defined in interaction with another, whether the other is a particular person or a generalized other (to use Mead's concept). I think that Kohut, by recognizing the importance of the selfobject throughout the life span, is implicitly subscribing to this type of interpersonal perspective. In this respect, as Bacal and Newman (1990) point out, the self-psychological approach might more accurately be thought of as a self-selfobject psychology.

As I have suggested elsewhere (Safran 1990a, Safran and Segal 1990), implicit in Sullivan's (1953) interpersonal theory is the notion that one's self-esteem at any point in time is a function of one's subjective sense of potential relatedness. To the extent that one has a generalized expectation that interpersonal relatedness is attainable, one's self-esteem will be less dependent on any particular person. One will thus have less of a need for a particular selfobject to regulate one's self-esteem.

And to the extent that one does not believe that relatedness is contingent on being some narrowly defined way, one will be better able to integrate a full range of different internal experiences (e.g., anger, sadness, lust) without experiencing a threat to one's subjective sense of self-cohesiveness. In other words, the person will be less likely to experience different emotions and associated action dispositions as alien and threatening to the self. Such a person will be less dependent on the reflected appraisals of a particular other in order to maintain a subjective experience of self as cohesive, and in fact will have less of a need to cling to a fixed concept of self. As Sullivan (1953) recognized, the self-system ultimately serves a defensive function by protecting one from anxiety resulting from the anticipated disintegration of interpersonal situations.

THE ALLIANCE RUPTURE AS AN ARENA FOR NEGOTIATING RELATEDNESS

Ruptures in the therapeutic alliance are breaches in relatedness. They are what Buber (1973) referred to as "misencounters," or "mis-meetings," that is, rifts that prevent true encounters from taking place. Alliance ruptures thus provide an opportunity to explore the barriers to relatedness that may occur for the client in everyday life. They also provide valuable opportunities to work on the task of being both separate and connected.

Breaches in the therapeutic alliance are inevitable. First, as Kohut (1984) has pointed out, it is inevitable that the therapist will at times fail the client empathically. As we have seen, this situation is exacerbated when clients disown important aspects of their inner experience or have a strong interpersonal pull that ensnares others in particularly pernicious vicious cycles. Second, the therapist will inevitably fail to fill whatever fantasies the client has about eliminating the fundamental sense of separateness and incompleteness that we all live with. A breach in the alliance highlights the reality of the client's separateness. If the therapist is able to empathize with the client's disappointment sufficiently well to establish a mutual sense of relatedness in context of this separateness, it will begin an important process of learning.

While in some cases clients will directly acknowledge their anger or dissatisfaction when an alliance rupture has taken place, in many cases they will have difficulty doing so or will do so indirectly (Safran, Crocker et al. 1990). As Rank (1945) suggested early on, angry, self-assertive feelings are perhaps the most difficult ones to learn to express because they are inherently separating in nature. And yet it is the expression of these very feelings that allows the individual to develop a sense of agency. The process of expressing dissatisfaction with the therapist when an alliance rupture takes place can thus play an important role in helping clients to develop a sense of themselves as responsible and creative agents who can influence their own destinies.

Learning to will, and to express one's will, however, is only half the battle. The other half consists of coming to accept that the world and people in it exist independent of one's will; that the events in the world run according to their own plan, and that other people have wills of their own. As Winnicott (1965) pointed out, an important part of the maturational process consists of seeing that the other is not destroyed by one's anger (or, I would add, controlled by one's expression of will), because this establishes the other as having a real, independent existence as a subject, rather than as an object. While this type of learning is a difficult and painful part of the disillusionment process, it ultimately helps to establish the other as capable of confirming oneself as real. In this way the groundwork is laid for relationships in which reciprocal confirmation can take place.

The processes of coming to accept both self and other are thus mutually dependent ones that can be facilitated by working through ruptures in the therapeutic alliance. The therapist, by empathizing with the client's experience of and reaction to the breach, demonstrates that potentially divisive feelings (e.g., anger, disappointment) are acceptable, and that relatedness is not contingent on disowning part of oneself. He or she demonstrates that relatedness is possible in the very face of separateness.

At the same time, however, the process of working through the alliance rupture does not undo the therapist's initial contribution to it, nor does it mean that he or she will not contribute to misencounters in the future. If the therapist is, however, to borrow Winnicott's descriptor, good enough, the client will gradually come to accept the therapist with all of his or her imperfections. The exploration and working through of alliance ruptures thus paradoxically entail an exploration and affirmation of both the separateness and potential togetherness of self and other.

As the client increasingly comes to accept his or her own separateness and the separateness of the therapist, the client has less of a desperate need to maintain some semblance of relatedness at all costs. This in turn allows clients to have more authentic moments of relatedness in which they relate to the therapist in a more spontaneous way and come closer to accepting the therapist as he or she is rather than as a character in their own drama. This helps to develop an appreciation of what is referred to in the Zen tradition as "suchness," that is, an acceptance and appreciation of things as they are. This is not a passive acceptance of whatever transpires, but rather a letting go of one's attempts to manipulate self and others in pursuit of perfection.

As clients' acceptance of their own fundamental aloneness increases as well as their faith that moments of contact or encounter are possible, they become less relentless in their pursuit of relatedness, and this permits them to be receptive to true moments of relatedness when they emerge. To quote Buber (1958): "The Thou meets me through grace—it is not found by seeking. But my speaking of the primary word to it as an act of my being, is indeed *the* act of my being" (p. 11).

CONCLUSIONS

As we have seen, the conceptualization of psychotherapy as "a new beginning" and the recognition that this new beginning often starts with a type of rupture in the client–therapist relationship have a long-standing history in psychotherapy theory. I believe, however,

that the movement of the therapeutic *zeitgeist* in a more interpersonal/
relationally oriented direction provides a framework within which
some significant technical and theoretical shifts are taking place.

Kohut's (1984) focus on the importance of working through
empathic failures in therapy is, as we have seen, similar in important
respects to Ferenczi's (1931) original thinking regarding the importance of working through the client's traumatic response to his or
her disillusionment with the therapist. The self-psychological perspective, however, appears to place a greater emphasis on understanding and empathizing with the client's experience of the
therapist's empathic failures as they take place on an ongoing basis.
This emphasis on the importance of continuously detecting disruptions in the relationship and understanding both parties' contributions to them is particularly evident in Stolorow's (1988) writing.
Thus, from a technical perspective, the therapeutic focus appears to
be shifting away from the exploration and working through of a
major traumatic event with the therapist, which is viewed as a
reenactment of a historical trauma, toward an ongoing exploration
of what are often subtle fluctuations in the quality of client–
therapist relatedness and the clarification of factors obstructing it
(cf. Safran and Segal 1990).

At a theoretical level, there has been a tendency for psychoanalytic thinking that emphasizes the corrective emotional experience
to use the metaphor of the infant to understand the client in
therapy. Eagle (1984) refers to this as metapsychological infantilizing and Mitchell (1988) refers to this as the "developmental tilt."
The assumption is that analysis induces a regressive process through
which existing but buried infantile longings are reactivated and that
the therapeutic relationship facilitates the resumption of an inter-
rupted developmental process. One of the problems with this type
of metaphor is the tendency to assume that these longings exist only
in clients (and not in therapists) or in particular types of clients. As
I have argued, however, the longing for union with other people and
the difficulties involved in accepting our separateness and negotiating relatedness are issues that we all struggle with throughout our
lives. For most of us the moments of true I–Thou relatedness, in

which we allow the other to reveal themselves to us as they really are in that moment, are few and far between.

Second, the assumption that an arrested developmental process resumes, as Eagle (1984) points out, assumes that an adult can go through the same type of developmental process that a child can. It thus fails to take into account that the clients are adults with adult abilities and capabilities, who will go through their own unique type of maturational process if the conditions are right. This type of conceptualization thus results in a type of infantilizing that fails to recognize that the therapeutic relationship is a meeting between two adults. As Menaker (1989) argues, while certain therapeutic practices (e.g., lack of self-disclosure, use of a couch) can establish a role relationship that can artificially induce childlike feelings and behaviors to emerge, it is a mistake to view these as feelings from the past, which are inappropriately transferred onto the therapist.

Hoffman (1991) has recently suggested that there is a paradigm shift taking place in psychoanalytic theory, toward what he terms a social-constructivist perspective. This perspective recognizes that therapy involves the ongoing construction of reality through the client–therapist interaction (through both dialogue and action), rather than the discovery of some objective truth. This shift toward a constructivist perspective is also consistent with current developments in cognitive therapy (e.g., Guidano 1991, Mahoney 1991) and experiential approaches (Gendlin 1991).

A growing number of theorists are viewing therapy as a meeting between two human beings who inevitably become trapped in a noncreative, fixed rut of interpersonal relatedness and who with goodwill and fortune are able to work themselves out of this rut into a new, more progressive mode of relatedness (Cashdan 1988, Levenson 1983, Mitchell 1988, Strupp and Binder 1984). Consistent with this view of things, I am suggesting a greater emphasis on the use of the ongoing breaches in the therapeutic alliance that are inevitable, as opportunities for negotiating the fundamental issues of human separateness versus relatedness in an ongoing and creative fashion. These inevitable ruptures in the therapeutic alliance—mismeetings—provide an ideal opportunity to explore and work out authentic modes of attaining human contact in the face of separateness.

Breaches in the therapeutic alliance provide an opportunity to work on the task of developing the capacity to be both separate and connected. They provide an opportunity to learn that the possibility of relatedness exists despite the fact that self and other have separate and independent needs, wills, and existences, and that true relatedness only occurs in the meeting of two separate human beings. As Rilke (1903) put it:

> For one human being to love another human being: that is perhaps the most difficult task that has been entrusted to us, the ultimate task, the final test and proof, the work for which all other work is merely preparation. That is why young people, who are beginners in everything, are not yet capable of love: it is something they must learn. With their whole being, with all their forces, gathered around their solitary, anxious upward-beating hearts, they must learn to love. But learning time is always a long, secluded time, and therefore loving, for a long time ahead and far on into life, is solitude, a heightened and deepened aloneness for the person who loves. Loving does not at first mean merging, surrendering, and uniting with another person (for what would a union be of two people who are unclarified, unfinished, and still incoherent?). It is a high inducement for the individual to ripen, to become something in himself, to become world, to become world in himself for the sake of another person. [pp. 68–69]

Part IV

Psychotherapy Integration

12

Barriers to Psychotherapy Integration

In recent years there has been a strong movement toward transcending traditional boundaries between different schools of psychotherapy and the development of perspectives that are more integrative in nature. One impetus for this development has been the failure of psychotherapy research to consistently demonstrate the superiority of one type of psychotherapy over others (Smith and Glass 1977). This has led many to recognize the importance of transcending interschool rivalries in the pursuit of a collaborative search for those processes leading to change. Another factor influencing this movement has been, I would suggest, a general cultural shift toward a postmodern perspective, entailing a more relativistic conception of reality and a healthy skepticism of ideology of any kind. In this chapter I will explore some of the practical and psychological barriers obstructing the process of psychotherapy integration and will point to ways of dealing with such obstacles.

SACRED COWS

The first barrier to creative integration is what can be conceptualized as cherished beliefs or, to use a colloquial expression, "sacred cows." Here the issue is that different therapeutic traditions adhere to certain core assumptions, rules, or prescriptions that become so intertwined with the identity of the tradition that they become sacred, inviolate, and unchallengeable. Like the proverbial cows of India, they become deified.

Often these sacred cows develop initially for very good reasons. They arise from valid intuitions about the nature of change and the therapeutic process. For example, the psychoanalytic prescription of therapist neutrality reflects the important intuition that gratifying the client's immediate wishes may in some cases impede the accurate understanding of underlying concerns. By rigidly adhering to the ideal of therapist neutrality, however, one can fail to recognize that the therapist inevitably contributes to the interpersonal field. This can prevent the type of flexibility that permits the therapist to respond creatively to the demands of the particular context.

The traditional cognitive-behavioral eschewal of the analysis of transference reflects a valid intuition that the therapeutic relationship does not necessarily parallel important situations in the client's life and a valid concern that insights and changes generated in the therapeutic relationship will not necessarily generalize to the client's everyday experience. By refusing to subject the therapeutic relationship to analysis, however, we fail to harness one of the potentially most powerful mechanisms of change.

Rigid adherence to positions of this type thus takes on a life of its own. Adherents of a tradition can become invested in a position, at least in part, because of the role the position plays as a core tenet in a belief system through which adherents achieve a sense of identity. I am reminded here of the institutionalized ritual in Kafka's "In the Penal Colony," in which the prisoner has the name of his or her crime tattooed into his or her flesh. The participants subject others and submit themselves to this crippling and torturous ritual whose real purpose has been shrouded by the mists of time but which has acquired a ritualistic significance because of its long history.

As Feyerabend (1962) has pointed out, scientific theories are no different than myths in this respect. Both have core tenets that are sacred and inviolable. Given the resistance of tenets of this type to change, I would suggest that an important step should consist of the identification by adherents of different orientations of those tenets that serve an important ideological function in their respective systems. This should help to clarify those situations in which debates about the advisability of various therapeutic practices are surface manifestations of deeper-level ideological concerns of a more fundamental nature that may be implicit, but not articulated as part of the dialogue. This in turn should enable a shift to a level of discourse that more directly confronts the concerns underlying the debate.

CARICATURING AND MISUNDERSTANDING OTHER TRADITIONS: THE STRAW MAN APPROACH

Another major barrier to psychotherapy integration consists of a lack of true familiarity with other traditions and a tendency to caricature them. Related to this is a lack of familiarity with more recent developments in other traditions. For example, cognitive-behaviorally oriented theorists who critique psychoanalytic theory and practice are often unfamiliar with contemporary developments in object relations theory, Lacanian analysis, or self psychology. They level many of their criticisms at a classical psychoanalytic perspective that is rejected by many contemporary psychoanalytic theorists.

Psychoanalytic theorists often fault cognitive-behavioral theorists for failing to deal adequately with the role of emotion in human functioning or for failing to deal adequately with transference–countertransference issues, without recognizing that newer developments in cognitive-behavioral theory have made extensive attempts to fill in these lacunae (e.g., Guidano 1991, Mahoney 1991, Safran and Segal 1990).

If criticism of another tradition is to be an informed one having the potential for stimulating new thinking rather than simply serving as a self-affirming rhetorical exercise, it is imperative for critics to recognize that the targets they are firing at are moving ones. In some respects, the mistakes being made by critics with a superficial understanding of other therapeutic traditions may be likened to the distorted understanding of other cultures characteristic of anthropologists of the Victorian era, who had no understanding of the role their ethnocentric attitudes played in their understandings of other cultures. In order to obtain a more accurate understanding of other psychotherapy traditions, it is necessary to recognize the way in which our preconceptions distort our understanding. It may also be necessary to spend a considerable amount of time observing the way in which theory is implemented in practice, rather than confining our analysis to the level of theoretical constructs, that are disembedded from practical context.

To carry this analogy a little further, I suggest that the practice of cross-cultural anthropology can provide us with a useful model for therapists wishing to learn from other therapeutic orientations. In this respect, the concept of *thick description* (e.g., Geertz 1973, Shweder 1991) may be particularly relevant. A thick description consists of a careful, nuanced, and contextualized description of other cultures as embodied in everyday practice. Many anthropologists argue that it is only through this type of careful ethnography that we can understand other cultures sufficiently well in their uniqueness to permit us to develop a more general understanding of humankind. In the same way, I suggest that the task of psychotherapy integration will be most profitably advanced through a type of careful cross-cultural ethnography, rather than through premature attempts to critique other approaches or to integrate diverse approaches at a superficial level.

REINVENTING THE WHEEL AND REPEATING OLD MISTAKES

A by-product of theoretical insularity and a lack of in-depth familiarity with other traditions is a failure of adherents of one tradition to take advantage of the knowledge that has been acquired in other traditions when working in areas or with techniques that have been more fully explored and developed by proponents of other traditions. For example, cognitive-behavioral therapists who are beginning to experiment with the analysis of the transference often fail to take advantage of the years of experience and clinical wisdom that have been acquired in this domain by their analytic colleagues. Such issues as timing of interpretations, depth of interpretation, and so on that have been explored in the psychoanalytic literature are often ignored by cognitive-behavioral colleagues who are then placed in the position of acquiring this knowledge in a slow and painstaking fashion through their own experience.

Another example would be the growing tendency for cognitive-behaviorists to experiment with the technique of historical reconstruction in therapy. After many years of rejecting the psychoanalytic focus on the past, some cognitive-behaviorists are now emphasizing the importance of historical reconstruction as a therapeutic tool (e.g., Guidano 1991, Mahoney 1991). Ironically, many psychoanalytic theorists are now questioning the emphasis upon historical reconstruction as a therapeutic intervention and are placing more emphasis on the exploration of the therapeutic interaction in the here and now. Both Gill (1982) and Strupp and Binder (1984), for example, question the extensive use of historical reconstruction and caution against the indiscriminate use of genetic transference interpretations. Contemporary analysts with an object relations or interpersonal bent criticize the archaeological metaphor implicit in the classical psychoanalytic practice of unearthing repressed memories and, instead, emphasize the importance of the corrective emotional experience that takes place in the therapeutic relationship (e.g., Mitchell, 1988). Spence (1982) has offered a compelling criticism of the archaeological metaphor from a hermeneutic perspective and, in so doing, has challenged aspects of the theoretical bedrock for this emphasis on historical reconstruction. Is this shift toward a more here-and-now focus in psychoanalytic practice merely a fashion, or is it at least partially a reflection of clinical experience? If it is the latter, it would be unfortunate if cognitive-behavioral therapists did not take advantage of whatever insights have been developed in this area by their psychoanalytic colleagues.

Conversely, psychoanalytic therapists who are beginning to experiment with behavioral interventions should be able to take advantage of whatever technical expertise in this area has been acquired by their behavioral colleagues over the years. For example, behaviorists have demonstrated experimentally that duration of exposure time plays a critical role in whether a phobic or obsessive client habituates to a stimulus situation or becomes sensitized. This suggests that psychoanalytic therapists who experiment with enactive techniques without this knowledge risk negative therapeutic effects in certain situations. To quote Santayana's oft-cited warning: "Those who forget the past are doomed to repeat its mistakes."

FAILING TO RECOGNIZE GENUINELY NEW DEVELOPMENTS

The converse of the previous point is a tendency for therapists adhering to a particular tradition to treat new theoretical and technical developments in another tradition with disdain, believing that they are simply recyclings of concepts and techniques that have been associated with their own tradition. For example, psychoanalytically oriented theorists and therapists may dismiss the current interest amongst cognitive therapists in experimenting with the use of the therapeutic relationship for exploring and challenging dysfunctional beliefs as a poor imitation of the transference analysis that has been central to psychoanalytic practice from its inception.

Client-centered therapists may dismiss many of the developments in self psychology as belated attempts to recognize what client-centered therapists have always insisted was primary, that is, the importance of empathy as a central therapeutic tool. In so doing, however, they may miss some of the subtle and important differences between client-centered and self psychological theory and practice.

The tendency to assimilate new developments to old models blinds therapists and clinicians to any genuinely new and creative developments that may emerge. A useful analogy to apply here is the translation of concepts from one language into another. In the same sense that there can be no exact translation from one language into another, there can never be an exact translation of concepts from one therapeutic tradition into another. Just as the translation of Dostoyevsky from Russian into English changes the meaning in subtle and important ways, the translation of concepts from psychoanalytic theory into cognitive-behavioral theory, or vice versa, changes the concepts.

An even more apt analogy, perhaps, can be found if we consider the way in which religious ideas and practices change as they become absorbed by different cultures. Consider, for example, the radical transformations that have taken place in Christianity as it spread from its roots in the Jewish tradition and became absorbed and transformed by a variety of indigenous cultures—Roman, Anglo-Saxon, Latin American, and so on. Or consider the fascinating transformations that took place in Buddhism as it migrated from India to countries such as China, Japan, and Tibet.

The meaning of a particular concept, and the particular way in which it will evolve and be put into practice, is thus inevitably transformed by the superordinate belief system within which it becomes embedded. The process of integration by its very nature creates novel forms, which are more than a simple additive combination of their component parts.

FUNDAMENTAL INCOMPATIBILITIES AMONG DIFFERENT THERAPEUTIC TRADITIONS

I want to touch now on the question of what can and cannot be integrated from different therapeutic traditions. Different theorists have taken different positions on this issue. Some, for example, have argued that behavioral and psychoanalytic traditions are fundamentally incompatible, because the active stance of the behavior therapist will in some fashion contaminate the transference relationship.

I think that this assertion is arguable. It depends on the assumption that there is some type of "pure" transference to be contaminated. This assumption is challenged by more interpersonal or social-constructivist (to use Hoffman's [1991] term) perspectives that view the experience in the therapeutic hour as a co-construction of both therapist and client rather than as an exclusive function of what the client brings to the situation.

Another position on this issue has recently been taken by Blatt (1991), who argues that certain aspects of psychoanalytic and cognitive behavioral theory are fundamentally incompatible, because psychoanalytic practice focuses on the transference relationship and on unconscious processes whereas cognitive-behavioral approaches focus on conscious cognitive processes. But surely these differences are more at the levels of technique and midlevel (and potentially reconcilable) theory, rather than fundamental incompatibilities. The fact that some cognitive therapists are now focusing on the transference relationship and on unconscious processes makes it clear that these differences are by no means insurmountable (e.g., Guidano 1991, Mahoney 1991, Safran and Segal 1990).

One of the more thoughtful positions on this issue has been taken by Messer and Winokur (1980) who argued that any incompatibilities between behavioral and psychoanalytic perspectives are at the level of fundamental underlying worldviews or philosophical perspectives. They suggest that psychoanalysis traditionally has more of a tragic worldview in which conflict is recognized as part of the fabric of life. Therapy, as Freud suggested, can at best transform neurotic misery into ordinary unhappiness. In contrast, behavior therapy is seen as having a comic worldview in which problems are seen as transient clouds in the blue sky of life.

Another example of a metatheoretical difference that borders on one of fundamental philosophical significance would be the difference between drive metapsychology, which views humans as inherently in conflict with society, and interpersonal metatheory, which views the individual as having a biologically innate propensity for interpersonal relatedness.

A third example would be the behavioral metatheoretical perspective, which emphasizes the importance of controlling problematic emotions with behavioral techniques, versus the humanistic perspective, which emphasizes the adaptive nature of emotional experience and the importance of allowing oneself to be as one is rather than attempting to manipulate oneself through self-control strategies.

While I do not agree that differences of this type are ultimately irreconcilable, I do believe that they lie at the heart of the most important and heated debates regarding the usefulness of different techniques and the appropriateness of different strategies. As long as a particular concept or therapeutic intervention from another approach does not violate one's core assumptions about the nature of life and of therapeutic change, one is free to experiment with different concepts and techniques, retaining those that are most useful and discarding others.

Techniques can be integrated and theoretical concepts can be integrated. Worldviews or fundamental philosophical perspectives, however, cannot be integrated because they are by their very nature mutually exclusive. I believe, however, that it is possible to move beyond the position of mutual exclusivity at this level if one has a superordinate worldview that views all worldviews as partial and inadequate in nature and recognizes the importance of viewing reality from the perspective of multiple lenses.

While it may be impossible to develop a single unifying worldview, I believe that integration can nevertheless proceed, through engaging in a dialectical process in which adherents of the different worldviews discuss their relative positions in an open-minded way, ultimately leading to a broadening and elaborating of both perspectives. The simultaneous apprehension of two different worldviews may be impossible in the same way that the perception of one gestalt in an ambiguous perceptual figure interferes with the perception of an incompatible one. The individual who has had the experience of apprehending both perceptions, however, can alternate back and forth between the two at will. Similarly, the therapist who is able to appreciate more than one worldview can alternate back and forth between different perspectives, thus broadening his or her options for helping the client.

Thus the answers to questions such as "Should I work at the level of surface issues or underlying dynamic conflicts?" "Should my approach be supportive in nature or more exploratory?" "Should I use behavioral interventions or will they interfere with the process of analysis?" can be decided on a case-by-case basis, rather than on the basis of inflexible philosophical principles, which are often not explicitly articulated.

CONCLUSIONS

In this chapter I have explored a number of common barriers to creative dialogue among theorists, researchers, and clinicians of different therapeutic orientations and have offered a number of suggestions for transcending these barriers. The analogy of cultural anthropology seems to be a useful one in this respect. Different therapeutic orientations are in essence different cultures, and one of the major obstacles to learning what there is to learn from different therapeutic orientations is a type of therapeutic ethnocentricism.

In his recent book on cultural psychology, Richard Shweder (1991) makes the following observations:

> If there is a piety in cultural anthropology it is the conviction that astonishment deserves to be a universal emotion. Astonishment and the assortment of feelings that it brings with it—surprise, curiosity, excitement, enthusiasm, sympathy—are probably the affects most distinctive of the anthropological response to the difference and strangeness of "others." Anthropologists encounter witchcraft trials, suttee, ancestral spirit attack, fire walking, body mutilation, the dream time, and how do they react? With astonishment. While others respond with horror, outrage, condescension, or lack of interest, the anthropologists flip into their world-revising mood. [p. 1]

I would like to suggest that this consciously inculcated stance of astonishment is one of the most valuable things that can come out of the psychotherapy integrative movement. I believe that the development and maintenance of a truly integrative spirit should be the goal of the integrative movement rather than the creation of a unitary, static, integrative paradigm.

To the extent that confronting alternative therapeutic paradigms and techniques flips us into a "world-revising mood," to use
Shweder's phrase, rather than the more common stance of outrage
and condescension that we are all too familiar with, the possibility of
radically deepening our understanding of the human change
process, rather than simply defending our existing worldviews,
emerges.

13

Psychotherapy Integration: A Postmodern Critique*

Jeremy D. Safran and Stanley B. Messer

The last two decades have witnessed the beginning of an important shift away from the prevailing climate of factionalism and parochialism among the psychotherapies toward one of dialogue and rapprochement (Arkowitz 1992, Bergin and Garfield 1994, Norcross and Goldfried 1992, Stricker and Gold 1993). Integrative links have been forged, for example, among psychodynamic, behavioral, and family system therapies (e.g., Wachtel and McKinney 1992), and among experiential, cognitive, and interpersonal approaches (e.g., Safran and Segal 1990). Commonalities across the different therapies have been distilled into single therapies (e.g., Garfield 1992, Prochaska 1995), and techniques from several sources have been employed eclectically in connection with the differing needs of individual clients (Beutler and Hodgson 1993, Lazarus 1992). A poll that surveyed clinical psychologists, marriage and family therapists, psychiatrists, and social workers has documented that from 59

---

*This chapter represents the equal participation of both authors.

percent to 72 percent endorse eclecticism as their preferred approach (Jensen et al. 1990).

In this chapter we adopt a postmodern perspective to critique common approaches to psychotherapy integration and to highlight the more radical implications of the integration movement for shaping our attitudes toward psychotherapy. A recurring theme in postmodern discourse, deriving originally from Hegel (1910), is that self-identity emerges only through the construction of "the other." The unfortunate effect of this construction is that "the self" always gets defined in contrast to "the other," who is thereby deprived of genuine standing. This functions to validate and maintain the privilege of the self or of the dominant group. Foucault (1967), for example, argues that during the eighteenth century the insane (the "irrational") were placed in the category of "the other" as part of the process of protecting and enshrining the rationalistic values of the enlightenment. An important function of postmodern critique is to challenge constructions of reality that have the effect of marginalizing "the other."

One way to view the recent trend toward psychotherapy integration is as a response to confrontation with "the other." In the conventional discourse that has taken place among therapeutic traditions, each approach has defined itself in contrast to the other. For example, psychoanalysis is defined in contrast to behavior therapy by its emphasis on the unconscious, and behavior therapy is defined in contrast to psychoanalytic therapy by its emphasis on social influence. As in the case of racial, ethnic, or cultural differences, perceived positive qualities of one's own group take on ritualistic significance whereas other traditions are assigned a negative, caricatured quality. The other is thus appropriated and used to define and enshrine the values of the self (Sampson 1993).

From a postmodern perspective, one of the most important functions that the psychotherapy integration movement can serve is to help theorists and practitioners move beyond the attitude of superiority, contempt, and aversion that frequently arises from the confrontation of adjoining therapeutic "cultures" toward a sense of surprise and eagerness to learn, which is also a natural human response to difference (Feyerabend 1987). One can compare the task of the psychotherapy integrationist with that of the cultural anthropologist. The anthropologist's task consists of struggling to understand and appreciate new cultures in their own unique terms, rather than dismissing them as inferior, reacting with moral outrage, or assimilating them to familiar categories. As Shweder (1991) suggests, it is vital for anthropologists to approach their subject matter with an attitude of openness and *astonishment*. He refers to this as a "world-revising mode," that is, a stance that is conducive to revising their fundamental assumptions.

Similarly, this type of consciously inculcated stance of astonishment is one of the most valuable attitudes that can emerge from the psychotherapy integration movement. To the extent that confronting alternate therapeutic paradigms and techniques flips us into a "world-revising mode," versus the more common stance of outrage and condescension, there is the possibility of its leading to a dialogue that can truly deepen our understanding of the human change process. The importance of dialogue of this type is a recurring theme throughout this chapter, and later we will explore the central role that it plays in the scientific enterprise.

In the following, we critically examine the three most frequently employed strategies for psychotherapy integration—technical eclecticism, common factors, and theoretical integration—in light of two defining characteristics of the postmodern attitude: contextualism and pluralism. We also explore the obstacles to integration that emerge at metatheoretical and epistemological levels of discourse. The chapter concludes with the implications of contextualism and pluralism for psychotherapy theory, practice, and research.

Contextualism is the hypothesis that an event cannot be studied as an isolated element, but only within its setting. Every event is said to have quality and texture. Quality is the total meaning of the phenomenon, and texture refers to the parts that make it up (Pepper 1942). Quality entails a fusion of the textural details; for example, "Lemon, sugar, and water are the details of the taste, but the quality of lemonade is such a persistent fusion of these that it is very difficult to analyze out its components" (Pepper 1942, p. 243,

after William James). The postmodern notion that there is more
than one correct theory or perspective by which to view any
phenomenon is known as *pluralism.* It is an antidote to parochialism
and the attitude that absolute certainty is attainable. Seeing how
other theories get a grip on the world can lead to enhanced
understanding and improvement of the theoretical ground on
which one stands (Nozick 1981). While contextualism notes that
context often determines which of many possible interpretations or
meanings we give to an event, pluralism acknowledges that there are
multiple perceptions of truth, each one influenced by the context
out of which the perceiver arises in making his or her judgments.

TECHNICAL ECLECTICISM

There has been discussion in the psychotherapy integration literature as to whether integrative efforts should have a more applied or
a more theoretical emphasis (Garfield 1994). Technical eclecticism
holds that theoretical integration involves fusing theories that are
irreconcilable, and that techniques should be combined pragmati-
cally on the basis of observed or presumed clinical efficacy (Lazarus
1996, Lazarus et al. 1992). Lazarus's multimodal therapy is a good
example of this approach. Techniques from Gestalt, cognitive,
behavioral, psychodynamic, and family systems therapy all may be
applied in one individual's therapy.

    One of the problems with this form of eclecticism is that it often
proceeds as if a therapeutic technique is a disembodied procedure
that can be readily transported from one context to another, much
like a medical technique, without consideration of its new psychotherapeutic context (Lazarus and Messer 1991). The problem can
be illustrated by reference to the hermeneutic circle, which stresses
the contextual nature of knowledge (Messer et al. 1988). Within this
view, a fact can be evaluated only in relation to the larger structure
of theory or argument of which it is a part, even while the larger
structure is dependent on its individual parts. Thus, a therapeutic
procedure such as an interpretation or empathic response does not

stand on its own, independent of the framework of meaning created by the entire therapeutic system.

This part–whole interdependence can be illustrated in various ways. For example, a client whose treatment has been primarily cognitive-behavioral may experience a therapist's shift to empathic/ reflective responding as a withholding of needed psychological expertise. Conversely, a client whose treatment has been client-centered or psychoanalytic may experience a shift to cognitive-behavioral interventions as controlling. Although such interventions have the potential to be effective, their meaning and impact should be explored in their new context (e.g., see Frank 1993, Messer 1992).

In a second type of technical eclecticism, different therapists or techniques are prescribed as optimal for different kinds of problems or clients, rather than combined in one client's treatment. This is known as prescriptive matching (Beutler and Clarkin 1990, Beutler and Harwood 1995), differential therapeutics (Frances 1984), or selective eclecticism (Messer 1992). In asking which therapy is best for which type of client, selective eclecticism is a movement toward greater contextualization of therapy.

The prescriptive matching approach, however, ignores the fact that two clients with the same diagnosis often have very different case formulations (Collins and Messer 1991, Persons 1991). Moreover, clients change both within one session and over the course of therapy. This requires the skilled clinician to constantly modify interventions in a context-sensitive fashion in attunement with a changing process diagnosis, rather than applying a therapy module in response to a static diagnosis or formulation (Rice and Greenberg 1984, Safran, Greenberg et al. 1988). The failure to conduct psychotherapy research in a sufficiently context-sensitive manner is probably one of the factors underlying the difficulty of demonstrating a consistent pattern of therapist–client interactions (Beutler 1991, Omer and Dar 1992). It is thus important for psychotherapy researchers to conceptualize relevant variables in more process-oriented, phase-specific terms that take ongoing context into account.

COMMON CHANGE PRINCIPLES AS INTEGRATION

A second form of psychotherapy integration consists of the discernment of common principles of change across different therapies (e.g., Frank and Frank 1991, Goldfried 1980, Weinberger 1995). For example, a common principle in many forms of psychotherapy consists of helping clients to become aware of and challenge their self-criticism. A closer look at the ways in which this is accomplished in different therapies, however, reveals important distinctions. In the scientific and rationalistic spirit of cognitive therapy, clients are encouraged to challenge self-criticism by treating their negative thoughts as hypotheses to be tested through examining relevant evidence, or by considering alternative perspectives. In Gestalt therapy, by contrast, self-criticism is challenged by means of eliciting an emotional experience through what is known as "the empty chair" exercise. In this approach, clients' self-criticism is expressed while sitting in one chair and then confronted by their emotional reaction to it while sitting in a second chair.

Although both of these techniques share the common principle of challenging self-criticism, important differences emerge when we take into account the theoretical context in which interventions are employed (Goldfried and Safran 1986). The hypothesis-testing intervention in cognitive therapy takes place within a theoretical framework that views self-criticism as maladaptive thinking to be recognized, controlled, and eliminated (Messer and Winokur 1984). It is embedded in a modernist worldview that values rationality, objectivity, and pragmatism (Woolfolk and Richardson 1984). Gestalt therapy, by contrast, regards self-criticism as an aspect of the self that must be recognized and then integrated with other parts of the self. In this therapy, the values of emotional experiencing, subjectivity, and the complexity of personality are paramount.

Because different therapies convey different overarching values or messages (Beutler et al. 1986, Kelly and Strupp 1992), any intervention must be understood as part of a general process through which such values are transmitted to the client. In the attempt to extract common principles, one can lose sight of important features of the overall therapeutic system and the process through which it works. As Wittgenstein (1953) once remarked, it is a mistake to try to get to the essence of an artichoke by divesting it of its leaves.

We are not arguing that there is never any value to extracting common principles. The utility of the specific common principle that is articulated, however, depends on the function that it serves in the phase of dialogue between systems of therapy. In early stages of integration, the articulation of common principles can play an important role in facilitating dialogue where none previously existed. In this way it can help to reduce the sense of "otherness." As the dialogue progresses, however, it becomes more critical to explore similarities *and* differences between orientations from a more nuanced perspective. Anthropologists refer to this type of contextualized exploration as *thick description* (Geertz 1973). Thick description provides a corrective to older forms of anthropological investigation that are more likely to assimilate aspects of new cultures into existing knowledge structures (Schwartz et al. 1992). Geertz has argued that it is only by understanding each culture in its uniqueness that we can learn something new about the human condition. Similarly, the exploration of other therapeutic systems in a refined, contextualized fashion can lead to new understanding of both other systems and our own.

Thus, differences among therapies in their higher-level theoretical constructs should not be ignored. Theories have a trickle-down effect on clinical practice. To return to our earlier example, challenging self-criticism may convey a different message in the approach of a therapist who subscribes to a theory that self-critical thoughts are distortions to be eliminated than it will in the approach of a therapist who views them as reflecting a part of the self containing the seeds of important strengths.

THEORETICAL INTEGRATION

In this form of integration, different theories are combined in the attempt to produce a superior, overarching conceptual framework.

Wachtel's (1977) joining of psychoanalytic and behavioral theories within an interpersonal psychodynamic framework and Safran and Segal's (1990) wedding of cognitive, experiential, and interpersonal approaches within a single theory of therapy are good examples of this genre. Such superordinate integrative theories are said to lead to new forms of therapy that capitalize on the strengths of each of their elements.

While the integration of pure form theories into one that is superordinate may bring certain advantages, the integrative theory could lose some of the practical wisdom that has evolved over time in its component therapeutic systems. In the same sense that interventions cannot be understood outside the context of the theory in which they are embedded, a theory of therapy cannot be fully comprehended without reference to the details of its clinical implementation. As Geertz (1983) suggests, in order to truly understand a culture there must be "a continuous dialectical tacking between the most local of local details and the most global of global structures in such a way as to bring them into simultaneous view" (p. 69). Similarly, a proper appreciation of a therapeutic approach requires a tacking back and forth between theory and the specifics of its implementation.

Organicism versus Pluralism

There are other potential problems with theoretical integration, to which a postmodern outlook alerts us. The task is sometimes approached as if there were one correct integration waiting in the wings to be discovered. Labeled *organicist* by the philosopher Stephen Pepper (1942), this perspective (or "world hypothesis" as he calls it) presumes that by organizing data at a higher level, the appearance of conflict between ideas or findings is resolved by their incorporation into an organic whole. Organicism posits that in the world we encounter fragments of experience, such as the observation of a school of therapy. These appear with certain contradictions, gaps, or opposition from other fragments of experience such as the observations of other theories of therapy. The various fragments tend to be resolved by incorporation into an organic whole that, all the while, was implicit in the fragments and that transcends them. In this view, progress in theoretical integration is achieved by including more and more of the fragments into a single, integrated, and unified whole.

There is an alternative view to organicism, namely, that psychology, by its very nature, is pluralistic: "Paradigms, theories, models (or whatever one's label for conceptual ordering devices) can never prove preemptive or preclusive of alternate organizations" (Koch 1981, p. 268). The pluralistic perspective holds that all theories are necessarily limited and that the best way of approaching the truth is through the ongoing confrontation of multiple, competing theories with data and with each other.

Integration as Translation

Theoretical integration typically involves some element of reconceptualization or translation from one framework into another. For example, in an attempt to place the insights of psychoanalytic theory on a firmer scientific footing, Dollard and Miller (1950) translated psychoanalytic concepts into learning theory. Contemporary examples include drawing on concepts from cognitive psychology to refine psychoanalytic theory, such as efforts to account for the phenomenon of transference in terms of schema theory (Safran and Segal 1990, Singer and Singer 1992, Westen 1988) and attempts to reformulate the psychoanalytic theory of the unconscious by means of cognitive theory (Erdelyi 1985). Within a contexualist view, however, language and theory are inextricably intertwined, which forces us to consider carefully what has been added by the translation. Psychological meanings only make sense by virtue of their interrelations to other terms within their conceptual setting. Thus, for example, while attempts to translate a concept from one theory into the terms of another may result in ease of empirical testability, some of the concept's richness and subtlety could be lost.

Translation can also lead to the reductionistic fallacy, which holds that theory A (regarded as nonscientific) is more adequately explained in terms of theory B (regarded as scientific). For example, it is a mistake to assume, a priori, that the principles of Chinese medicine can be better explained in terms of the principles of Western medicine. As Sampson (1983) argues,

> [T]o examine a culture's own system of understanding requires us to become familiar with the culture in *its* terms, rather than our own. This requires a dialogic rather than a monologic approach. We must carry on a dialogue with the other culture. In this dialogue our framework and theirs meet. Out of that meeting a newly cast understanding of both them and us is likely to emerge. [p. 185]

METATHEORETICAL INTEGRATION

In comparing the visions of reality contained within psychoanalytic, behavioral, and humanistic therapies, Messer and Winokur (1984) have illustrated the difficulties of integration at the metatheoretical level. They argued that psychoanalytic therapy is guided primarily by a tragic view of reality in which people are subject to forces not of their knowing and that can be only partially ameliorated. Behavior therapy, by contrast, falls more within the comic vision, where conflicts are viewed as external and more readily resolvable. Empirical findings on the process of these two therapies are consistent with this description (Goldfried 1991). The humanistic therapies, by contrast, are characterized by a romantic vision, which prizes individuality, spontaneity, and unlimited possibilities in life.

Fundamental differences in worldview are not readily integrated because they are mutually exclusive in many respects and are typically held as unquestionable presuppositions. Nor can they be resolved by reference to the data. What Kuhn (1970) has said about the incommensurability of different paradigms applies here: There is no set of rules to tell us how rational agreement can be reached or to settle all conflicts between paradigms or worldviews. It is tempting to think that the relative value of different therapeutic systems can be resolved definitively through psychotherapy research. However, the evaluation of therapeutic outcome is inextricably tied to values and shades of meaning (Messer and Warren 1990). This is unlike the situation in engineering where a bridge will collapse if the correct method of building it is not employed, or in medicine where a child will die if an incorrect procedure is applied to repair a heart valve.

For example, if an individual comes to accept her shyness and finds meaning in it, can we consider it a good outcome, or does there have to be a substantial reduction in her shyness? Gandhi (1957) maintained that his own shyness had become one of his greatest assets because it forced him to think before he spoke. If an individual loses his phobic symptoms upon joining a cult, should this be considered a good outcome? Rilke, one of the great poets of the twentieth century, chose to cultivate his pain and solitude in order to deepen his art. Would Wittgenstein's life have been "better" if he had been happy in the conventional sense? Of course there are some outcomes on which most, if not all, clinicians will agree. For example, few clinicians would argue that reducing suicidal behavior is not a desirable outcome in the treatment of a severely depressed client. Differences will, however, emerge when it comes to other types of outcome with the same client. For example, the existentially oriented therapist is likely to be more concerned than the cognitive therapist with helping a client to live authentically.

Metatheoretical systems are best thought of as multiple lenses, each of which can bring into sharper focus different phenomena and different aspects of the same phenomenon. For example, while tragic and comic visions cannot easily be integrated, they can each be usefully brought to bear in different clinical contexts and in highlighting different dimensions of one person's experience. This can be conceptualized as a type of dialectical thinking that allows one to take into account the paradoxes and contradictions that are inherent in life.

A long-term psychoanalytic therapist may be suspicious of the good outcomes reported by short-term behavior therapists, seeing these as superficial and unenduring. From a short-term behavioral perspective, the psychoanalytic emphasis on structural change may be viewed as presumptuous insofar as the therapist claims to know what changes clients need to make. Dialogue about this type of issue can lead to questions such as the following: How ambitious should the therapist be regarding change? How should the therapist and client negotiate differences in desired outcome? When should a reemergence of a problem be considered a relapse, and when should it be considered a new problem? What types of change should health insurance pay for?

This is not to say that research is irrelevant or that clinicians should feel free to define outcome as they will. Rather, different kinds of outcomes emphasized by different therapists must be viewed within the context of the values and visions of life each holds to be true, and this multiplicity of values is merely a reflection of the complex nature of life. Psychotherapy integration does not solve this problem but serves to highlight it. A postmodern perspective directs us to confront this complexity rather than to gloss over it or ignore it. It encourages us to engage in ongoing dialogue with colleagues who hold different worldviews. It also encourages dialogue with clients about the tasks and goals of therapy. This type of negotiation constitutes an important part of the process of establishing a therapeutic alliance (Bordin 1979).

The recent shift in behaviorally oriented theory toward an emphasis on self-acceptance rather than self-control (Jacobson 1994) provides an example of the type of metatheroretical elaboration that can result from dialogue among different theoretical traditions. Although it has not been uncommon for behavior therapists to borrow techniques and concepts from other traditions, they are usually assimilated into a fundamental worldview that emphasizes the importance of self-control. By explicitly proposing that change be viewed as self-acceptance, an outlook typically associated with the experiential tradition, Jacobson is challenging the underlying paradigm through which change is understood. The resulting shift does not necessarily have to radically change the specific techniques that are employed, but the different ends to which they are put may affect their ultimate impact.

Messer (1992) has referred to this kind of importation of concepts as *assimilative integration* (pp. 151–155). It is the incorporation of attitudes, perspectives, or techniques from one therapy into another in a way that is cognizant of how context shapes the meaning of foreign elements. This mode of integration favors a firm grounding in any one system of psychotherapy, but with a willingness to incorporate or assimilate perspectives or practices from other schools (see also Stricker and Gold 1996). This is an evolutionary process in which the contact with difference leads to a de facto, even if unacknowledged, integration. However, to carry on such a dialogue with the other in a meaningful fashion, one must be knowledgeable about and firmly rooted in at least one tradition, and know where one stands.

INTEGRATION AT THE EPISTEMOLOGICAL LEVEL

Different therapeutic traditions tend to be associated with different epistemological stances, and this also creates an obstacle to integration. A survey by Morrow-Bradley and Elliott (1986) found that, in general, practicing therapists find little of value in psychotherapy research, and that psychodynamically oriented therapists are less likely to make use of psychotherapy research findings than are their behavioral peers. The behavioral tradition subscribes to the epistemological stance of logical empiricism (Scriven 1969) and its associated methodology of experimental research. The empirical/experimental method of truth-seeking, which psychologists have adopted from the natural sciences, relies heavily on observation, laboratory studies, elementism, and objectivism (Kimble 1984, Krasner and Houts 1984). It stems from the philosophy of scientific modernism, which includes the belief that nature has an existence independent of the observer and is accessible to the operations of the human mind (Schrodinger 1967). Findings are presumed to be context-free and lead to universal, nomothetic laws.

Psychoanalysis, by contrast, has traditionally been associated with an epistemological stance, which is more hermeneutic in nature (Messer et al. 1988). Under Brentano's influence, Freud distinguished psychology from the natural sciences and instead developed a "descriptive science based on the direct observation of psychological life, with a focus on its meaning" (Wertz 1993). Psychoanalysis was thus originally understood to be a descriptive and interpretive science rather than an experimental one.

Proponents of psychoanalysis have, to some degree, accommodated themselves to the canons of experimental research. But, as Hornstein (1993) has stated, "American psychologists did to psychoanalysis what they did to every *verstehen*-based psychology that arrived on the boat from Europe—they ignored its underlying assumptions, skimmed off what they could use, and repackaged the remaining content in the sparkling language of positivist science" (p. 586). Even while this synthesis of psychoanalysis and experimental method took place, there was never any extensive debate about the fundamentals of scientific practice (Hornstein 1993). This may account, at least in part, for the failure of experimental research to have had a substantial impact on the practice of psychoanalytic therapy.

For some time now, there has been a call for methodological pluralism in psychology (Polkinghorne 1984), which we endorse as an important feature of postmodernism. Cook (1985), for example, recommends agreement from independent epistemological perspectives as the best foundation for approximating truth. Similarly, Bevan (1991) warns us to be wary of rule-bound methodology: "Use any method with a full understanding of what it does for you but also what constraints it may place on you. . . . Be mindful of the potential value of methodological pluralism" (p. 479). Such methods may include traditional experimental research, case analysis (both quantitative and qualitative), skilled reflection (Hoshmand and Polkinghorne 1992), phenomenological descriptions, anthropological field studies, action research, and narrative approaches.

Calls for methodological pluralism, however, come up against strong emotional barriers. Hudson (1972), in a book with the ironic title, *The Cult of the Fact,* suggests that experimentalists (the "tough-minded") tend to think of nonexperimentalists (the "soft-minded") as sloppy, even morally remiss, in their unwillingness to treat hard data seriously. Nonexperimentalists, on their part, tend to view experimentalists as mechanistic, dehumanizing, and simpleminded. Part of what is at stake here is the question of what constitutes "science." A number of philosophers of science from Kuhn (1970) onward have demonstrated that the process through which science evolves is very different from the picture portrayed in the "standard view" of science (Manicas and Secord 1983). Science has an irreducibly social and interpretive character. Data are only one element in a rhetorical process through which members of a scientific community attempt to persuade one another (Weimer 1979).

The rules and standards of scientific practice are worked out by members of a scientific community and are modified over time. Many contemporary philosophers and sociologists of science assert that the demarcation criteria between science and nonscience are not as clear-cut as they were once thought to be. They argue that the logical empiricist view of science is a reconstruction according to certain criteria of rationality rather than an accurate portrait of the way science really works (Bernstein 1983, Feyerabend 1975, Houts 1989, Kuhn 1970, Safran and Muran 1994, Weimer 1979). The "research-practice split" is thus, in part, fueled by the same type of marginalization of the "other" associated with the contest between different therapeutic orientations.

BEYOND RELATIVISM

The appreciation of the relative merits of different psychotherapies within a pluralist outlook and the willingness to engage in informed debate about philosophical and epistemological issues can lead to the conclusion that all are equal and anything goes. That is, one can confuse openness to other approaches with a kind of intellectual anarchy or wishy-washiness. A relativistic position is said to characterize our culture in this postmodern era in general. It has led critics (e.g., Bloom 1987) to argue that our culture lacks fundamental moral and political convictions and, in the current relativistic climate, there is "no enemy other than the man who is not open to everything" (p. 27).

Finding a stance that is both pluralistic and nonrelativistic is a central concern for many contemporary philosophers, and a new understanding of the nature of science is emerging (Bernstein 1983, Gadamer 1980, Habermas 1979, Rorty 1982). A central theme in this understanding is the importance of dialogue among members of the scientific community. This emphasis on dialogue should not be confused with sentimentalism. The point is an epistemological one. A central theme in the contemporary philosophy of science is that our understanding of things is inevitably shaped by our preconceptions. There are no theory-free observations (Hanson 1958). The reason that dialogue is critical is because it provides a means of moving beyond our preconceptions toward a better understanding of the things themselves (Gadamer 1980). Through the process of recognizing our preconceptions and engaging in dialogue with that which is alien, the possibility of seeing beyond our preconceptions emerges. True dialogue involves seeking to listen to and understand what the other is saying and a willingness to test our opinions through such encounters. Rather than a facile acceptance of alternative positions, true dialogue involves an active engagement in the process of truth seeking.

This recognition of the importance of dialogue emerges out of historical and sociological analyses of the way science actually operates rather than the way it should operate. Scientific practice involves deliberation among members of the scientific community, interpretation of existing research, and application of agreed-upon criteria for making judgments and debate about which criteria are relevant. The absence of absolute foundations is not equivalent to arbitrariness. Bernstein (1993) refers to the underlying philosophical position as one of "engaged fallibilistic pluralism." This means "taking our own fallibility seriously—resolving that however much we are committed to our own styles of thinking, we are willing to listen to others without denying or suppressing the otherness of the other" (p. 336).

A parallel can be drawn between scientific practice and the process of making judicial decisions (Bernstein 1983, Polanyi 1958).

Principles of judicial arbitration evolve over time through rational deliberation and precedent. Evidence plays a critical role, but this evidence is always subject to interpretation. Each case must be dealt with in its particularities. Rather than applying universal principles, general rules of argument are given more or less weight depending on the specific nature and circumstances of the case. These contextual features of common law do not make judicial decisions irrational or nihilistic, but they do make it impossible to adequately model them through universally applicable algorithms.

We are thus advocating ongoing dialogue at all levels of analysis—empirical, theoretical, metatheoretical, and epistemological—and not an uncritical acceptance of all therapeutic orientations and techniques. The challenge that psychotherapy theorists and researchers face as we enter the twenty-first century is one of learning to live with an irreducible ambiguity, without ignoring it and without wallowing in it (Bernstein 1993).

IMPLICATIONS FOR THEORY, PRACTICE, AND RESEARCH

What are the implications of pluralism and contextualism for psychotherapy theory, practice, and research? At a *theoretical level* we have highlighted, in accordance with pluralism, the importance of maintaining a continuing dialogue among multiple perspectives. Rather than aspiring to one superordinate theory, such a dialogue leads over time to a degree of assimilation of ideas and techniques from one theory or therapy into another.

One might argue that there is a contradiction between stressing appreciation for the otherness of the other, all the while critiquing the different forms of integration and advocating some assimilation of them. Critical analysis, however, is part of the dialogue. Although there is an inherent tension between appreciation of difference versus a critique or assimilation of differences, we have argued for a dialectical process between them, and not a facile or wholesale acceptance or rejection of difference.

In line with a contextualist viewpoint, theoretical dialogue must be grounded in the specifics of clinical practice. Just as study of a culture requires tacking back and forth between theory and observational detail, a theory of therapy has to be embodied in the particularities of practice. It is not enough, for example, to discuss the differences between transference and stimulus generalization in theoretical terms. Comparison on the theoretical level must be grounded in clinical material. Cultivating an attitude of astonishment among psychotherapy researchers and clinicians can play a critical role in creating a climate conducive to presenting videotapes and audiotapes of actual clinical material in public forums, thereby facilitating clinically grounded dialogue across theoretical orientations.

An implication of pluralism for *practice* and *training* in psychotherapy is that we should be fluent in more than one therapy language and mode of practice (Andrews et al. 1992, Messer 1987). In the same way that one has to spend time in other cultures in order to truly understand them, one has to immerse oneself in other therapeutic orientations in order to be able to appreciate their strengths and recognize their limitations. Clinical psychology programs are too often conducted within one theoretical perspective, which does not allow students to be multilingual and multicultural in relation to the multiplicity of existing therapeutic languages and cultures. Aside from book knowledge, the best way of learning about other approaches is to be supervised in their practice or to experience them as a client.

While pluralism emphasizes our attaining knowledge of several approaches, contextualism highlights the need for clinicians to evaluate a technique they incorporate from a different orientation in the ongoing context of therapy. A technique takes on the coloring of its surround and it must be assimilated in such a fashion that it fits comfortably within the theoretical and clinical framework into which it is imported. One must attend carefully to the effect on clients of such a change in the therapist's manner, perspective, or technique.

Regarding the implications of postmodernism for *research*, it is important to find ways to take into account the context and complexity of clinical phenomena. A finding from a randomized clinical trial that a treatment approach is effective with singly diagnosed clients does not speak sufficiently to the practicing clinician who has to work with complicated (often dual-diagnosed) clients whose nuances of personality and psychopathology are not readily captured by their diagnosis or the research protocols (Fensterheim and Raw 1996, Goldfried and Wolfe 1996, Safran and Muran 1994, 1996). Group designs that study subject variability are unable to mine the context-rich information that can be extracted from the study of *intra*subject variability. Although it is difficult to generalize from such single-subject research, this can be accomplished by multiple replications or by combining intensive and extensive analysis (Barlow 1981, Greenberg 1986, Kazdin 1982, Safran, Greenberg et al. 1988).

Thus, research comparing different treatment modalities at a global level (e.g., cognitive therapy vs. interpersonal therapy), or examining clients by treatment interactions, should be augmented by research that investigates specific interventions that are effective in specific contexts and the processes that underlie such change. For example, Safran and colleagues (Safran, Crocker et al. 1990, 1994, Safran and Muran 1996) have developed an empirically based model of the processes that lead to the resolution of ruptures in the therapeutic alliance. This model specifies which specific therapist interventions will be effective in the context of specific client processes along the pathway to resolution.

Messer and his students have studied the effect of therapists' competence and their adherence to a psychodynamic focus on the ongoing progress of individual clients. Raters had access to the flow of clinical material, thus allowing context to affect their ratings (Messer et al. 1992, Tishby and Messer 1995). Collins and Messer (1991) adapted Plan Formation methodology (Curtis et al. 1994) to study how case formulations are influenced by the context of a rater's favored theory.

A fruitful strategy for promoting the development of integrative knowledge can consist of identifying important therapeutic contexts or markers (Rice and Greenberg 1984) that may be responded to differently by therapists with different orientations (Safran and Inck 1995). For example, how do different traditions respond to instances of client self-criticism or to defensive maneuvers? Are there markers that are favored by, or unique to, specific orientations? By working with these smaller units of analysis (i.e., intervention A in context B), there is an opportunity to get beyond brand-name theories, allowing the results to become more accessible and relevant across traditions. It is also closer to a level that is meaningful to clinicians and therefore can be used to guide practice in a way complementary to randomized clinical trials.

Thus, research programs consistent with the spirit of integration need not necessarily evaluate the effectiveness of integrative treatment programs per se. When researchers dialogue with one another, within a spirit of pluralism, around the kind of process research just described, they can more readily absorb results stemming from other viewpoints because it gets around their emotional attachment to a brand-name therapy.

Another implication of pluralism for research is the importance of being open-minded about methods other than those that are experimental or correlational. Each method has its assets and shortcomings, but too often we sacrifice richer, contextual meaning for exactness and narrowly focused certitude. Some combination of quantitative and qualitative methods employed within the same research paradigm, for example, may lead to a better understanding of the complexities of psychotherapy than either approach alone.

CONCLUSIONS

In summary, the development of an open and engaged stance toward integration among theorists can lead to more fruitful cross-theoretical dialogue rather than the advocacy of a premature, unified paradigm (see Mahoney 1993, Stricker 1994). The greatest value of the psychotherapy integration movement lies in the creative and growth-oriented confrontation with and dialogue about difference, and it is in this process that the payoff lies.

Our call for a more contextually based, pluralistic approach toward psychotherapy integration may seem to some to invite unnecessary complication into a field that is already complex enough. To be sure, there are times when the strategy of simplification through ignoring context or alternative perspectives is the most appropriate way to proceed. Ultimately, it may be best to pursue an ongoing dialectic between the strategy of simplification and that of thick description (cf. Elliott and Anderson 1994).

The search for a single, unified therapeutic model and laments about the preparadigmatic and unscientific state of psychotherapy theory stem from a misunderstanding of the nature of science. In the natural sciences it is recognized that multiple, contradictory theories are necessary to capture different aspects of the underlying phenomena, and that a given theory captures some of these aspects at the expense of others (Nozick 1981). Moreover, contemporary philosophers of science state that science evolves through methodological pluralism rather than a uniform set of procedures and criteria.

Over a century ago, John Stuart Mill (Cohen 1961), a strong advocate of empirical methods in scientific procedure, argued that a plurality of views is critical for the following reasons:

1. A view that one rejects may be true nevertheless, and to reject it assumes one's own infallibility.
2. A problematic view may contain some portion of the truth because the prevailing view is never the whole truth. It is only by collision with contrary opinions that the remainder of the truth has a chance of being recognized.
3. A point of view that is wholly true, but not subjected to challenge, will be held as a prejudice rather than on a rational basis.
4. Someone holding a particular point of view without considering alternative perspectives will not really understand the meaning of the view he or she holds.
5. Decisive evidence against a perspective can only be articulated once an alternative perspective is advanced. This results from the fact that evidence in the absence of theory is meaningless.

Both psychotherapy integration and science flourish in an atmosphere of confronting and discussing difference rather than shunning it. Once an integrative system becomes codified, creativity and openness wither. Once can become an adherent of an integrative system in the same way that one becomes a cognitive therapist, a Freudian, or a Jungian. A theoretical system is always in danger of becoming a fossilized remnant of what was once a vital insight, even in the hands of the person who developed it. It was presumably for this reason that Jung once remarked (in Progoff 1953): "I am not a Jungian and I never could be."

Part V

An Interview

An Interview with Jeremy Safran

Christine Maguth Nezu and Lisa DelliCarpinni

INTRODUCTION

The following is a dialogue or interview with Jeremy D. Safran, Ph.D., as narrated by the first author, Christine M. Nezu.

I have followed Jeremy Safran's work since the early-to-mid-1980s when, as a psychology intern, I was urgently trying to integrate what I was learning from a wide array of clinical supervisors. My behavioral training had provided me with a worldview toward psychotherapy. This typically included an attempt to understand the functional relationships among the various clinical variables that existed with a particular clinical case. The mysterious process of psychotherapy clearly appeared more than an educational didactic experience for the client. It was an investigational relationship for both therapist and client, and each theoretical aspect of psychology seemed to add another piece to my understanding of how this relationship worked. Upon hearing of Dr. Safran's current work at

Beth Israel Medical Center in New York City, through one of the psychology interns (a student of mine, Lisa DelliCarpinni), and because of the cognitive provocation and integrative help provided by Jeremy Safran's publications during my own training years, Lisa and I decided to contact him for an interview. In addition to indulging my own questions that I've stored for several years, I am hopeful that the following interview excerpts will serve to interest readers who are still evolving in their understanding of this unique and complex relationship called psychotherapy.

BACKGROUND

After recently completing three years as the director of the Clinical Psychology Program at the New School for Social Research in New York, Jeremy Safran continues to focus his efforts on investigating aspects of the therapeutic relationship in psychotherapy. I interviewed him on a blustery winter afternoon in 1996, at Beth Israel Medical Center, where he has been engaged in a six-year project in collaboration with J. Christopher Muran, Psychology Chief in the Department of Psychiatry. Their research is currently focused on investigating two important areas of the therapeutic alliance: (1) the examination of the therapeutic alliance over the course of therapy, and (2) the processes involved in repairing ruptures in the therapeutic alliance. Safran and Muran, along with other investigators, report that research supports the proposition that once an alliance is developed, it becomes "both the context and part of the content of therapy" (Horvath 1995). As such, we were eager to engage Dr. Safran regarding his own thoughts concerning the process of an effective therapeutic alliance.

INTERVIEW

Chris Nezu (CN): While reading a recent article written by you and Christopher Muran (Safran and Muran 1995), I thought you seem to be working on the assumption that therapists will have a sensitivity to pick up a rupture that is occurring in the therapeutic alliance and identify certain nuances of client–therapist interaction. It seems that some therapists have more of a natural ability to do this than others. How do you train someone in these skills?

JEREMY SAFRAN (JS): As your question suggests, selection of trainees can be extremely important. It does seem that some individuals take more naturally to the approach than others. However, assuming that you're selecting people with some natural or inherent ability, then the training involves a balance between a structured, didactic approach and working with trainees' exploration of their own issues—how they contribute to the therapy relationship. The difficulty inherent in supervision is that the process involves trying to figure out the right balance between working with people to engage in self-exploratory process versus providing a more structured, didactic approach. Finally, there is a training issue involving another type of balance—the trainee's balance of learning through discovery of his or her own answers versus giving the trainee more concrete answers to questions.

CN: This would require, then, if I put myself in the role of the supervisor, training students in your approach, constantly trying to balance how much I'm picking up the trainee's own difficulties in self-exploration, versus actual didactic training that is reasonably required. This demands a significant degree of decision-making on the part of the supervisor.

JS: Right.

CN: As you describe the psychotherapy relationship, it is evident that you underscore the importance of a therapist being tuned in to her own emotional reactions. Specifically, clinicians probably need to ask themselves how reliably or effectively they can serve as a scientific instrument or participant-observer, or how much they are being reactive to their own interpersonal backgrounds. As a function of this required fine-tuning, is going through personal therapy an important part of the therapist training?

JS: Yes, I think so. I don't believe that this guarantees any-thing—there is a history of people being analyzed in the psycho-analytic tradition, and many people who have undergone this experience are not effective analysts. It is obviously only a part of the training and depends upon other things. I think the process of going through therapy can be useful if it is the right therapist and the right therapy.

CN: What type of therapy should they experience?

JS: By the right therapy, I don't mean a particular brand or orientation of psychotherapy, but that it may be important to be working with the right therapist. Variables such as personality style are so important, so if someone seeks therapy and it ends up being a helpful experience that leads them to look more carefully at themselves, deal with their own issues, and ultimately develop and maintain an increased openness, then I think that can be a useful process.

LISA DELLICARPINNI (LDC): What role do you think supervision plays in complementing individual therapy?

JS: I think that the extent to which this takes place depends upon the particular therapist and supervisor and their relationship. Supervision is analogous to therapy in the sense that one therapist–supervisor dyad may engage in more self-exploration than another. As a supervisor, you have to respect the individual needs of each student and work with them at a level at which they are willing to work—finding the balance. However, having said that, even with those therapists and supervisors who are comfortable engaging in self-exploration in supervision, there is a difference between therapy and supervision.

LDC: How so?

JS: There are important points at which to draw the line and acknowledge the constraints of the relationship. For example, in a therapist–supervisor relationship, the trainee is being evaluated as well as also being the one who is engaging in self-exploration. Given that, where do the people involved mutually agree to draw the line and acknowledge constraints specific to any situation?

CN: That brings us to another question that I wanted to ask you. In speaking with people who have attended your workshops, or read your articles, the question comes up as to how you would define your theoretical orientation.

JS: I've always resisted defining myself.

CN: I know.

JS: I can certainly tell you the ways in which I've been influenced. I went to a behavioral school and was trained in a very behavioral tradition, but at the same time I was receiving clinical training "on the sly" in a more experiential tradition.

CN: Why was your experiential training "on the sly"? Why do you suppose other behavioral colleagues to whom I have spoken have made similar statements and tend to, at least early in their behavioral training, seek additional training "on the sly"?

JS: Your guess is as good as mine. I can say that the people who were teaching when I went to school regarded those traditions that were not behavioral as unscientific, intangible, and devalued them in the same way that some of my experiential colleagues always seemed to devalue traditional behavioral training. Here in New York, where there is a predominance of psychoanalytic professionals, people significantly devalue both behavioral and experiential traditions. I suppose people become threatened by other approaches.

CN: The analogy that comes to mind is the traditional medical model that can be very restrictive or critical toward students who are seeking information concerning alternative approaches to Western medicine. It's surprising how students can be placed in such positions, at a time when options to learning could be open, and critical analysis of many different viewpoints could be exercised.

JS: It's especially ironic when you consider the psychotherapy experience. We often say that we are teaching therapists to be open in order to see another person's perspective and understand their worldview, but my experience is that clinical training often does precisely the opposite.

CN: I've heard many differences of opinion regarding the "ownership" of your orientation to treatment. Some describe you as cognitive-behavioral, others cognitive-interpersonal, others say psychoanalytic or object relations-based, and others describe your work as Sullivanian.

JS: Do these people want to own or disown me?

CN: I tend to frame things positively.

JS: Very strategic. You mentioned Sullivan. I was very influenced by that tradition, not so much in my clinical training, but as an undergraduate. There was something about the interpersonal theory that I really took to. When I started practicing after I earned my Ph.D., I began to write about the interface between Sullivan's work and cognitive approaches as I tried to understand the experience of being a therapist. For example, in my first job I worked with Brian Shaw (who co-authored *The Cognitive Therapy of Depression* with Aaron Beck and trained the cognitive therapists for the NIMH collaborative study on depression), and I really tried to practice the standard cognitive therapy but realized that it just didn't work for me. Now, obviously, cognitive strategies have been shown to be effective and work very well for many therapists in many situations, but somehow, for me, I had difficulty implementing them effectively, because there was something about the sensibility that I just didn't quite have. In the therapy situation, I'd try to change someone's thoughts, and what would happen is . . . the client kind of backed off and it wouldn't work.

CN: It felt as though you were attacking the person?

JS: Exactly. This emerged as very interesting to me, because I was trying to do things a certain way and the strategies were not working. I think that was one of the many variables that influenced me in terms of being more interested in the relationship and the ruptures that can occur in the therapeutic alliance. Actually, my interests go back even earlier than that because, as I mentioned before, I was interested in Sullivan from the very beginning. I remember when I first started conducting therapy, I noted early on that there was something fascinating about those moments when I felt, to use Sullivan's terms, a deterioration in the quality of the communication. I began to get a sense that working with that aspect of treatment really seemed very important. Thus some of it had to do with certain training experiences, and some of it had to do with my own personality. So to go back to your original question of how would I define myself, I suppose that I have resisted defining myself because of the fact that there is certain rigidity to people's need to classify others and classify themselves. That has always bothered me. The other thing is that I have always found it kind of stimulating to be working on the boundary in some way, to never completely be working within just one tradition . . . it gives me something to react against.

CN: I view things from a behavioral, or functional, perspective. It's easy for me to translate, for example, when I look at the therapeutic alliance, to say: here's an example of interpersonal behavior. Or looking at a corrective experience in terms of exposure to distress and response prevention of previously learned coping responses. I can remember making sense out of some of the brief psychodynamic strategies during my own training in this way, so that I might be open to new ideas but at the same time maintain a way or framework from which I could understand how it all worked. What guides your thinking and helps you organize what you accept and what you choose to leave out of your belief system or worldview? That can be a real challenge.

JS: There is no one tradition that provides an orienting framework for me. I include bits and pieces of many different viewpoints.

CN: Has your way of integrating these various viewpoints changed over the years? Are you a different clinician or clinical theorist now than you were five years ago?

JS: I think that in some ways I am a more flexible clinician than I was when the interpersonal process book came out (Safran and Segal 1990). The therapy transcripts in that book probably represent a less flexible therapy than I conduct now. I had a clearer sense then about what was right and what was wrong or what was good versus bad process. I think there's probably a way now in which I'm both more flexible and also in certain ways less disciplined than I was back then. I think that would be a primary difference. To be specific, years ago there was a lot of focus in my work on exploring the client's moment-by-moment experiencing, feeling, awareness of what was interfering with that experience in any way, and a lot of focus on exploring the subtleties of the therapeutic relationship. I suppose that what I have found over time is that too relentless a focus of that kind can really get in the way. You know, it can be really an inhibiting factor or can create problems, so I think that I'm probably much more willing now to just follow clients wherever they're going and sort of work in a roundabout kind of way. I'll sometimes spend a session just talking if I have a sense this is something the client needs to do for one reason or another.

LDC: How do you make those decisions?

JS: Part of it has to do with the way in which I conceptualize the case. Let me give you an example. If I was working with a young man, for instance, who never had the experience of having a father whom he could look up to and model himself after, and part of my conceptualization is that this could be an important part of the growth process for him, I may allow him to use me in that capacity at times. For example, I may be more willing to answer questions and talk about myself than I would be with someone else where I didn't have the same case conceptualization. So, part of it has to do with the case conceptualization and part of it has to do with the subtle feelings or intuitions that I have.

CN: This raises the question, however, regarding how one would know that was an interaction based on the case conceptualization, and therefore the idea of "just talking" may be in the client's best interest, versus the interpersonal response of a therapist, who may never, for example, have had a son with whom he or she could share things.

JS: You're making a good point, and I think that therapists may not realize at the moment why they are doing what they're doing . . . and for reasons that they may not immediately be aware of. That is why there has to be an ongoing willingness on the part of the therapist to explore why we're doing what we're doing. It's important to be open to the possibility that, as a therapist, you are doing something for another reason, whether through personal exploration or feedback from others.

CN: Regarding the way in which you formulate cases, what is your viewpoint about assessment tools in forming case conceptualization? Do you use self-report instruments, or standardized tests? Do you think there is any place for projective measures? What tools do you use to formulate a case conceptualization?

JS: First of all, I think anything that people can use to help them conceptualize a case is good. Personally, I don't use standard psychological instruments and I never found them particularly useful. I rely on what goes on in the therapeutic relationship, and the person's report of what is going on in their life in general, and what has gone on historically. However, I think it's important to distinguish the way in which I work in this respect from the way in which many others work. I place more emphasis on what's happening in the here and now of the therapeutic relationship than many others would. My sense is that any information I get about the client's history and what's happening outside of session is useful, but I don't then try to fit my sense of what is going on in the therapeutic relationship into some kind of frame that I extract from standardized testing information. It's more likely that whatever information I acquire about what's happening outside of therapy or in the past is a kind of background information that is there at some level, but I'm attending most fully to what is happening in the here and now of the therapy relationship. The organization of this information takes place at a somewhat unconscious level, kind of like a pattern-recognition experience. I remember struggling with this question when I was writing the book with Segal, *Interpersonal Process in Cognitive Therapy* (Safran and Segal 1990). At the time, we had a Swiss psychologist, Franz Caspar, working with us on a sabbatical. He was writing a book on case conceptualization. Franz has a very elaborate case conceptualization procedure; he gets it all laid out and nailed down and he was very critical of my tendency to be less formal and more intuitive in the case conceptualization process. And so I struggled with how I could defend a more intuitive case conceptualization. The model that I came up with came from research that has been conducted with expert systems, particularly expert chess players—you know, the difference between the way in which expert chess players work versus computers. The view is that for expert chess players, much of their ability involves a kind of pattern recognition, where they have all the data in front of them, and it is organized by overall pattern.

CN: Sounds almost like a right-hemispheric kind of "Aha—I'm seeing the whole concept" kind of phenomenon.

JS: That's right! And I do think that in terms of the way in which I work, that plays an important role. Unless you have some understanding of what's happening in the here and now of the therapeutic relationship and a way of including this in your formulation, you're inevitably going to have a distorted view of the client. It's important to be very attentive to the current therapeutic relationship and then combine that information with whatever is known about the client's out-of-therapy or past experiences.

Before ending our interview, I provided Dr. Safran with the opportunity to talk about what was important to him. He responded by saying that he was curious about the current conventional wisdom among AABT (Association for the Advancement of Behavior Therapy) members concerning the topics we were discussing. My response was that I believe that scientists and clinicians who call themselves cognitive-behavioral have some differing viewpoints. I related to him the changes in emphasis that I have observed over the years at AABT conventions and the more recent popularity of symposia and workshops that incorporate an acknowledgment of emotional and interpersonal factors, as well as focus on therapist reactions to clients. I shared my own and others' views of a synergy existing between cognitive-behavioral therapies and the type of work he writes about (Kuehlwein and Rosen 1993). To summarize, it is my view that there exist identifiable functions regarding the way individuals think, feel, and behave interpersonally, based largely on what is important to them. It is quite plausible to accept an ethological perspective of understanding interpersonal social relations as survival behaviors and, as such, a type of primary reinforcement. The difficulty has always resided in the demands of science to empirically demonstrate the importance of such variables.

We completed our discussion with a mutual agreement that cognitive-behavioral clinicians probably focus on the therapeutic relationship as an important part of treatment, probably more than most nonbehavioral professionals realize. This is not surprising because behavior therapists have always defined their focus in the here and now and have always viewed reciprocal interpersonal reactions as important tenets of social learning theory.

We thanked Dr. Safran for his openness and willingness to share his views regarding the therapeutic relationship and implications for case conceptualization, treatment, and supervision. The therapeutic relationship appears to hold a transtheoretical importance that has not received the empirical attention it deserves in the literature. Investigations of such complex and meaningful clinical phenomena are not easily constructed or funded. We eagerly await the results of his current research in collaboration with Christopher Muran.

References

Abelson, R. P. (1963). Computer simulation of "hot cognitions." In *Computer Simulations of Personality*, ed. S. Tomkins and S. Messick. New York: Wiley.

—— (1981). Psychological status of the script concept. *American Psychologist* 36:715–729.

Alden, L., and Cappe, R. (1981). Nonassertiveness: Skill deficit or selective self-evaluation? *Behavior Therapy* 12:107–114.

Alexander, F., and French, T. M. (1946). *Psychoanalytic Therapy: Principles and Application.* New York: Ronald.

Alexander, L. B., and Luborsky, L. (1986). The Penn helping alliance scales. In *The Psychotherapeutic Process: A Research Handbook*, ed. L. S. Greenberg and W. M. Pinsof. New York: Guilford.

Anchin, J. C. (1982). Sequence, pattern, and style: integration and treatment implications of some interpersonal concepts. In *Handbook of Interpersonal Psychotherapy*, ed. J. C. Anchin and D. Kiesler, pp. 95–131. New York: Pergamon.

Anderson, J. R., and Bower, G. H. (1973). *Human Associative Memory.* Washington, DC: Winston.

Andrews, J. D., Norcross, J. C., and Halgin, R. P. (1992). Training in psychotherapy integration. In *Handbook of Psychotherapy Integration*, ed. J. C. Norcross and M. R. Goldfried, pp. 563–592. New York: Basic Books.

Arbus, D. (1972). *Diane Arbus*. Millerton, NY: An Aperture Monograph.

Arkowitz, H. (1992). Integrative theories of therapy. In *History of Psychotherapy: A Century of Change*, ed. D. K. Freedheim, H. J. Freudenberger, J. W. Kessler, et al., pp. 261–304. Washington, DC: American Psychiatric Association.

Arkowitz, H., and Hannah, M. T. (1989). Cognitive, behavioral and psychodynamic therapies: Converging or diverging pathways to change? In *Comprehensive Handbook of Cognitive Therapy*, ed. A. Freeman, K. M. Simon, and L. E. Butler, pp. 143–167. New York: Plenum.

Arkowitz, H., Holliday, S., and Hutter, M. (1982). *Depressed women and their husbands: a study of marital interaction and adjustment.* Paper presented at the annual meeting of the Association for the Advancement of Behavior Therapy, Los Angeles, CA, November.

Arnkoff, D. (1980). Psychotherapy from the perspective of cognitive theory. In *Psychotherapy Process*, ed. M. Mahoney, pp. 339–362. New York: Plenum.

———— (1983). Common and specific factors in cognitive therapy. In *Psychotherapy and Patient Relationships*, ed. M. J. Lambert, pp. 85–125. Homewood, IL: Dorsey.

Arnold, M. B. (1960). *Emotion and Personality.* New York: Columbia University Press.

Atthowe, J. M. (1973). Behavior innovation and persistence. *American Psychologist* 28:34–41.

Bacal, H. A., and Newman, K. M. (1990). *Theories of Object Relations: Bridges in Self Psychology.* New York: Columbia University Press.

Balint, M. (1935). Pregenital organization of the libido. In *Primary Love and the Psychoanalytic Techniques.* New York: Liveright.

Bandura, A. (1977). Self-efficacy: towards a unifying theory of behavior change. *Psychological Review* 84:191–215.

———— (1978). The self system in reciprocal determinism. *American Psychologist* 33:344–358.

Barlow, D. H. (1981). On the relation of clinical research to clinical practice: current issues, new directions. *Journal of Consulting and Clinical Psychology* 49:142–155.

Barlow, D. H., and Hersen, M. (1984). *Single Case Experimental Designs: Strategies for Studying Behavior Change*, 2nd ed. New York: Pergamon.

Baron, R. M. (1980). Contrasting approaches to social knowing: an ecological perspective. *Personality and Social Psychology* 6:591–600.

Bartlett, F. (1932). *Remembering: A Study in Experimental and Social Psychology*. London and New York: Cambridge University Press.

Batchelor, S. (1979). *A Guide to the Bodhisattva's Way of Life*. English translation of Shantideva's *Bodhisattvacharyavatara*. New Delhi: Indraprastha Press.

Beck, A. T. (1976). *Cognitive Therapy and the Emotional Disorders*. New York: International Universities Press.

———— (1983). Cognitive therapy of depression: new perspectives. In *Treatment of Depression: Old Controversies and New Approaches*, ed. P. J. Clayton and J. E. Barrett. New York: Raven.

Beck, A. T., Rush, A., Shaw, B., and Emery, G. (1979). *Cognitive Therapy of Depression*. New York: Guilford.

Bedrosian, R. C. (1981). Ecological factors in cognitive therapy: the use of significant others. In *New Directions in Cognitive Therapy*, ed. G. Emery, S. D. Hollon, and R. C. Bedrosian, pp. 239–254. New York: Guilford.

Beebe, B. (1985). Mother–infant mutual influence and precursors of self and object representations. In *Empirical Studies of Psychoanalytic Theories*, vol. 2, ed. J. Masling. Hillsdale, NJ: Lawrence Erlbaum.

Beidel, D. C., and Turner, S. M. (1986). A critique of the theoretical bases of cognitive-behavioral theories and therapy. *Clinical Psychology Review* 6:177–197.

Beier, E. G. (1966). *The Silent Language of Psychotherapy: Social Reinforcement of Unconscious Processes*. New York: Pergamon.

Benjamin, L. S. (1974). Structural analysis of social behavior. *Psychological Review* 81:392–425.

Bergin, A. E. (1970). The deterioration effect: a reply to Braucht. *Journal of Abnormal Psychology* 75:300–302.

Bergin, A. E., and Garfield, S. L., eds. (1994). *Psychotherapy and Behavior Change*, 4th ed. New York: Wiley.

Bernstein, R. (1983). *Beyond Objectivism and Relativism: Science, Hermeneutics and Praxis*. Philadelphia: University of Pennsylvania Press.

———— (1993). *The New Constellation*. Cambridge, MA: MIT Press.

Beutler, L. E. (1991). Have all won and must all have prizes? Revisiting Luborsky et al.'s verdict. *Journal of Consulting and Clinical Psychology* 59:226–232.

Beutler, L. E., and Clarkin, J. (1990). *Systematic Treatment Selection*. New York: Brunner/Mazel.

Beutler, L. E., Crago, M., and Arizmendi, T. G. (1986). Therapist variables in psychotherapy process and outcome. In *Handbook of Psychotherapy and Behavior Change*, ed. S. L. Garfield and A. E. Bergin, 3rd ed., pp. 257–310. New York: Wiley.

Beutler, L. E., and Harwood, T. M. (1995). Prescriptive psychotherapies. *Applied and Preventive Psychology* 4:89–100.

Beutler, L. E., and Hodgson, A. B. (1993). Prescriptive psychotherapy. In *Comprehensive Handbook of Psychotherapy Integration*, ed. G. Stricker and J. R. Gold, pp. 151–163. New York: Plenum.

Bevan, W. (1991). Contemporary psychology: a tour inside the onion. *American Psychologist* 46:475–483.

Bhaskar, R. (1979). *The Possibility of Naturalism*. Brighton, England: Harvester.

Bibring, E. (1937). Therapeutic results of psychoanalysis. *International Journal of Psycho-Analysis* 18:170–189.

Biran, M. (1988). Cognitive and exposure treatment for agoraphobia: reexamination of the outcome research. *Journal of Cognitive Psychotherapy: An International Quarterly* 2:165–178.

Blatt, S. J. (1991). *What can and cannot be integrated between dynamic-interpersonal and cognitive-behavioral approaches to depression*. Paper presented at the annual Society for Psychotherapy Integration Conference, London, England, June.

Bloom, A. (1987). *The Closing of the American Mind*. New York: Simon & Schuster.

Bollas, C. (1989). *Forces of Destiny: Psychoanalysis and Human Idiom*. London: Free Association Books.

Bordin, E. (1979). The generalizability of the psychoanalytic concept of the working alliance. *Psychotherapy: Theory, Research, and Practice* 16:252–260.

——— (1994). Theory and research in the therapeutic working alliance: new directions. In *The Working Alliance: Theory, Research, and Practice*, pp. 13–37. New York: Wiley.

Borkevec, T., and Sides, J. (1979). The contribution of relaxation and expectancy to fear reduction. *Behaviour Research and Therapy* 17:529–540.

Bower, G. H. (1978). Contacts of cognitive psychology with social learning theory. *Cognitive Therapy and Research* 3:249–262.

——— (1981). Mood and memory. *American Psychologist* 36:129–148.

Bower, G. H., and Mayer, J. D. (1985). Failure to replicate mood-dependent retrieval. *Bulletin of the Psychonomic Society* 23:30–42.

Bowers, K. S., and Meichenbaum, D., eds. (1984). *The Unconscious Reconsidered.* New York: Wiley.

Bowlby, J. (1969). *Attachment and Loss: Vol. 1. Attachment.* New York: Basic Books.

——— (1973). *Attachment and Loss: Vol. 2. Separation, Anxiety, and Anger.* New York: Basic Books.

——— (1980). *Attachment and Loss: Vol. 3. Loss: Sadness and Depression.* London: Hogarth.

Bretherton, I. (1985). Attachment theory: retrospect and prospect. In *Monographs of the Society for Research in Child Development*, 209, vol. 50, nos. 1–2. Chicago: University of Chicago Press.

Breuer, J., and Freud, S. (1895). Studies on hysteria. *Standard Edition* 2:1–170.

Brewer, W. F., and Nakamura, G. V. (1984). The nature and functions of schemas. In *Handbook of Social Cognition*, ed. R. S. Wyer and T. K. Srull, pp. 119–160. Hillsdale, NJ: Lawrence Erlbaum.

Broadbent, D. E. (1958). *Perception and Communication.* New York: Pergamon.

Buber, M. (1958). *I and Thou*, trans. R. Gregor Smith, 2nd ed. New York: Scribner.

——— (1973). *Meetings*, trans. M. Friedman. LaSalle, IL: Open Court.

Bucci, W. (1988). Converging evidence for emotional structures: theory and method. In *Psychoanalytic Process Research Strategies*, ed. H. Dahl, H. Kächele, and H. Thomä, pp. 29–49. New York: Springer.

Butler, S. F., and Strupp, H. H. (1986). Specific and nonspecific factors in psychotherapy: a problematic paradigm for psychotherapy research. *Psychotherapy* 23:30–40.

Cacioppo, J. T., Glass, C. R., and Merluzzi, T. V. (1979). Self-statements and self-evaluations: a cognitive response analysis of heterosocial anxiety. *Cognitive Therapy and Research* 3:249–262.

Cantor, N., and Mischel, W. (1977). Traits as prototypes: effects on recognition memory. *Journal of Personality and Social Psychology* 35:38–48.

Carson, R. C. (1969). *Interaction Concepts of Personality*. Chicago: Aldine.

——— (1982). Self-fulfilling prophecy, maladaptive behavior, and psychotherapy. In *Handbook of Interpersonal Psychotherapy*, ed. J. C. Anchin and D. J. Kiesler, pp. 64–77. New York: Pergamon.

Cashdan, S. (1973). *Interactional Psychotherapy: Stages and Strategies in Behavioral Change*. New York: Grune & Stratton.

——— (1988). *Object Relations Therapy*. New York: Norton.

Caston, J., Goldman, R., and McClure, M. M. (1987). The immediate effects of psychoanalytic interventions. In *The Psychoanalytic Process: Theory, Clinical Observation, and Empirical Research*, ed. J. Weiss, H. Sampson, and the Mount Zion Psychotherapy Research Group, pp. 277–298. New York: Guilford.

Chapman, A. H. (1978). *The Treatment Techniques of Harry Stack Sullivan*. New York: Brunner/Mazel.

Chassan, J. B. (1979). *Research Design in Clinical Psychology and Psychiatry*, 2nd ed. New York: Irvington.

Cherry, E. C. (1953). Some experiments on the recognition of speech, with one and with two ears. *Journal of the Acoustical Society of America* 25:975–979.

Chrzanowski, G. (1982). Interpersonal formulations of psychotherapy: a contemporary model. In *Handbook of Interpersonal Psychotherapy*, ed. J. C. Anchin and D. J. Kiesler. New York: Pergamon.

Cohen, C. E. (1981). Person categories and social perception: testing some boundaries of the processing effects of prior knowledge. *Journal of Personality and Social Psychology* 40:441–452.

Cohen, M., ed. (1961). *The Philosophy of John Stuart Mill.* New York: Modern Library.

Collins, A. M., and Loftus, E. F. (1975). A spreading activation theory of semantic processing. *Psychological Review* 82:407–428.

Collins, W. D., and Messer, S. B. (1988). *Transporting the plan diagnosis method to a different setting: reliability, stability, adaptability.* Paper presented to the Annual Conference of the Society for Psychotherapy Research, Santa Fe, NM, June.

——— (1991). Extending the plan formulation method to an object relations perspective: reliability, stability and adaptability. *Psychological Assessment: A Journal of Consulting Clinical Psychology* 3:75–81.

Conrad, C. (1974). Context effects in sentence comprehension: a study of the subjective lexicon. *Memory and Cognition* 2:130–138.

Cook, T. D. (1985). Postpositivist critical multiplism. In *Social Science and Social Policy*, ed. R. L. Scotland and M. M. Marks, pp. 21–62. Beverly Hills, CA: Sage.

Corteen, R. S., and Dunn, D. (1974). Shock associated words in a nonattended message: a text for momentary awareness. *Journal of Experimental Psychology* 102:1143–1144.

Corteen, R. S., and Wood, B. (1972). Autonomic responses to shock associated words. *Journal of Experimental Psychology* 94:308–313.

Coyne, J. C. (1976). Depression and the response of others. *Journal of Abnormal Psychology* 90:286–297.

——— (1982). A critique of cognitions as causal entities with particular reference to depression. *Cognition Therapy and Research* 6:3–13.

Coyne, J. C., and Gotlib, I. H. (1983). The role of cognition in depression: a critical appraisal. *Psychological Bulletin* 94:472–505.

——— (1986). Studying the role of cognition in depression: well-trodden paths and cul-de-sacs. *Cognitive Therapy and Research* 10:695–705.

Craighead, W. E., Kimball, W. H., and Rehak, P. J. (1979). Mood changes, physiological response, and self-statements during social rejection imagery. *Journal of Consulting and Clinical Psychology* 47:385–396.

Curtis, J. T., Silberschatz, G., Sampson, H. and Weiss, J. (1994). The plan formulation method. *Psychotherapy Research* 4:197–207.

Dawes, R. M. (1976). Shallow psychology. In *Cognition and Social Behavior*, ed. J. S. Carroll and J. W. Payne, pp. 3–11. Hillsdale, NJ: Lawrence Erlbaum.

Dawson, M. C., and Schell, A. M. (1982). Electrodermal responses to attended and nonattended significant stimuli during dichotic listening. *Journal of Experimental Psychology: Human Perception and Performance* 8:315–324.

Derogatis, L. R. (1977). SCL-90 administration, scoring and procedure manual. Baltimore: Johns Hopkins University School of Medicine.

Derry, P. A., and Kuiper, N. A. (1981). Schematic processing and self-referents in clinical depression. *Journal of Abnormal Psychology* 90:286–297.

Deutsch, J. A., and Deutsch, D. (1963). Attention: some theoretical considerations. *Psychology Review* 70:80–90.

Dixon, F. (1971). *Subliminal Perception: The Nature of Controversy*. New York: McGraw-Hill.

Dixon, N. (1981). *Preconscious Processing*. New York: Wiley.

Dollard, J., and Miller, N. E. (1950). *Personality and Psychotherapy: An Analysis in Terms of Learning, Thinking and Culture*. New York: McGraw-Hill.

Eagle, M. N. (1984). *Recent Developments in Psychoanalysis*. New York: McGraw-Hill.

——— (1987). The psychoanalytic and the cognitive unconscious. In *Theories of the Unconscious and Theories of the Self*, ed. R. Stern, pp. 155–190. Hillsdale, NJ: Analytic.

Ekman, P., ed. (1972). *Darwin and Facial Expression: A Century of Research in Review*. New York: Academic.

Ekman, P., and Friesen, W. V. (1975). *Unmasking the Face*. Englewood Cliffs, NJ: Prentice-Hall.

Elkin, I., Shea, T., Watkins, J., et al. (1989). NIMH treatment of depression collaborative research program: I: general effectiveness of treatments. *Archives of General Psychiatry* 46:971–982.

Elliott, R. (1984). A discovery oriented approach to significant change events in psychotherapy: interpersonal process recall and comprehensive process analysis. In *Patterns of Change: Intensive Analysis*, ed. L. N. Rice and L. S. Greenberg, pp. 249–286. New York: Guilford.

Elliott, R., and Anderson, C. (1994). Simplicity and complexity in psychotherapy research. In *Psychotherapy Research: Assessing and Redirecting the Tradition*, ed. R. L. Russell, pp. 65–113. New York: Guilford.

Ellis, A. (1962). *Reason and Emotion in Psychotherapy*. New York: Stuart.

Ellis, A., and Greiger, R. (1977). *Handbook of Rational-Emotional Therapy*. New York: Springer.

Erdelyi, M. H. (1985). *Psychoanalysis: Freud's Cognitive Psychology*. San Francisco: Freeman.

Fairbairn, W. R. D. (1952). *Psychoanalytic Studies of the Personality*. London: Tavistock and Routledge and Kegan Paul.

Fensterheim, H., and Raw, S. D. (1996). Psychotherapy research is not psychotherapy practice. *Clinical Psychology: Science and Practice* 3:168–171.

Ferenczi, S. (1931). Child analysis in the analysis of adults. In *Final Contributions to the Problems and Methods of Psychoanalysis*, pp. 126–142. London: Karnac.

Feyerabend, P. K. (1962). Explanation, reduction, and empiricism. In *Minnesota Studies in the Philosophy of Science*, vol. III, ed. H. Feigl and G. Maxwell. Minneapolis: University of Minnesota Press.

———— (1975). *Against Method. An Outline of an Anarchistic Theory of Knowledge*. London: Verso.

———— (1987). *Farewell to Reason*. London: Verso.

Fiske, S. T., and Linville, P. W. (1980). What does the schema concept buy us? *Personality and Social Psychology Bulletin* 6:543–557.

Folkman, S., Schaefer, C., and Lazarus, R. (1979). Cognitive processes as mediators of stress and coping. In *Human Stress and Cognition: An Information Processing Approach*, ed. V. Hamilton and D. Warburton, pp. 265–298. Chichester: Wiley.

Foreman, S. A., and Marmar, C. R. (1985). The therapist actions that address initially poor therapeutic alliances in psychotherapy. *American Journal of Psychiatry* 142:922–926.

Foucault, M. (1967). *Madness and Civilization*. London: Tavistock.

Frances, A., Clarkin, J., and Perry, S. (1984). *Differential Therapeutics in Psychiatry*. New York: Brunner/Mazel.

Frank, J. D., and Frank, J. B. (1991). *Persuasion and Healing: A*

Comparative Study of Psychotherapy. Baltimore: Johns Hopkins University Press.

Frank, K. A. (1993). Action, insight, and working through: outlines of an integrative approach. *Psychoanalytic Dialogues* 3:535–578.

Freud, S. (1896). The aetiology of hysteria. *Standard Edition* 3:187–221, 1963.

Gadamer, H. (1980). *Dialogue and Dialectic*, trans. P. C. Smith. New Haven: Yale University Press.

Gandhi, M. K. (1957). *The Story of My Experience with Truth*. Boston: Beacon.

Garfield, S. L. (1992). Eclectic psychotherapy: a common factors approach. In *Handbook of Psychotherapy Integration*, ed. J. C. Norcross and M. R. Goldfried, pp. 169–210. New York: Basic Books.

———— (1994). Eclecticism and integration in psychotherapy: developments and issues. *Clinical Psychology: Science and Practice* 1:123–137.

Gaston, L., and Marmar, C. R. (1990). Reliability and criterion-related validity of the California Psychotherapy Alliance Scales—Patient Version. *Psychological Assessment* 3:63–74.

Geertz, C. (1973). *Interpretation of Cultures*. New York: Basic Books.

———— (1983). *Local Knowledge: Further Essays in Interpretive Anthropology*. New York: Basic Books.

Gendlin, E. T. (1962). *Experiencing and the Creation of Meaning*. New York: Free Press.

———— (1978). *Focusing*. New York: Bantam.

———— (1991). On emotion in therapy. In *Emotion, Psychotherapy and Change*, ed. J. D. Safran and L. S. Greenberg. New York: Guilford.

Gibson, J. J. (1966). *The Senses Considered as Perception Systems*. Boston: Houghton Mifflin.

———— (1979). *The Ecological Approach to Visual Perception*. Boston: Houghton Mifflin.

Gill, M. M. (1976). Metapsychology is not psychology. In *Psychology Versus Metapsychology: Essays in Memory of George S. Klein*, ed. M. M. Gill and P. S. Holzman. New York: International Universities Press.

——— (1982). *Analysis of Transference I: Theory and Technique.* New York: International Universities Press.

Gill, M. M., and Hoffman, I. Z. (1982). A method of studying the analysis of aspects of the patient's experience of the relationship in psychoanalysis and psychotherapy. *Journal of the American Psychoanalytic Association* 30:137–167.

Glass, C. R., Merluzzi, T. V., Biever, J. L., and Larsen, K. M. (1982). Cognitive assessment of social anxiety: development and validation of a self-statement questionnaire. *Cognitive Therapy and Research* 6:37–55.

Goldfried, M. R. (1979). Anxiety reduction through cognitive-behavioral intervention. In *Cognitive-Behavioral Interventions*, vol. 2, ed. P. C. Kendall and S. D. Hollon. New York: Academic.

——— (1980). Toward delineation of therapeutic change principles. *American Psychologist* 35:991–999.

——— (1982). Resistance and clinical behavior therapy. In *Resistance: Psychodynamic and Behavioral Approaches*, ed. P. L. Wachtel, pp. 95–114. New York: Plenum.

——— (1991). Research issues in psychotherapy integration. *Journal of Psychotherapy Integration* 1:5–25.

Goldfried, M. R., and Davison, G. C. (1976). *Clinical Behavior Therapy.* New York: Holt, Rinehart and Winston.

——— (1994). *Clinical Behavior Therapy.* New York: Wiley.

Goldfried, M. R., Padawer, N., and Robins, C. (1984). Social anxiety and the semantic structure of heterosocial interaction. *Journal of Abnormal Psychology* 93:87–97.

Goldfried, M. R., and Robins, C. (1983). Self-schemas, cognitive bias, and the processing of therapeutic experiences. In *Advances in Cognitive Behavioral Research and Therapy*, vol. 2, ed. P. C. Kendall. New York: Academic.

Goldfried, M. R., and Safran, J. D. (1986). Future directions in psychotherapy integration. In *Handbook of Eclectic Psychotherapy*, ed. J. C. Norcross, pp. 463–483. New York: Brunner/Mazel.

Goldfried, M. R., and Wolfe, B. E. (1996). Psychotherapy practice and research: repairing a strained alliance. *American Psychologist* 51:1007–1016.

Goldstein, A. P., Heller, K., and Sechrest, L. (1966). *Psychotherapy and the Psychology of Behavior Change*. New York: Wiley.

Gray, J. A., and Wedderburn, A. A. (1960). Grouping strategies with simultaneous stimuli. *Quarterly of the Journal of Experimental Psychology* 12:180–184.

Greenberg, J. R. (1991). Countertransference and reality. *Psychoanalytic Dialogues* 1(1):52–73.

Greenberg, J. R., and Mitchell, S. A. (1983). *Object Relations in Psychoanalytic Theory*. Cambridge, MA: Harvard University Press.

Greenberg, L. S. (1979). Resolving splits: the two-chair technique. *Psychotherapy: Theory, Research, and Practice* 16:310–318.

———— (1984a). A task analysis of intrapersonal conflict resolution. In *Patterns of Change: Intensive Analysis of Psychotherapy Process*, ed. L. N. Rice and L. S. Greenberg, pp. 67–123. New York: Guilford.

———— (1984b). Task analysis: the general approach. In *Patterns of Change*, ed. L. N. Rice and L. S. Greenberg, pp. 124–148. New York: Guilford.

———— (1986). Change process research. *Journal of Consulting and Clinical Psychology* 54:4–11.

Greenberg, L. S., Elliott, R. K., and Lietaer, G. (1994). Research on experiential psychotherapies. In *Handbook of Psychotherapy and Behavior Change*, ed. A. Bergin and S. Garfield, pp. 509–542. New York: Wiley.

Greenberg, L. S., and Pinsof, W. M. (1986). *The Psychotherapeutic Process: A Research Handbook*. New York: Guilford.

Greenberg, L. S., Rice, L. N., and Elliott, R. (1994). *Process-Experiential Therapy: Facilitating Emotional Change*. New York: Guilford.

Greenberg, L. S., and Safran, J. D. (1980). Encoding, information processing and cognitive behaviour therapy. *Canadian Psychologist* 21:59–66.

———— (1981). Encoding and cognitive therapy: changing what clients attend to. *Psychotherapy: Theory, Research, and Practice* 18:163–169.

———— (1984a). Hot cognition: emotion coming in from the cold: a reply to Rachman and Mahoney. *Cognitive Therapy and Research* 8:591–598.

——— (1984b). Integrating affect and cognition: a perspective on therapeutic change. *Cognitive Therapy and Research* 8:559–578.

——— (1986a). *Emotion in Psychotherapy.* New York: Guilford.

——— (1986b). Hot cognition and psychotherapy process: an information-processing/ecological perspective. In *Advances in Cognitive-Behavioral Research and Therapy*, vol. 5, ed. P. C. Kendall, pp. 143–177. New York: Academic.

——— (1987). *Emotion in Psychotherapy: Affect, Cognition and the Process of Change.* New York: Guilford.

——— (1989). Emotion in psychotherapy. *American Psychologist* 44:19–29.

Greenson, R. R. (1967). *The Technique and Practice of Psychoanalysis*, vol. 1. New York: International Universities Press.

Guidano, V. F. (1987). *Complexity of the Self: A Developmental Approach to Psychopathology and Therapy.* New York: Guilford.

——— (1991). Affective change events in a cognitive therapy system approach. In *Emotion, Psychotherapy and Change*, ed. J. D. Safran and L. S. Greenberg, pp. 50–80. New York: Guilford.

Guidano, V. F., and Liotti, G. (1983). *Cognitive Processes and Emotional Disorders.* New York: Guilford.

Guntrip, H. (1969). *Schizoid Phenomena: Object Relations and the Self.* New York: International Universities Press.

Habermas, J. (1979). *Communication and the Evolution of Society*, trans. T. McCarthy. Boston: Beacon.

Hanson, N. R. (1958). *Patterns of Discovery.* Cambridge: Cambridge University Press.

Harvey, A. (1988). *Love's Fire: Re-creations of Rumi.* Ithaca, NY: Meeramma.

Hasher, L., and Zacks, R. T. (1984). Automatic processing of fundamental information: the case frequency of occurrence. *American Psychologist* 38:1372–1388.

Hayek, F. A. (1978). *New Studies in Philosophy, Politics, Economics and the History of Ideas.* Chicago: University of Chicago Press.

Haynal, A. (1988). *Controversies in Psychoanalytic Method.* New York: New York University Press.

Hegel, G. W. F. (1910). *The Phenomenology of Mind.* London: George Allen and Unwin.

Henry, W. P., Schacht, T. E., and Strupp, H. H. (1986). Structural analysis of social behavior: application to a study of interpersonal process in differential psychotherapeutic outcome. *Journal of Consulting and Clinical Psychology* 54:27–31.

———— (1990). Patient and therapist introject, interpersonal process, and differential psychotherapy outcome. *Journal of Consulting and Clinical Psychology* 58(6):768–774.

Higgins, E. T. (1987). Self discrepancy: a theory relating self and affect. *Psychological Review* 3:319–340.

Hill, C., and Safran, J. D. (1994). Assessing interpersonal schemas: anticipated responses of significant others. *Journal of Social and Clinical Psychology* 13:366–379.

Hoffman, I. Z. (1991). Discussion: toward a social-constructivist view of the psychoanalytic situation. *Psychoanalytic Dialogues* 1(1):74–105.

Hollon, S. D., and Beck, A. T. (1979). Cognitive therapy of depression. In *Cognitive-Behavioral Interventions: Theory, Research and Procedures*, ed. P. C. Kendall and S. D. Hollon. New York: Academic.

Holt, R. R. (1976). Drive or wish? A reconsideration of the psychoanalytic theory of motivation. In *Psychology Versus Metapsychology: Essays in Memory of George S. Klein*, ed. M. M. Gill and P. S. Holzman. New York: International Universities Press.

Horney, K. (1945). *Our Inner Conflicts*. New York: Norton.

Hornstein, G. A. (1993). Freud is not the Dilthey of psychology (at least not in America). *American Psychologist* 48:585–586.

Horowitz, M. J. (1979). *States of Mind*. New York: Plenum.

———— (1988). *Introduction to Psychodynamics: A New Synthesis*. New York: Basic Books.

Horowitz, M. J., Marmar, C., Krupnick, J., et al. (1984). *Personality Styles and Brief Psychotherapy*. New York: Basic Books.

Horvath, A. O. (1995). Therapeutic relationship: from transference to alliance. *In Session: Psychotherapy in Practice* 1:7–18.

Horvath, A. O., and Greenberg, L. (1989). Development and validation of the working alliance inventory. *Journal of Counseling Psychology* 36:223–233.

Horvath, A. O., and Symonds, B. D. (1991). Relation between working alliance and outcome in psychotherapy: a meta-analysis. *Journal of Counseling Psychology* 38:139–149.

Hoshmand, A. L., and Polkinghorne, D. E. (1992). Redefining the science-practice relationship and professional training. *American Psychologist* 47:55–66.

Houts, A. C. (1989). Contributions of the psychology of science to metascience: a call for explorers. In *Psychology of Science: Contributions to Metascience*, ed. W. R. Shadish, R. A. Neimeyer, and A. C. Houts, pp. 47–88. Cambridge: Cambridge University Press.

Hudgins, M. K., and Kiesler, D. J. (1987). Individual experiential psychotherapy: an analogue validation of the intervention module of psychodynamic doubling. *Psychotherapy* 24:245–255.

Hudson, L. (1972). *The Cult of the Fact.* New York: Harper Torchbooks.

Izard, C. E. (1977). *Human Emotions.* New York: Plenum.

Jacobson, N. S. (1989). The therapist–client relationship in cognitive behavior therapy: implications for treating depression. *Journal of Cognitive Psychotherapy* 3:85–96.

———— (1994). Behavior therapy and psychotherapy integration. *Journal of Psychotherapy Integration* 4:105–119.

James, W. (1890). *The Principles of Psychology.* New York: Holt.

Janet, P. (1907). *The Major Symptoms of Hysteria.* New York: Hafner, 1965.

Jensen, J. P., Bergin, A. E., and Greaves, D. W. (1990). The meaning of eclecticism: new survey and analysis of components. *Professional Psychology* 21:124–130.

Johnson-Laird, P. N., Herrmann, D. J., and Chaffin, F. (1984). Only connections: a critique of semantic networks. *Psychological Bulletin* 96:292–315.

Kahn, J., Coyne, J. C., and Margolin, G. (1985). Depression and marital agreement: the social construction of despair. *Journal of Social and Personal Relationships* 2:447–461.

Kahneman, D. (1973). *Attention and Effort.* Englewood Cliffs, NJ: Prentice-Hall.

Kazdin, A. E. (1982). *Single-case Research Designs: Methods for Clinical and Applied Settings.* New York: Oxford University Press.

———— (1986). Comparative outcome studies of psychotherapy: methodological issues and strategies. *Journal of Consulting and Clinical Psychology* 54:95–105.

Kelly, G. A. (1955). *The Psychology of Personal Constructs*. New York: Norton.

Kelly, T., and Strupp, H. (1992). Patient and therapist values in psychotherapy. *Journal of Consulting and Clinical Psychology* 60:34–40.

Kendall, P. C., and Bemis, K. M. (1984). Thought and action in psychotherapy: the cognitive-behavioral approaches. In *Handbook of Clinical Psychology*, ed. M. Hersen, A. E. Kazdin, and A. Bellack. New York: Pergamon.

Kendall, P. C., and Hollon, S. D., eds. (1981). *Assessment Strategies for Cognitive-Behavioral Interventions*. New York: Academic.

Kernberg, O. (1976). *Object Relations Theory and Clinical Psychoanalysis*. New York: Jason Aronson.

Kiesler, D. J. (1966). Some myths of psychotherapy research and the search for a paradigm. *Psychological Bulletin* 65:110–136.

——— (1982a). Confronting the client–therapist relationship in psychotherapy. In *Handbook of Interpersonal Psychotherapy*, ed. J. C. Anchin and D. J. Kiesler, pp. 274–295. New York: Pergamon.

——— (1982b). Interpersonal theory for personality and psychotherapy. In *Handbook of Interpersonal Psychotherapy*, ed. J. C. Anchin and D. J. Kiesler. New York: Pergamon.

——— (1983). The 1982 interpersonal circle: a taxonomy for complementarity in human transactions. *Psychological Review* 90:185–214.

——— (1986). Interpersonal methods of diagnosis and treatment. In *Psychiatry*, ed. J. O. Cavenar, pp. 1–23. Philadelphia: Lippincott.

——— (1987). Research manual for the Input Message Inventory. Palo Alto, CA: Consulting Psychologist Press.

——— (1988). *Therapeutic Metacommunication: Therapist Impact Disclosure as Feedback in Psychotherapy*. Palo Alto, CA: Consulting Psychologist Press.

Kiesler, D. J., Bernstein, A. J., and Anchin, J. C. (1976). *Interpersonal Communication, Relationship and the Behavior Therapies*. Richmond, VA: Virginia Commonwealth University.

Kiesler, D. J., and Watkins, L. M. (1989). Interpersonal complementarity and the therapeutic alliance: a study of relationship in psychotherapy. *Psychotherapy* 26:183–194.

Kimble, G. A. (1984). Psychology's two cultures. *American Psychologist* 39:833–839.

Kivlighan, D. M., and Schmitz, P. J. (1992). Counselor technical activity in cases with improving working alliances and continuing-poor working alliances. *Journal of Counseling Psychology* 39:32–38.

Klein, G. S. (1976). *Psychoanalytic Theory: An Exploration of Essentials.* New York: International Universities Press.

Klein, M., Mathieu, P., Gendlin, E. T., and Kiesler, D. (1969). *The Experiencing Scale.* Madison, WI: Wisconsin Psychiatric Institute.

Koch, S. (1981). The nature and limits of psychological knowledge: lessons of a century qua "science." *American Psychologist* 36:257–269.

Kohut, H. (1984). *How Does Analysis Cure?* ed. A. Goldberg and P. Stephansky. Chicago: University of Chicago Press.

Kostandov, E., and Arzamanov, Y. (1977). Averaged cortical evoked potentials to recognized and non-recognized verbal stimuli. *Acta Neurobiologiae Experimentalis* 37:311–324.

Krantz, S. E. (1985). When depressive cognitions reflect negative realities. *Cognitive Therapy and Research,* 9:595–610.

Krasner, L., and Houts, A. C. (1984). A study of the "value" systems of behavioral scientists. *American Psychologist* 39:840–850.

Kuehlwein, K. T., and Rosen, H., eds. (1993). *Cognitive Psychotherapies in Action: Evolving Innovative Practice.* San Francisco: Jossey-Bass.

Kuhn, T. (1970). *The Structure of Scientific Revolutions,* 2nd ed. Chicago: University of Chicago Press.

Kuiper, N. A., and Olinger, L. J. (1986). Dysfunctional attitudes and a self-worth contingency model of depression. In *Advances in Cognitive-Behavioral Research and Therapy,* ed. P. C. Kendall, pp. 115–142. Orlando, FL: Academic Press.

LaBerge, D. (1981). Automatic information processing: a review. In *Attention and Performance,* vol. 9, ed. J. Long and A. Baddeley, pp. 173–186. Hillsdale, NJ: Lawrence Erlbaum.

Lacan, J. (1964). *The Four Fundamental Concepts of Psychoanalysis,* ed. J. A. Miller, trans. A. Sheridan. New York: Norton.

Lakatos, I. (1978). The methodology of scientific research programs. In *Philosophical Papers,* vol. I. Cambridge: Cambridge University Press.

Lambert, M. J. (1986). Implications of psychotherapy outcome research for eclectic psychotherapy. In *Handbook of Eclectic Psychotherapy*, ed. J. C. Norcross, pp. 536–561. New York: Brunner/Mazel.

——— (1989). The individual therapist's contribution to psychotherapy process and outcome. *Clinical Psychology Review* 9:469–485.

Lambert, M. J., ed. (1983). *Psychotherapy and Patient Relationships.* Homewood, IL: Dorsey.

Lambert, M. J., Shapiro, D. A., and Bergin, A. E. (1986). The effectiveness of psychotherapy. In *Handbook of Psychotherapy and Behavior Change*, ed. L. Garfield and A. E. Bergin, 3rd ed., pp. 157–216. New York: Wiley.

Landau, R. J., and Goldfried, M. R. (1981). The assessment of schemata: a unifying framework for cognitive, behavioral and traditional assessment. In *Assessment Strategies for Cognitive Behavioral Interventions*, ed. P. C. Kendall and S. D. Hollon, pp. 363–399. New York: Academic.

Lang, P. J. (1977). Imagery and therapy. *Behavior Therapy* 8:862–886.

——— (1983). Cognition in emotion: concept and action. In *Emotion, Cognition and Behavior*, ed. C. Izard, J. Kagan, and R. Zajonc, pp. 192–226. London and New York: Cambridge University Press.

——— (1985). The cognitive psychopathology of emotion, fear and anxiety. In *Anxiety and the Anxiety Disorders*, ed. A. Tuma and J. Maser. Hillsdale, NJ: Lawrence Erlbaum.

Lang, P. J., Levin, D., Miller, G., and Kozak, M. (1983). Fear behavior, fear imagery, and the psychophysiology of emotion: the problem of affective response integration. *Journal of Abnormal Psychology* 92:276–306.

Langs, R. (1975). Therapeutic misalliances. *International Journal of Psychoanalytic Psychotherapy* 4:77–105.

Lapoint, K. A., and Harrel, T. H. (1978). Thoughts and feelings: correlational relationships and cross-situational consistence. *Cognitive Therapy and Research* 2:311–322.

Lazarus, A. A. (1980). Psychotherapy process. *Special Issue of Cognitive Therapy and Research*, ed. M. Goldfried, 4:269–306.

——— (1992). Multimodal therapy: technical eclecticism with minimal integration. In *Handbook of Psychotherapy Integration*, ed. J. C. Norcross and M. R. Goldfried, pp. 231–263. New York: Basic Books.

——— (1996). The utility and futility of combining treatments in psychotherapy. *Clinical Psychology: Science and Practice* 3:59–68.

Lazarus, A. A., Beutler, L. E., and Norcross, J. C. (1992). The future of technical eclecticism. *Psychotherapy* 29:11–20.

Lazarus, A. A., and Messer, S. B. (1991). Does chaos prevail? An exchange on technical eclecticism and assimilative integration. *Journal of Psychotherapy Integration* 1:143–158.

Lazarus, R. S. (1984). On the primacy of cognition. *American Psychologist* 39:124–129.

Lazarus, R. S., Coyne, J., and Folkman, S. (1982). Cognition, emotion and motivation: the doctoring of Humpty-Dumpty. In *Psychological Stress and Psychopathology*, ed. R. W. J. Neufeld. New York: McGraw-Hill.

Leary, T. (1957). *Interpersonal Diagnosis of Personality*. New York: Ronald.

Levenson, E. (1983). *The Ambiguity of Change*. New York: Basic Books.

Leventhal, H. (1979). A perceptual motor processing model of emotion. In *Advances in the Study of Communication and Affect: Perception of Emotion in Self and Others*, vol. 5, ed. P. Pliner, K. R. Blankstein, and J. M. Spigel. New York: Plenum.

——— (1982). The integration of emotion and cognition: a view from the perceptual-motor theory of emotion. In *Affect and Cognition*, ed. M. S. Clarke and S. T. Fiske, pp. 121–156. Hillsdale, NJ: Lawrence Erlbaum.

——— (1984). A perceptual-motor theory of emotion. In *Advances in Experimental Social Psychology*, ed. L. Berkowitz, pp. 117–182. New York: Academic.

Linehan, M. (1993). *Cognitive Behavioral Treatment of Borderline Personality Disorder*. New York: Guilford.

Liotti, G. (1984). Cognitive therapy, attachment theory, and psychiatric nosology: a clinical and theoretical inquiry into their interdependence. In *Cognitive Psychotherapies: Recent Development in Theory, Research and Practice*, ed. M. A. Reda and M. J. Mahoney, pp. 211–232. Cambridge, MA: Ballinger.

——— (1987). The resistance to change of cognitive structures: a counterproposal to psychoanalytic metapsychology. *Journal of Cognitive Psychotherapy* 2:87–104.

———— (1988). Attachment and cognition: a guideline for the recon-struction of early pathogenic experiences in cognitive psycho-therapy. In *Handbook of Cognitive Psychotherapy*, ed. C. Perris, I. Blackburn, and H. Perris, pp. 62–79. New York: Springer.

Lorenz, K. (1973). *Behind the Mirror.* New York: Harcourt Brace Jovanovich.

Lowen, A. (1967). *The Betrayal of the Body.* London: Collier.

Luborsky, L. (1984). *Principles of Psychoanalytic Psychotherapy.* New York: Basic Books.

Luborsky, L., Crits-Christoph, P., McClellan, A. T., et al. (1986). Do therapists vary much in their success? *American Journal of Ortho-psychiatry* 56:501–512.

Luborsky, L., McClellan, A.T., Woody, G. E., et al. (1985). Therapist success and its determinants. *Archives of General Psychiatry* 42:602–611.

Luborsky, L., Mintz, J., Auerbach, A., et al. (1980). Predicting the outcome of psychotherapy: findings of the Penn psychotherapy project. *Archives of General Psychiatry* 37:471–481.

Luborsky, L., Singer, B., and Luborsky, L. (1975). Comparative studies of psychotherapies: Is it true that "everyone has won and all must have prizes?" *Archives of General Psychiatry* 32:995–1008.

Mace, W. M. (1977). James J. Gibson's strategy for perceiving: ask not what's inside your head, but what you head's inside of. In *Per-ceiving, Acting, and Knowing: Toward an Ecological Psychology*, ed. R. Shaw and J. Bransford, pp. 43–65. Hillsdale: NJ: Lawrence Erl-baum.

Mahler, M. (1974). Symbiosis and individuation: the psychological birth of the human infant. In *The Selected Papers of Margaret S. Mahler*, vol. 2. New York: Jason Aronson.

Mahoney, M. J. (1974). *Cognition and Behavior Modification.* Cam-bridge, MA: Ballinger.

———— (1980). Psychotherapy and the structure of personal revo-lutions. In *Psychotherapy Process: Current Issues and Future Directions*, ed. M. J. Mahoney, pp. 157–180. New York: Plenum.

———— (1982). Psychotherapy and human change processes. In *Psy-chotherapy Research and Behavior Change*, vol. 1, pp. 73–122. Washington, DC: American Psychiatric Association.

——— (1984). Integrating cognition, affect and action: a comment. *Cognitive Therapy and Research* 8:585–589.

——— (1991). *Human Change Processes.* New York: Basic Books.

——— (1993). Diversity and the dynamics of development in psychotherapy integration. *Journal of Psychotherapy Integration* 3:1–14.

Mahoney, M. J., and Thoresen, C. E. (1974). *Self-Control: Power to the Person.* Belmont, CA: Brooks/Cole.

Main, M., Kaplan, N., and Cassidy, J. (1985). Security in infancy, childhood, and adulthood: a move to the level of representation. *Monographs of the Society for Research in Child Development*, 209, vol. 50, nos. 1–2. Chicago: University of Chicago Press.

Manicas, P. T., and Secord, P. F. (1983). Implications for psychology of the new philosophy of science. *American Psychologist* 38:399–413.

Marcel, A. J. (1980). Conscious and preconscious recognition of polysemous words: locating the selective effects of prior verbal context. In *Attention and Performance*, vol. 8, pp. 435–457, ed. R. S. Nickerson. Hillsdale, NJ: Lawrence Erlbaum.

Markus, H. (1977). Self-schemata and processing information about the self. *Journal of Personality and Social Psychology* 35:63–78.

——— (1983). Self-knowledge: an expanded view. *Journal of Personality* 51:543–565.

Markus, H., and Nurius, P. (1986). Possible selves. *American Psychologist* 41:954–969.

Marlatt, G. A. (1978). Craving for alcohol, loss of control and relapse: a cognitive-behavioral analysis. In *Alcoholism: New Directions in Behavioral Research and Treatment*, ed. P. E. Nathan, G. A. Marlatt, and T. Loberg. New York: Plenum.

Marlatt, G. A., and Gordon, J. R. (1979). Determinants of relapse: implications for the maintenance of behavior change. In *Behavioral Medicine: Changing Health Lifestyles*, ed. P. Davison, pp. 410–452. New York: Plenum.

Marmar, C. R., Horowitz, M. J., Weiss, D. S., et al. (1986). The development of the therapeutic alliance rating system. In *The Psychotherapy Process: A Research Handbook*, pp. 367–390. New York: Guilford.

Marmar, C. R., Weiss, D. S., and Gaston, L. (1989). Towards the validation of the California Therapeutic Alliance Rating System. *Journal of Consulting and Clinical Psychology* 57:46–52.

McArthur, L. Z., and Baron, R. M. (1983). Toward an ecological theory of social perception. *Psychological Review* 90:215–238.

McCullough, J. P. (1984a). Single-case investigative research and its relevance for the nonoperant clinician. *Psychotherapy* 21:382–388.

—— (1984b). Cognitive-behavioral analysis system of psychotherapy: an interactional treatment approach for dysthymic disorder. *Psychiatry* 47:234–250.

McCullough, J. P., and Carr, K. F. (1987). Stage process design: a predictive confirmation structure for the single case. *Psychotherapy* 24:759–767.

Mead, G. H. (1934). *Mind, Self and Society.* Chicago: University of Chicago Press.

Meddin, J. (1982). Cognitive therapy and symbolic interactionism: expanding clinical potential. *Cognitive Therapy and Research* 6:151–165.

Mehrabian, A. (1972). *Nonverbal Communication.* Chicago: Aldine-Atherton.

Meichenbaum, D. (1977). *Cognitive-Behavioral Modification.* New York: Plenum.

Meichenbaum, D., and Gilmore, J. B. (1984). The nature of unconscious processes: a cognitive-behavioral perspective. In *The Unconscious Reconsidered,* ed. K. S. Bowers and D. Meichenbaum, pp. 273–298. New York: Wiley.

Menaker, E. (1989). *Appointment in Vienna.* New York: St. Martin's.

Merluzzi, T. V., and Rudy, T. E. (1982). *Cognitive assessment of social anxiety: a "surface" and "deep" structure analysis.* Paper presented at the American Psychological Association Annual Meeting, Washington, DC, August.

Merluzzi, T. V., Rudy, T. E., and Glass, C. (1981). The information-processing paradigm: implication for clinical science. In *Cognitive Assessment,* ed. T. Merluzzi, C. Glass, and M. Genest. New York: Guilford.

Messer, S. B. (1987). Can the tower of Babel be completed? A critique of the common language proposal. *Journal of Integrative and Eclectic Psychotherapy* 6:195–199.

—— (1992). A critical examination of belief structures in integrative and eclectic psychotherapy. In *Handbook of Psychotherapy Integra-*

tion, ed. J. C. Norcross and M. R. Goldfried, pp. 130–165. New York: Basic Books.

Messer, S. B., Sass, L. A., and Woolfolk, R. L., eds. (1988). *Hermeneutics and Psychological Theory: Interpretive Perspectives on Personality, Psychotherapy, and Psychopathology*. New Brunswick, NJ: Rutgers University Press.

Messer, S. B., Tishby, O., and Spillman, A. (1992). Taking context seriously in psychotherapy research: relating to patient progress in brief psychodynamic therapy. *Journal of Consulting and Clinical Psychology* 60:678–688.

Messer, S. B., and Warren, S. (1990). Personality change and psychotherapy. In *Handbook of Personality: Theory and Research*, ed. L. A. Pervin, pp. 371–398. New York: Guilford.

Messer, S. B., and Winokur, M. (1980). Some limits to the integration of psychoanalytic therapy and behavior therapy. *American Psychologist* 35:818–827.

———— (1984). Ways of knowing and visions of reality in psychoanalytic therapy and behavior therapy. In *Psychoanalytic Therapy and Behavior Therapy: Is Integration Possible?* ed. H. Arkowitz and S. B. Messer, pp. 53–100. New York: Plenum.

Michotte, A. E. (1950). The emotions regarded as functional connections. In *Feelings and Emotions*, ed. M. L. Reymart, pp. 114–146. New York: McGraw-Hill.

Mischel, W. (1973). Toward a cognitive social learning reconceptualization of personality. *Psychological Review* 80:252–283.

Mitchell, S. A. (1988). *Relational Concepts in Psychoanalysis: An Integration*. Cambridge, MA: Harvard University Press.

Moray, N. (1959). Attention in dichotic listening: affective cues and the influence of instructions. *Quarterly of the Journal of Experimental Psychology* 11:56–60.

Morrow-Bradley, C. O., and Elliott, J. R. (1986). Utilization of psychotherapy research by practicing psychotherapists. *American Psychologist* 41:188–197.

Moyne, J., and Barks, C. (1986). *Unseen Rain: Quatrains of Rumi*. Putney, VT: Threshold.

Murphy, C. M., and Messer, D. J. (1977). Mothers, infants and pointing: a study of gesture. In *Studies in Mother–Infant Interaction*, ed. H. R. Schaffer. London: Academic.

Neely, J. H. (1977). Semantic priming and retrieval from lexical memory. *Journal of Experimental Psychology* 106:226–254.

Neimeyer, R. A. (1985). Personal constructs in clinical practice. In *Advances in Cognitive-Behavioral Research and Therapy*, vol. 4, pp. 275–339, ed. P. C. Kendall. New York: Academic.

Neisser, U. (1967). *Cognitive Psychology*. New York: Appleton-Century-Crofts.

———— (1976). *Cognition and Reality: Principles and Implications of Cognitive Psychology*. San Francisco: Freeman.

———— (1980). Three cognitive psychologies and their implications. In *Psychotherapy Process*, ed. M. J. Mahoney. New York: Plenum.

———— (1981). John Dean's memory: a case study. *Cognition* 9:1–22.

Nelson, K., and Greundel, J. M. (1981). Generalized event representations: basic building blocks of cognitive development. In *Advances in Developmental Psychology*, vol. 1, pp. 131–158, ed. M. E. Lamb and A. L. Brown. Hillsdale, NJ: Lawrence Erlbaum.

Nemiah, J. C. (1984). The unconscious and psychopathology. In *The Unconscious Reconsidered*, ed. K. S. Bowers and D. Meichenbaum, pp. 49–87. New York: Wiley.

Newtson, D. (1973). Attribution and the unit of perception of ongoing behavior. *Journal of Personality and Social Psychology* 28:28–38.

Nisbett, R., and Ross, L. (1980). *Human Inference: Strategies and Shortcomings of Social Judgment*. Englewood Cliffs, NJ: Prentice-Hall.

Norcross, J. C., and Goldfried, M. R., eds. (1992). *Handbook of Psychotherapy Integration*. New York: Basic Books.

Norman, D. A., and Bobrow, D. G. (1975). On data-limited and resource-limited processes. *Cognitive Psychology* 7:44–64.

Nozick, R. (1981). *Philosophical Explanations*. Cambridge, MA: Harvard University Press.

O'Banion, K., and Arkowitz, H. (1977). Social anxiety and selective memory for affective information about the self. *Social Behavior and Personality* 5:321–328.

Ogden, T. H. (1986). *The Matrix of the Mind*. Northvale, NJ: Jason Aronson.

Omer, H., and Dar. R. (1992). Changing trends in three decades of psychotherapy research: the flight from theory into pragmatics. *Journal of Consulting and Clinical Psychology* 60:88–93.

Orenstein, H., and Carr, J. (1975). Implosion therapy by tape recording. *Behaviour Research and Therapy* 13:177–182.

Orlinsky, D. E., and Howard, K. I. (1986). The relation of process to outcome in psychotherapy. In *Handbook of Psychotherapy and Behaviour Change*, ed. S. L. Garfield and A. E. Bergin, 3rd ed., pp. 283–330. New York: Wiley.

Osgood, G. E. (1953). *Method and Theory in Experimental Psychology*. New York: Oxford University Press.

Parloff, M. B. (1986). Placebo controls in psychotherapy research: A sine qua non or a placebo for research problems? *Journal of Consulting and Clinical Psychology* 51:79–87.

Paulhus, D. L., and Martin, C. L. (1988). Functional flexibility: a new conception of interpersonal flexibility. *Journal of Personality and Social Psychology* 1:88–101.

Pepper, S. P. (1942). *World Hypotheses: A Study of Evidence*. Berkeley, CA: University of California Press.

Perls, F. (1973). *The Gestalt Approach and Eye Witness Therapy*. Palo Alto, CA: Science and Behavior Books, Bantam.

Perls, F., Hefferline, R., and Goodman, P. (1951). *Gestalt Therapy*. New York: Dell.

Persons, J. B. (1991). Psychotherapy outcome studies do not represent current models of psychotherapy: a proposed remedy. *American Psychologist* 46:99–106.

Piaget, J. (1954). *Construction of Reality in the Child*. New York: Basic Books.

Plutchik, R. (1980). *Emotion: A Psychoevolutionary Synthesis*. New York: Harper & Row.

Polanyi, M. (1958). *Personal Knowledge*. Chicago: University of Chicago Press.

——— (1966). *The Tacit Dimension*. New York: Doubleday.

Polkinghorne, D. E. (1984). Further extensions of methodological diversity for counseling psychology. *Journal of Counseling Psychology* 31:416–429.

Posner, M. I., and Snyder, R. R. (1975a). Attention and cognitive control. In *Information Processing and Cognition*, ed. R. L. Solso. Hillsdale, NJ: Lawrence Erlbaum.

——— (1975b). Facilitation and inhibition in the processing of signals. In *Attention and Performance*, ed. P. M. A. Rabbitt and S. Dornic, pp. 669–682. New York: Academic.

Prochaska, J. O. (1995). An eclectic and integrative approach: transtheoretical therapy. In *Essential Psychotherapies: Theory and Practice*, ed. A. S. Gurman, and S. B. Messer, pp. 403–440. New York: Guilford.

Progoff, I. (1953). *Jung's Psychology and Its Social Meaning*. New York: Dialogue House Library.

Quillian, M. R. (1968). Semantic memory. In *Semantic Information Processing*, ed. M. L. Minsky, pp. 227–259. Cambridge, MA: Massachusetts Institute of Technology Press.

Rachman, S. (1981). The primacy of affect: some theoretical implications. *Behavior, Research and Therapy* 19:273–290.

——— (1983). Irrational thinking with special reference to cognitive therapy. *Advances in Behavioral Research and Therapy* 5:63–88.

——— (1984). A reassessment of the "primacy of affect." *Cognitive Therapy and Research* 8:579–584.

Racker, H. (1968). *Transference and Countertransference*. New York: International Universities Press.

Raimy, V. (1975). *Misunderstandings of the Self*. San Francisco: Jossey-Bass.

Rank, O. (1929). *The Trauma of Birth*. New York: Harper & Row.

——— (1936). *Truth and Reality: The Central Statement of Rank's Ideas*. New York: Norton.

——— (1945). *Will Therapy and Truth and Reality*. New York: Knopf.

Reber, A. S., and Lewis, S. (1977). Implicit learning: an analysis of the form and structure of a body of tacit knowledge. *Cognition* 5:333–361.

Reda, M. A. (1984). Cognitive organization and antidepressants: attitude modification during amitriptyline treatment in severely depressed individuals. In *Cognitive Psychotherapies*, ed. M. A. Reda and M. J. Mahoney, pp. 119–140. Cambridge, MA: Ballinger.

Reich, W. (1942). *The Function of the Orgasm*. New York: Orgone Institute.

——— (1949). *Character Analysis*. New York: Noonday.

Rice, L. N. (1984). Client tasks in client-centered therapy. In *Client-Centered Therapy and the Person-Centered Approach: New Directions in*

Theory, Research and Practice, ed. R. F. Levant and J. M. Shlien, pp. 182–202. New York: Praeger.

Rice, L. N., and Greenberg, L. S. (1984). *Patterns of Change: Intensive Analysis of Psychotherapeutic Process.* New York: Guilford.

Ricks, D. F. (1974). Supershrink: methods of a therapist judged successful on the basis of adult outcomes of adolescent patients. In *Life History Research in Psychopathology*, ed. D. F. Ricks, M. Roff, and A. Thomas. Minneapolis: University of Minnesota Press.

Rilke, R. M. (1903). *Letters to a Young Poet*, ed. and trans. S. Mitchell. New York: Vintage, 1986.

Rogers, C. R. (1951). *Client-Centered Therapy.* Boston: Houghton Mifflin.

———— (1961). *On Becoming a Person.* Boston: Houghton Mifflin.

Rogers, T. B., Rogers, P. J., and Kuiper, N. A. (1979). Evidence for the self as a cognitive prototype: the "false alarms effect." *Personality and Social Psychology Bulletin* 5:53–56.

Rorty, R. (1982). *Consequences of Pragmatism.* Minneapolis: University of Minnesota Press.

Roth, D., and Rehm, L. P. (1980). Relationships among self-monitoring processes, memory and depression. *Cognitive Therapy and Research* 4:149–158.

Rothbart, M., Evans, M., and Fulero, S. (1979). Recall for nonconfirming events: memory processes and the maintenance of social stereotypes. *Journal of Experimental Psychology* 15:343–355.

Rumelhart, D. E., Lindsay, P. H., and Norman, D. A. (1972). A process model for long-term memory. In *Organization of Memory*, ed. E. Tulving and W. Donaldson, pp. 198–246. New York: Academic.

Rush, A. J., Weissenberger, J., and Eaves, G. (1984). *Do thinking patterns predict depressive symptoms?* Unpublished manuscript, University of Texas.

Safran, J. D. (1984a). Assessing the cognitive-interpersonal cycle. *Cognitive Therapy and Research* 8:333–348.

———— (1984b). Some implications of Sullivan's interpersonal theory for cognitive therapy. In *Cognitive Psychotherapies: Recent Developments in Theory, Research and Practice*, ed. M. A. Reda and M. J. Mahoney, pp. 251–272. Cambridge, MA: Ballinger.

———— (1986). *A critical evaluation of the schema construct in psycho-*

therapy research. Paper presented at the Society for Psychotherapy Research Conference, Boston, June.

——— (1990a). Towards a refinement of cognitive therapy in light of interpersonal theory: I. Theory. *Clinical Psychology Review* 10:87–105.

——— (1990b). Towards a refinement of cognitive therapy in light of interpersonal theory: II. Practice. *Clinical Psychology Review* 10:107–121.

——— (1993). Breaches in the therapeutic alliance: an arena for negotiating authentic relatedness. *Psychotherapy* 30:111–124.

Safran, J. D., Crocker, P., McMain, S., and Murray, P. (1990). Therapeutic alliance rupture as a therapy event for empirical investigation. *Psychotherapy* 27:154–165.

Safran, J. D., and Greenberg, L. S. (1982a). Cognitive appraisal and reappraisal: implications for clinical practice. *Cognitive Therapy and Research* 6:251–258.

——— (1982b). Eliciting "hot cognitions" in cognitive behavior therapy: rationale and procedural guidelines. *Canadian Psychology* 23:83–87.

——— (1986). Hot cognition and psychotherapy process: an information-processing ecological approach. In *Advances in Cognitive-Behavioral Research and Therapy,* vol. 5, pp. 143–177, ed. P. C. Kendall. New York: Academic.

——— (1987). Affect and the unconscious: a cognitive perspective. In *Theories of the Unconscious,* ed. R. Stern, pp. 191–212. Hillsdale, NJ: Analytic.

——— (1988). Feeling, thinking and acting: a cognitive framework for psychotherapy integration. *Journal of Cognitive Psychotherapy: An International Quarterly* 2:109–130.

——— (1989). The treatment of anxiety and depression: the process of affective change. In *Anxiety and Depression: Distinctive and Overlapping Features,* ed. P. C. Kendall and D. Watson, pp. 455–489. Orlando, FL: Academic.

——— (1993). The therapeutic alliance rupture as a transtheoretical phenomenon: definitional and conceptual issues. *Journal of Psychotherapy Integration* 3:33–49.

Safran, J. D., and Greenberg, L. S., eds. (1991). *Emotion, Psychotherapy and Change.* New York: Guilford.

Safran, J. D., Greenberg, L. S., and Rice, N. L. (1988). Integrating psychotherapy research and practice: modeling the change process. *Psychotherapy* 25:1–17.

Safran, J. D., Hill, C., and Ford, C. (1988). *A self-report measure of the interpersonal schema.* Unpublished manuscript.

Safran, J. D., and Inck, T. A. (1995). Psychotherapy integration: implications for the treatment of depression. In *Handbook of Depression,* ed. E. E. Beckham and W. R. Leber, pp. 425–434. New York: Guilford.

Safran, J. D., and Muran, J. C. (1994). Toward a working alliance between research and practice. In *Psychotherapy Research and Practice,* ed. P. F. Talley, H. H. Strupp, and J. F. Butler, pp. 206–226. New York: Basic Books.

———— (1995). Resolving therapeutic alliance ruptures: diversity and integration. *In Session: Psychotherapy in Practice* 1:81–92.

———— (1996). The resolution of ruptures in the therapeutic alliance. *Journal of Consulting and Clinical Psychology* 64:447–458.

Safran, J. D., Muran, J. C., and Samstag, L. W. (1994). Resolving therapeutic alliance ruptures: a task analytic investigation. In *The Working Alliance: Theory, Research and Practice,* ed. A. O. Horvath and L. S. Greenberg, pp. 225–255. New York: Wiley.

Safran, J. D., Muran, J. C., and Wallner, L. K. (1991). *Research on therapeutic alliance ruptures.* Symposium presented at the Society for Psychotherapy Research Conference.

Safran, J. D., and Segal, Z. V. (1987). An investigation of the processes mediating schematic effects on the acquisition of social knowledge. *Canadian Journal of Behavioral Science* 19:137–150.

———— (1990). *Interpersonal Process in Cognitive Therapy.* New York: Basic Books.

Safran, J. D., Segal, Z. V., Hill, C., and Whiffen, V. (1990). Refining strategies for research on self-representations in emotional disorders. *Cognitive Therapy and Research* 14:143–160.

Safran, J. D., Vallis, T. M., Segal, Z. V., and Shaw, B. F. (1986). Assessment of core cognitive processes in cognitive therapy. *Cognitive Therapy and Research* 10:509–526.

Safran, J. D., and Wallner, L. K. (1991). The relative predictive validity of two therapeutic alliance measures in cognitive therapy. *Psychology Assessment* 3:188–195.

Sampson, E. E. (1993). *Celebrating the Other: A Dialogic Account of Human Nature*. Boulder, CO: Westview.

Sandler, J., and Sandler, A. M. (1978). On the development of object relationships and affects. *International Journal of Psycho-Analysis* 59:285–296.

Schachtel, E. G. (1959). *Metamorphosis*. New York: Basic Books.

Schachter, S., and Singer, J. E. (1962). Cognitive, social, and physiological determinants of emotional state. *Psychological Review* 69:377–399.

Schafer, R. (1976). *A New Language of Psychoanalysis*. New Haven, CT: Yale University Press.

——— (1983). *The Analytic Attitude*. New York: Basic Books.

Schank, R. C., and Abelson, R. P. (1977). *Scripts, Plans, Goals, and Understanding*. Hillsdale, NJ: Lawrence Erlbaum.

Schlenker, B., and Leary, M. (1982). Social anxiety and self-presentation: a conceptualization and model. *Psychological Bulletin* 92:641–785.

Schrodinger, E. (1967). *Mind and Matter*. New York: Cambridge University Press.

Schwartz, T., White, G. M., and Lutz, C. A., eds. (1992). *New Directions in Psychological Anthropology*. New York: Cambridge University Press.

Scriven, M. (1969). Logical positivism and the behavioral sciences. In *The Legacy of Logical Positivism*, ed. P. Achinstein and S. Barker, pp. 195–209. Baltimore: Johns Hopkins University Press.

Segal, Z. V. (1984). *Shifting cognitive assessment strategies from a state to trait focus: the case of self-schema measures*. Paper presented at the meeting of the Association for Advancement of Behavior Therapy, Philadelphia.

Segal, Z. V., and Shaw, B. F. (1986). Cognition in depression: a reappraisal of Coyne and Gotlib's critique. *Cognitive Therapy and Research* 10:671–693.

Shapiro, D. A. (1985). Recent applications of meta-analysis in clinical research. *Clinical Psychology Review* 5(1):13–34.

Shaw, R., and Bransford, J. (1977). *Perceiving, Acting and Knowing:*

Toward an Ecological Psychology. Hillsdale, NJ: Lawrence Erl-baum.

Shevrin, H. (1973). Brain wave correlates of subliminal stimulation, unconscious attention, primary and secondary process thinking and repressiveness. *Psychological Issues* 8:56–87.

Shevrin, H., and Dickman, S. (1980). The psychological unconscious: A necessary assumption for all psychological theory? *American Psychologist* 35:421–434.

Shiffrin, R. M., and Schneider, W. (1977). Controlled and automatic human information processing: II. Perceptual learning, automatic attending, and a general theory. *Psychology Review* 84:127–190.

Shweder, R. A. (1991). *Thinking Through Cultures: Expeditions in Cultural Psychology.* Cambridge, MA: Harvard University Press.

Silberschatz, G. (1987). Testing pathogenic beliefs. In *Theory, Clinical Observation and Empirical Research,* ed. J. Weiss, H. Sampson, and The Mount Zion Psychotherapy Research Group. New York: Guilford.

Silberschatz, G., Fretter, P. B., and Curtis, J. T. (1986). How do interpretations influence the process of psychotherapy? *Journal of Consulting and Clinical Psychology* 54:646–652.

Simons, A., Murphy, G., Levine, J., and Wetzel, R. (1984). *Sustained improvement one year after cognitive and/or pharmacotherapy of depression.* Paper presented at the meeting of the Society for Psychotherapy Research, Lake Louise, June.

Singer, J. A., and Singer, J. L. (1992). Transference in psychotherapy and daily life: implications of current memory and social cognition research. In *Interface of Psychoanalysis and Psychology,* ed. J. W. Barron, M. A. Eagle, and D. L. Wolitzky, pp. 516–538. Washington, DC: American Psychoanalytic Association Press.

Sloane, R. B., Staples, F. R., Cristol, A. H., et al. (1975). *Short Term Analytically Oriented Psychotherapy Versus Behaviour Therapy.* Cambridge, MA: Harvard University Press.

Smith, M. L., and Glass, G. V. (1977). Meta-analysis of psychotherapy outcome studies. *American Psychologist* 32:752–760.

Smith, M. L., Glass, G. V., and Miller, T. I. (1980). *The Benefits of Psychotherapy.* Baltimore, MD: Johns Hopkins University Press.

Spence, D. P. (1980). Lawfulness in lexical choice—A natural experiment. *Journal of the American Psychoanalytic Association* 28:115–132.

——— (1982). *Narrative Truth and Historical Truth: Meaning and Interpretation in Psychoanalysis.* New York: Norton.

Spitz, R. (1965). *The First Year of Life.* New York: International Universities Press.

Sterba, R. (1934). The fate of the ego in analytic therapy. *International Journal of Psycho-Analysis* 15:117–126.

Stern, D. N. (1985). *The Interpersonal World of the Infant.* New York: Basic Books.

Stiles, W. B., Shapiro, D. A., and Elliott, R. (1986). Are all psychotherapies equivalent? *American Psychologist* 41:165–180.

Stolorow, R. (1988). Intersubjectivity, psychoanalytic knowing and reality. *Contemporary Psychoanalysis* 24:331–338.

Stone, L. (1954). The widening scope of indications for psychoanalysis. *Journal of the American Psychoanalytic Association* 2:567–594.

——— (1961). *The Psychoanalytic Situation.* New York: International Universities Press.

Strack, S., and Coyne, J. C. (1983). Social confirmation of dysphoria: shared and private reactions to depression. *Journal of Personality and Social Psychology* 44:798–806.

Stricker, G. (1994). Reflections on psychotherapy integration. *Clinical Psychology: Science and Practice* 1:3–12.

Stricker, G., and Gold, J. R. (1996). Psychotherapy integration: an assimilative, psychodynamic approach. *Clinical Psychology: Science and Practice* 3:47–58.

Stricker, G., and Gold, J. R., eds. (1993). *Comprehensive Handbook of Psychotherapy Integration.* New York: Plenum.

Strupp, H. H. (1980). Success and failure in time-limited psychotherapy: further evidence. Comparison IV. *Archives of General Psychiatry* 37:947–954.

——— (1986). The nonspecific hypothesis of therapeutic effectiveness: a current assessment. *American Journal of Orthopsychiatry* 56:513–520.

Strupp, H. H., and Binder, J. L. (1984). *Psychotherapy in a New Key: A Guide to Time-Limited Dynamic Psychotherapy.* New York: Basic Books.

Suh, C. S., O'Malley, S. S., Strupp, H. H., and Johnson, M. E. (1989). The Vanderbilt Psychotherapy Process Scale (VPPS). *Journal of Cognitive Psychotherapy: An International Quarterly* 3:123–154.

Suh, C. S., Strupp, H. H., and O'Malley, S. S. (1986). The Vanderbilt process measures: the Psychotherapy Process Scale (VPPS) and the Negative Indicators Scale (VNIS). In *The Psychotherapeutic Process: A Research Handbook*, ed. L. S. Greenberg and W. M. Pinsoff, pp. 285–324. New York: Guilford.

Sullivan, H. S. (1940). *Conceptions of Modern Psychiatry*. New York: Norton.

——— (1953). *The Interpersonal Theory of Psychiatry*. New York: Norton.

——— (1954). *The Psychiatric Interview*. New York: Norton.

——— (1956). *Clinical Studies in Psychiatry*. New York: Norton.

Sutton-Simon, K., and Goldfried, M. R. (1979). Faulty thinking patterns in two types of anxiety. *Cognitive Therapy and Research* 3:193–203.

Swann, W. B., Jr., and Read, S. J. (1981a). Acquiring self-knowledge: the search for feedback that fits. *Journal of Personality and Social Psychology* 41:1119–1128.

——— (1981b). Self-verification processes: how we sustain our self-conceptions. *Journal of Experimental Social Psychology* 17:351–372.

Sweet, A. A. (1984). The therapeutic relationship in behavior therapy. *Clinical Psychology Review* 4:253–272.

Tansey, M. J., and Burke, W. F. (1989). *Understanding Countertransference*. Hillsdale, NJ: Analytic.

Teasdale, J., and Fogarty, S. (1979). Differential effects of induced mood on recall of pleasant and unpleasant events from episodic memory. *Journal of Abnormal Psychology* 88:235–241.

Tishby, O., and Messer, S. B. (1995). The relationship between plan compatibility of therapist interventions and patient progress: a comparison of two plans. *Psychotherapy Research* 5:76–88.

Titchener, E. B. (1908). *Lectures on the Elementary Psychology of Feeling and Attention*. New York: Macmillan.

Tomkins, S. S. (1980). Affect as amplification: some modifications in theory. In *Emotion: Theory, Research and Experience*, ed. R. Plutchik and H. Kelerman. New York: Academic.

Toulmin, S. (1972). *Human Understanding*. Princeton, NJ: Princeton University Press.

Treisman, A. M. (1960). Contextual cues in selective listening. *Quarterly of the Journal of Experimental Psychology* 12:242–248.

——— (1969). Strategies and models of selective attention. *Psychology Review* 76:282–299.

Trevarthen, C. B. (1968). Two mechanisms of vision in primates. *Psychologische Forschung* 31:299–337.

Trevarthen, C. B., and Hubley, P. (1978). Secondary intersubjectivity: Confidence, confiders and acts of meaning in the first year. In *Action, Gesture and Symbol*, ed. A. Lock. New York: Academic.

Tronick, E. Z. (1989). Emotions and emotional communication in infants. *American Psychologist* 44:112–119.

Tronick, E. Z., and Cohn, J. F. (1989). Infant–mother face to face interaction: age and gender differences in coordination and the occurrence of mis-coordination. *Child Development* 60:85–92.

Tulving, E. (1972). Episodic and semantic memory. In *Organization of Memory*, ed. E. Tulving and W. Donaldson. New York: Academic.

Turvey, M. T. (1977). Preliminaries to a theory of action with reference to vision. In *Perceiving, Acting and Knowing: Toward an Ecological Psychology*, ed. R. Shaw and J. Bransford. Hillsdale, NJ: Lawrence Erlbaum.

Underwood, G. (1977). Contextual facilitation from attended and unattended messages. *Journal of Verbal Learning and Verbal Behavior* 16:99–106.

——— (1978). Attentional selectivity and behavioral control. In *Strategies of Information Processing*, ed. G. Underwood. London and New York: Academic.

Van Den Bergh, O., and Eelen, P. (1984). Unsconscious processing and emotions. In *Cognitive Psychotherapies: Recent Developments in Theory, Research and Practice*, ed. M. A. Reda and M. J. Mahoney. Cambridge, MA: Ballinger.

Von Wright, J. M., Anderson, K., and Stenman, V. (1975). Generalization of conditioned GSR's in dichotic listening. In *Attention and Performance*, ed. P. M. A. Rabbitt and S. Domic, pp. 194–204. New York: Academic.

Wachtel, P. (1977). *Psychoanalysis and Behavior Therapy.* New York: Basic Books.

———— (1980). What should we say to our patients? On the wording of the therapists' comments. *Psychotherapy: Theory, Research, and Practice* 17:183–188.

———— (1982). *Resistance: Psychodynamic and Behavioral Approaches.* New York: Plenum.

———— (1987). *Action and Insight.* New York: Guilford.

Wachtel, P. L., and McKinney, M. K. (1992). Cyclical psychodynamics and integrative psychodynamic therapy. In *Handbook of Psychotherapy Integration,* ed. J. C. Norcross and M. R. Goldfried, pp. 335–370. New York: Basic Books.

Weimer, W. B. (1977). A conceptual framework for cognitive psychology: motor theories of the mind. In *Perceiving, Acting and Knowing: Toward an Ecological Psychology,* ed. R. Shaw and J. Bransford, pp. 267–311. Hillsdale, NJ: Lawrence Erlbaum.

———— (1979). *Notes on the Methodology of Scientific Research.* Hillsdale, NJ: Lawrence Erlbaum.

Weinberger, J. (1995). Common factors aren't so common: the common factors dilemma. *Clinical Psychology: Science and Practice* 2:45–69.

Weiss, J., Sampson, H., and The Mount Zion Psychotherapy Research Group (1987). *The Psychoanalytic Process: Theory, Clinical Observation, and Empirical Research.* New York: Guilford.

Weissman, A. N., and Beck, A. T. (1978). *Development and validation of the dysfunctional attitude scale: a preliminary investigation.* Paper presented at the meeting of the American Educational Research Association, Toronto, Canada, March.

Wertz, F. J. (1993). On psychoanalysis and academic psychology. *American Psychologist* 48:584–585.

Westen, D. (1988). Transference and information processing. *Clinical Psychology Review* 8:161–179.

White, M. (1952). Sullivan and treatment. In *The Contributions of Harry Stack Sullivan,* ed. P. Mullahy. New York: Hermitage.

Wiggins, J. S. (1979). A psychological taxonomy of trait-descriptive terms: the interpersonal domain. *Journal of Personality and Social Psychology* 3:395–412.

———— (1982). Circumplex models of interpersonal behavior in clinical psychology. In *Handbook of Research Methods in Clinical Psychology*, ed. P. C. Kendall and J. N. Butcher, pp. 183–221. New York: Wiley Interscience.

Wilkins, W. (1985). Therapy credibility is not a nonspecific event. *Cognitive Therapy and Research* 9:119–125.

Wilson, G. T. (1980). Toward specifying the nonspecific factors in behavior therapy: a social learning analysis. In *Psychotherapy Process: Current Issues and Future Directions*, ed. M. J. Mahoney, pp. 283–307. New York: Plenum.

———— (1984). Clinical issues and strategies in the practice of behavior therapy. In *Annual Review of Behavior Therapy and Practice*, ed. G. T. Wilson, C. M. Franks, K. D. Brownell, and P. C. Kendall, pp. 288–317. New York: Guilford.

Winnicott, D. W. (1965). *The Maturational Processes and the Facilitating Environment.* London: Hogarth.

Wittgenstein, L. (1953). *Philosophical Investigations.* Oxford: Basil Blackwell.

Wolpe, J. (1978). Cognition and causation in human behavior and its therapy. *American Psychologist* 35:437–446.

Woolfolk, R. L., and Richardson, F. C. (1984). Behavior therapy and the ideology of modernity. *American Psychologist* 39:777–786.

Zadny, J., and Gerard, H. B. (1974). Attributed intentions and informational selectivity. *Journal of Experimental Social Psychology* 10:34–52.

Zajonc, R. B. (1980). Feeling and thinking: preferences need no inferences. *American Psychologist* 35:171–175.

———— (1984). On the primacy of affect. *American Psychologist* 39:117–123.

Zajonc, R. B., and Markus, H. (1984). Affect and cognition: the hard interface. In *Emotions, Cognition and Behavior*, ed. C. E. Izard, J. Kagan, and R. B. Zajonc, pp. 73–102. Cambridge: Cambridge University Press.

Zetzel, E. (1956). Current concepts of transference. *International Journal of Psycho-Analysis* 37:369–376.

Credits

The author gratefully acknowledges permission to reprint material from the following sources:

"Assessing the Cognitive-Interpersonal Cycle," by J. D. Safran, in *Cognitive Therapy and Research* 8:333–348. Copyright © 1984 by Plenum Publishing Corporation.

"Assessment and Modification of Core Cognitive Process," here titled "Assessing Core Cognitive Processes in Cognitive Therapy," by J. D. Safran, T. M. Vallis, Z. V. Segal, and B. F. Shaw, in *Cognitive Therapy and Research* 10:509–526. Copyright © 1986 by Plenum Publishing Corporation and reprinted by permission of the publisher and the co-authors.

"Towards a Refinement of Cognitive Therapy in Light of Interpersonal Theory: I. Theory, II. Practice," by J. D. Safran, in *Clinical Psychology Review* 10:87–105; 107–121. Copyright © 1990 by Elsevier Science Ltd, The Boulevard, Langford Lane, Kidlington 0X5 1GB, UK.

Index

Abelson, R. P., 70, 79, 80, 172
Action, emotion and, unconscious, 162–167
Adaptive affect, as motivator, hot cognition, 130–136
Affect, in cognitive therapy, Sullivanian theory, 19–20
Alden, L., 6
Alexander, F., 230, 235
Alexander, L. B., 188, 213, 222, 231
Alliance rupture. *See* Therapeutic alliance rupture
Alvarez, H. F., xii
Anchin, J. C., 63
Anderson, C., 289
Anderson, J. R., 119
Andrews, J. D., 286
Anxiety
    affective processing dysfunctions, 180

therapeutic process and, cognitive-interpersonal cycle, 27–37
Arbus, D., 242
Arkowitz, H., 6, 82, 230, 269
Arnkoff, D., 59, 61, 86, 87, 110, 190, 230
Arnold, M. B., 123, 127, 128, 172
Arzamanov, Y., 7
Associative network models, hot cognition, 118–120
Atthowe, J. M., 17
Avoidance, affective processing dysfunctions, 180

Bacal, H. A., 247
Balint, M., 238, 239, 240, 243
Bandura, A., 10, 17, 109
Barks, C., 239